John Rook

Everyday English

PITMAN

PITMAN PUBLISHING LIMITED
128 Long Acre, London WC2E 9AN

A Longman Group Company

First published by Longman 1978

Reprinted 1986

© Longman Group Limited 1978

ISBN 0 273 02686 0

Produced by Longman Singapore Publishers Pte Ltd
Printed in Singapore

Contents

Acknowledgements

I am very grateful to the following authorities for allowing me to use questions from past examination papers:

Associated Examining Board
Joint Matriculation Board
University of London
Royal Society of Arts
London Chamber of Commerce and Industry
Institute of Bankers
Association of Medical Secretaries

Chapter 1

Writing in sentences

Written composition is a matter of deciding what you want to say and on the order in which you wish to say it, and then saying it — in well-planned sentences.

Unfortunately, many people appear not to know what a sentence is. They write in fragments of sentences or in sentences which run into each other. This often makes it difficult for them to express what they want to say and throws an unfair burden on anyone who wants to, or has to, read what they have written.

Accordingly, the main purposes of this opening chapter are: to try to give some indication of what a sentence is, to provide examples of groups of words which are not sentences, and to suggest ways in which short sentences can be expanded or combined with other sentences. We will not try to *define* a sentence (to say what a sentence is) since all adequate definitions of sentences are so academic that they can usually be understood only by those people who already know what a sentence is!

Those who know what a sentence is know it because they do a lot of reading. Such people may decide that our account of how sentences can be expanded and combined is somewhat unrealistic; and they will probably be familiar with a wide variety of sentence patterns not dealt with in this section. They should find the sentence-construction exercises at the end of this chapter very easy. Nevertheless, they may find parts of this chapter useful.

First, we will consider — rather briefly — nouns and verbs.

NOUNS are the names of things (objects, substances, feelings, ideas, arts, sciences, living creatures, places) or the names of people. Here are some examples:

table, banana, beauty, air, postman, newspaper, laughter, book, hatred, fire, beginning, end, architect, Parliament, Germany, honesty, physics, Christianity, Frank Sinatra, existence, Napoleon, Henry VIII, polygon, spider, stupidity, fox.

There are forty-eight nouns in the following twenty sentences.

1. The cat sat on the mat.
2. William likes romantic films.
3. My brother eats like a horse.
4. My father sleeps in a tent.
5. Sociology is the study of society.
6. My friend is not going to France for his holidays this year.
7. That boxer is the champion of the world.
8. A pantechnicon is a very large lorry.
9. Television is sometimes a great time-waster.
10. Marx was one of the first advocates of Communism.
11. Diamonds are a girl's best friend.
12. His house consists of three rooms.
13. Her beauty did not astonish him.
14. America was discovered by Columbus but was named after Amerigo Vespucci.
15. John is writing a letter.
16. The train will be arriving in two hours' time.
17. Imagine my horror when I heard the news!
18. The first artificial satellite was launched by the Russians.
19. Miss Jones is making the report.
20. The letter is being dictated to the Principal's secretary.

The underlined words in the above sentences are VERBS. Verbs may consist of a single word or of groups of words, e.g. *was bitten, will have been doing.* Usually, verbs express actions (e.g. *hits, chewed, was running, will have left, would have been eating*) but note that many verbs do not express actions — not physical actions, at any rate, e.g. *is, are, am, were, have, exist, possess, sleep, lie* (e.g. in bed), *hear, see, taste, smell, feel, think, understand, love, hate, appreciate, consist, comprise, believe, consider.* It will be noticed that some words can be used as nouns or verbs, according to the job those words are doing in a sentence, e.g. *sleep, smell, taste, love.*

There are ten verbs and seventeen nouns in the following sentences:

1. My friend loves ice-cream.
2. Rome is in Italy.
3. She will be arriving soon.
4. I would have liked to come.
5. The little town lies at the foot of the mountain.
6. The dog was bitten by the man.
7. We never listen to classical music.
8. Darwin propounded the theory of evolution.
9. The noise at the discotheque almost deafened me.
10. Man is still trying to eradicate disease.

The essentials of a sentence

A sentence must always have a *subject* and a *verb.*

The subject is the thing or person that does the action described by the verb or has it done to it or him (as in sentence 6 above).

Subjects are always nouns or groups of words that represent nouns (e.g. *What we want* is more money), or PRONOUNS (*I, you, he, she, it, we, they, one, this, that, these, those, yours, ours, theirs, mine*).

The following are examples of complete sentences, complete because they all have subjects and verbs.

1. London is the capital of the United Kingdom. (Contains two proper nouns.)
2. John loves Mary.
3. Mary was once loved by Peter.
4. She swims well.
5. Malcolm sneezed.
6. Those are mine.
7. The dog chased the cat.
8. I was not eating my lunch.
9. The Anti-Combination Acts were passed in 1799.
10. That is clear.
11. I like milk.
12. It does me good.
13. Russia was attacked by Germany in 1941.
14. Yours is smaller than ours.

3

15. One should practise caution. (Contains an <u>abstract noun</u>.)
16. Before the days of limited liability people were often not willing to invest their money.
17. <u>That he will come</u> is certain.
18. <u>What I want to say to you</u> can wait.
19. <u>Whether he will arrive</u> is not certain.
20. <u>Why she wants to take the examination</u> is not clear.

In the last four sentences the subjects, groups of words which we call noun clauses, have been underlined.

Note that a present participle (e.g. *eating*, on its own) or a past participle (e.g. *having eaten*, or *eaten*, on its own) cannot do the job of a verb. Nor can an *infinitive* (e.g. *to be, to go, to exist*, etc.).

If there is no complete verb there cannot be a sentence, even though there may appear to be a subject. The following groups of words are not sentences:

- With reference to your letter of March 6th. (No verb and no subject.)
- With reference to your letter of April 17th concerning a proposed visit of a group of your students to the Victoria and Albert Museum. (No verb and no subject.)
- Sausages frying in the pan. (No verb.)
- The Government resigning today. (No verb.)
- In answer to your enquiry. (No verb and no subject.)
- Blue-grey storm clouds scudding across the sky. Trees bending before the wind. People hurrying home. (No verbs.)
- Thanking you in anticipation. (No verb and no subject.)
- Having eaten my breakfast. (No verb and no subject.)
- Sipping cocktails by moonlight. (No verb and no subject.)
- Keeps my dentures sparkling clean! (No subject.)
- Makes you feel young again! (No subject.)

Combining sentences by means of conjunctions

Sentences, each of course containing a subject and a verb, cannot be hooked together with commas. This sort of thing is wrong:

- I was so tired, I fell asleep.
- I like milk, it does me good.

- Britain is in the Common Market, people argue about this, they will still be arguing in ten years' time.
- The most important cause of the increase in the size of England's population in the second half of the eighteenth century was not the rise in the birth-rate, it was the fall in the death-rate, this was largely due to a rise in living standards.

Such sentences can be joined only by CONJUNCTIONS — joining words. Some of the commonest conjunctions are: *and, but, so, although, since, because, as, before, after, if, unless, when, for* (when it introduces a reason for believing something already said) and *that* (when it introduces a result or something said, seen, or felt). For example:

- I was so tired that I fell asleep. (When the *that* is missed out from "result" sentences it is often a sign that the writer is writing down speech, because, through lack of reading, he has insufficient experience of written words.)
- I like milk because it does me good.
- Britain is in the Common Market and people argue about this and they will still be arguing in ten years' time. [What a poor style!]
- The most important cause of the increase in the size of England's population in the second half of the eighteenth century was not the rise in the birth-rate but the fall in the death-rate, and this was largely due to a rise in living standards.
- We played tennis although it was raining.
- The train was late so I was furious.
- I watched television after I had eaten my tea.
- You ought to be grateful to her for she has saved you a lot of trouble.
- John liked Jean because she looked beautiful.
- It rained so heavily that the streets were flooded.
- He said that she was happy.

It should be noted that *therefore, however,* and *then* should not be used as conjunctions, for they are not joining words. The following sentences are incorrectly joined:

- It was raining therefore we couldn't play tennis.
- Later it stopped however the courts were too wet.
- I watched television for a while, then I went to bed, however I couldn't get to sleep.

Many people seem extremely unwilling to use *but* when they

write, perhaps because they think that in writing one should never use the obvious word! People's fondness for *therefore* instead of *so* may perhaps be the result of their having been told at school not to overdo the use of *so*.

Try joining up the sentences in each of the following groups:

1. I like ice-cream. It is fattening.
2. The English team won. They were two men short. Circumstances did not favour them.
3. It is obvious that it is raining. That man is using his umbrella.
4. He met her on Thursday. They were married on Friday.
5. Pamela is an excellent typist. She works very hard.
6. You should clean your teeth. You go to bed.
7. Washington is the capital of the United States. New York is much bigger.
8. All elephants are animals. The converse is not true.
9. Oscar Wilde referred to two nations separated by the same language. He was alluding to England and America. (Try *starting* your sentence with a conjunction.)
10. Jean is a fast accurate typist. She is good at spelling. She does not have to spend time desperately searching through the dictionary.

Now that you have connected the simple sentences in each group, each group is a longer sentence, but it could not be linked with another sentence by means of a comma. Either another conjunction would have to be used, or the whole thing would have to be replanned so as to incorporate the new material.

Building more complicated sentences

Simple sentences can, as we have noted, be attached by conjunctions to other simple sentences to make longer sentences, but this is of course not the only way of making longer sentences. Another way is to add single words or groups of words to a simple sentence.

Without being put off by the rather childish topic, consider the following sentence:

- The dog chased the cat.

By adding ADJECTIVES (describing words), we could say:

- The big brown dog chased the lazy black cat.

By adding ADVERBS (which usually tell us how, how much, or how often), we might produce this sentence:

- The big brown dog angrily chased the disgracefully lazy black cat.

We could expand this sentence further by adding *clauses*, groups of words which contain complete verbs (or *finite verbs*, to use the correct grammatical term) but which cannot be treated as complete sentences.

By adding describing clauses (*adjectival clauses*), we might say:

The big brown dog that lived in the house next to mine angrily chased the disgracefully lazy black cat, who was notorious for her dishonesty.

This sentence might be expanded still further by adding *adverbial clauses*. Adverbial clauses may tell us how, why, when and where an action takes place or under what disadvantages it takes place (although) or under what conditions it might take place (if). For example:

Although he had just had a heavy lunch at the residence of a hospitable friend and was feeling in consequence rather sleepy, the big brown dog that lived in the house next to mine angrily chased the disgracefully lazy black cat, who was notorious for her dishonesty, because the cat had stolen his bone.

This last sentence is still basically the five-word sentence we started with. It could rather clumsily be extended still further by means of a conjunction, e.g. "and he caught her" or "but, weighed down with carbohydrates, he was unable to overhaul her".

A fairly complicated sentence of this sort could be thought of as a number of short statements, one of them forming the basic sentence, the remainder turned into subordinate (supporting) clauses.

Another way of combining sentences or, to put it differently, of reducing the number of sentences one has to use to express one's meaning is to make phrases (very short groups of words) or single words do the job of whole sentences. For example:

- The book had a green cover. John wanted to buy it.

This can become:

- John wanted to buy the book with the green cover.
- Muhammad Ali has won many fights. He used to be known as Cassius Clay. He has won his fights easily.

This can become:
- Muhammad Ali, formerly known as Cassius Clay, has won many fights easily.
- Britain in the twentieth century has many economic problems. These problems are very serious. They are difficult to solve.

This can be synthesized as follows:
- Twentieth-century Britain has many very serious economic problems which are difficult to solve.

Consider the following five sentences:
- My friend is called John.
- I shall see him tonight.
- I shall see him at his house.
- I shall see him at eight o'clock.
- He wants to discuss next year's holiday.

By avoiding repetition and using an adverbial clause of reason (a clause which explains *why*), we may express the information contained in the five sentences in one sentence:

At eight o'clock tonight I shall see my friend John at his house because he wants to discuss next year's holiday.

Very useful for reducing the number of sentences one has to use are present participles (*laughing, running, arriving*, etc.) and past participles (*disgusted, beaten, having said*, etc.) and infinitives (*to see, to inspect, to be able*, etc.). Infinitives may often be used to express purpose. For example:
- I have to catch a train. It leaves at six o'clock.
- I have to catch a train leaving at six o'clock.
- I was disgusted by the poorness of the meal. I refused to pay the bill.
- Disgusted by the poorness of the meal, I refused to pay the bill.
- I had tea. Then I watched television.
- Having had tea, I watched television.
  (Or, After I had had tea, . . . or, After tea, . . .)
- I wrote to the company. I wanted to ask them if they had any vacancies.
- I wrote to the company to ask them if they had any vacancies.
- I was leaving the cinema. Then I saw my friend.
- On leaving the cinema, I saw my friend.

When one uses participles, care should be taken to ensure that what is written makes sense. The action described by the participle should be that performed by the subject of the sentence. The use of unrelated or misrelated participles sometimes has unfortunate results. For example:

- Coming out of the cinema, a taxi drew up.
- Being a wet day, I took my umbrella.
- Passing the workhouse, his eyes encountered the bill on the gate. (Charles Dickens' *Oliver Twist*.)
- If selected for an audition, we should defray your expenses. (Letter from the BBC.)
- Shopping in the town centre, a dog bit me on the ankle.
- Having inspected our records, you owe us £5.
- Having bought this magazine, I hope you will enjoy it. (Remark by the Editor of *Nottingham University Rag Magazine*.)
- Rounding the bend at 35 m.p.h., the "Red Lion" came into view.
- Walking up the street, the house numbers went from 2 to 60.
- Cautiously opening the cupboard door, a skeleton toppled out.
- Having refunded the £10 m. to the trade unions, their answer could hardly be unequivocal. (*Daily Telegraph*.)

It should in fairness be said that the intended meaning of most of these sentences is clear enough and that in the eighteenth and nineteenth centuries very great authors occasionally used participles in this rather casual way.

Conclusion

Much of what has been said so far will seem obvious to many of the people who read this book. Moreover, as suggested earlier, the account of how sentences may be formed and combined may seem to them unrealistic, and it will certainly seem incomplete.

The fact is that most people who do a good deal of reading usually have no difficulty in writing in sentences, since they are used to *seeing* sentences; and they are probably familiar with a wide variety of sentence-patterns — those with multiple subjects, for example. The exercises which start on page 10 will probably be child's play to them.

There are many other benefits to be got from reading: a

knowledge of the main grammatical rules, improved spelling, an understanding of the function of punctuation, an ever-widening vocabulary (i.e. the words that one knows exactly how to use) including many quite common words which are nevertheless not used very often in speech, a knowledge of what sorts of expression are acceptable in the written language; the realization that when we write we should say exactly what we mean and not be content with a vague approximation; and an appreciation of tone and style.

Now certainly there are people who do a large amount of reading but who, for one reason or another, never develop the ability to express themselves well in writing. It cannot be said that if one reads well one will certainly write well. What, however, is certain is that those who never read or who read very little or whose reading is restricted to those publications which are written in short sentences and simple words will never derive any of the benefits mentioned above. This is because their experience of language is mainly experience of conversation.

When we talk we usually talk in short sentences, fragments of sentences, interrupted sentences and sentences which start by following one pattern and finish in another; we use too few words or too many; and because we can rely on our listeners' knowledge of the situation in which the conversation is taking place and can communicate by gestures and facial expressions and tone of voice we often say things which if written down would seem utter nonsense. We often have to have several "goes" at expressing our meaning because we have little time to prepare what we want to say.

Clearly, this is no kind of practice for written composition, for clear communication in writing. Even those who are most adept at expressing their meaning clearly and vigorously in speech will never acquire any proficiency in written composition unless they read widely, attentively and often.

Exercises in synthesis (combining sentences)

The following should perhaps be regarded not as exercises but as tests, tests of skill in sentence construction — skill acquired by reading and developed by practice in writing. As exercises, i.e. as ways of improving written composition, their value is limited.

1. Rewrite the following passage in not more than three sentences, without using "and" or "but" or "so".

Iceland is an island. It is volcanic. It lies in the North Atlantic Ocean. The area of Iceland is 40,000 square miles. The population is 200,000. Iceland was uninhabited before the 9th century. Then settlers came from Norway. Norway claimed authority there. For some centuries it was governed by Denmark. In 1944 Iceland became an independent republic. The main industry is fishing.

2. In each of the following combine the groups of short sentences into one good sentence. Do not use "and", "but", "so", "then", "therefore". You may change the order of the sentences, but do not change the meaning.

(a) I reached the river. It is near a little town. I was very frightened. I nearly trod on a snake. It was very large. It was crawling across the road. It had evidently been injured.

(b) Harry was deserted by his family. One brother did not desert him. He badly needed help. He did not despair.

3. Show your skill at sentence structure by combining the following, in the most suitable way:

The herring is a genus of fish. It is allied to the sprat. It is found near the land. This is in the North Atlantic area. It is not found in the Mediterranean. There are about sixty species. Most are available as food. The common herring is found in schools. These swim near the surface. They move constantly. They go from place to place. They are following their food. There is a result. Herring fishery is uncertain. A good fishing area may be suddenly deserted. There may seem to be no reason for this. The herring feeds on minute creatures. It filters them out of the water. It does this by gill-rakers. These are at the side of the throat. They act like a kind of sieve. The baleen of the whale acts in the same way.

(Royal Society of Arts, English Language II, 1963.)

4. Reduce the following passage to eight or fewer sentences:

The streamer-tail is the most beautiful bird in Jamaica. Some people say it is the most beautiful bird in the world.

11

It is also called the doctor humming bird. The cock bird is about nine inches long. Seven inches of it however are tail. The tail consists of two long feathers. They are black. The feathers curve across each other. The inner edges of the feathers are in the form of a scalloped design. The bird's head and crest are black. Its wings are dark green. The long bill is scarlet. The eyes are black. They are bright and confiding. The body is green. It is emerald coloured. The green is a dazzling green. Consequently, when the sun is on the breast you see the brightest green thing in nature. In Jamaica, birds that are loved are given nicknames. *Trochilus polytmus* is called "doctor bird". He is called "doctor bird" because his two streamers remind people of a black tail-coat. Black tail-coats were worn by old-time physicians.

(Adapted from *For Your Eyes Only* (a James Bond story) by Ian Fleming.)

5. Expand the following notes into a passage of good connected English:

Roman Britain

Latin name for Britain — Britannia. Regarded as mysterious island by Romans. Rumoured to be rich in minerals. Julius Caesar invaded S.E. Britain 55 BC. Left following year. Caligula considered invading Britain. Emperor Claudius began conquest AD 43. Island gradually conquered — most of it. Fierce resistance from some tribes. Overcome in time. Britons adopted Roman ways. Wall built by Hadrian. To keep out Picts and Scots. Built about AD 122—8. Later another barrier further north — called Antonine Wall. Most of Britain part of Roman Empire for over three centuries.

6. Rewrite the following passage in longer sentences so that the jerky effect is eliminated:

More slimmers are turning to drugs to lose weight. And taking astonishing trouble to get them. Often at the taxpayer's expense.

Women are getting hooked on slimming pills.

Doctors have been asked by the Health Department to cut down on the prescribing of anti-obesity medicines.

Not because of the cost. Because of what the drugs can do to a patient if they are not used sensibly.

In Italy, all but one kind of slimming drug — the ones containing fenfluramine — are banned.

Doctors there feel they are too dangerous to prescribe.

By comparison, Britain is a slimmer's pill paradise. It is too easy to get the drugs.

(From an article in a popular British newspaper.)

7. Use all of the following information to compose an article in continuous sentences on the city of Munich.

Munich — city in Germany — next in size to Berlin and Hamburg — situated S.E. of the country — stands on the R. Isar — about 1700 feet above sea level — flourished during 19th century — many institutions founded then for the encouragement of the arts and sciences — Nazi movement began there after World War I — suffered severely from bombing in World War II — facade of new town hall untouched — cathedral in Munich one of the largest Gothic churches in Germany — many parks and gardens in city — many new buildings now erected — centre of road, rail and air communications — site of Olympic Games 1972 — World Cup 1974 — pop. 950,000.

(English Language Ordinary Level Syll. 1, Associated Examining Board.)

8. Rewrite the following passage, incorporating all the information but using no more than EIGHT sentences:

The first English canal was the Sankey Brook Navigation. This was opened in 1757. It enabled coal to be carried by water from St Helens to Liverpool. But it was another canal which awakened public interest. This was the Bridgewater Canal. It ran from Worsley to Manchester. It was opened in 1761. The Duke of Bridgewater was a wealthy nobleman. He had been jilted. He wanted to forget his sorrows. To do this he turned his energies to business. He owned some collieries at Worsley. Worsley is seven miles from Manchester. The cost of carrying coal on horseback for seven miles was high. Therefore it was difficult to find customers. It was decided to cut a canal. The engineer was James Brindley. Brindley was illiterate. He was a Derbyshire millwright. He was also a genius. His canal was a masterpiece. It was immediately successful in its commercial purpose. The price of coal in Manchester fell by a half.

Fused and non-sentences

If you can see what is wrong with the following you probably have no difficulty in writing in complete sentences.

1. It is raining therefore we cannot play tennis.
2. In reply to your letter of March 17th, in which you applied for the post of Clerical Assistant.
3. Hoping to hear from you soon.
4. Miles of golden sands. Unspoilt countryside. A marvellous night-life. All these you will find. In Biarritz.
5. Haven't I seen you before, I seem to recognize your face, I'm sure we've met before.
6. Statistical evidence cannot be invalidated by a few startling exceptions, this is what many people do not realize, they think that if one heavy smoker lives to 100 it's all right for everyone to smoke.
7. Potatoes have gone up again, however I hear that they are coming down soon.
8. All I could see now of the holiday makers were their empty Coca Cola cans left stranded on the beach, somehow even these empty tin-cans seemed to fit into this beautiful place. (From a student's essay.)
9. I am nineteen years old and will be leaving college at the end of August after completing a three-year course in Retailing and I am taking four examinations in June and July, I do already have four "O" levels and eight C.S.E. exams from school, they are as follows:
10. Come here, I want to talk to you.
11. As an alternative to a house, perhaps you might like to consider a flat, we have a number of very reasonably priced flats on our register of properties. (From a letter written by a mature student.)
12. Our bank manager has informed us that he will not be selling any beers or spirits, for our part we have promised not to cash cheques or open a loan department. (Sign in a public house.)

Parts of speech

It could be reasonably said that even at a time when the teaching of formal grammar is in decline a knowledge of the four main types of words should be part of most people's general knowledge. Read the following passage:

Why the founders of St Merryn's Hospital chose to erect their institution at a main road crossing upon a valuable office-site and thus expose their patients' nerves to constant laceration, is a foible that I never properly understood. But for those fortunate enough to be suffering from complaints unaffected by the wear and tear of continuous traffic, it did have the advantage that one could lie abed and still not be out of touch, so to speak, with the flow of life. Customarily the west-bound buses thundered along trying to beat the lights at the corner; as often as not a pig-squeal of brakes and a salvo of shots from the silencer would tell that they hadn't. Then the released cross-traffic would rev. and roar as it started up the incline. And every now and then there would be an interlude: a good grinding bump, followed by a general stoppage — exceedingly tantalizing to one in my condition where the extent of the contretemps had to be judged entirely by the degree of profanity resulting. Certainly, neither by day nor during most of the night, was there any chance of a St Merryn patient being under the impression that the common round had stopped just because he, personally, was on the shelf for the moment.

(From *The Day of the Triffids* by John Wyndham.)

1. Pick out the fifteen finite (complete) verbs from the passage.
2. Pick out forty nouns.
3. Pick out ten adjectives.
4. Pick out eight adverbs.

Supplementary questions

1. Identify five metaphors from the above passage and explain why they are effective (consult Chapter 13).
2. Consult a good dictionary to find the derivation of "tantalize".

Definitions

In some examinations candidates (i.e. people taking the examination) are asked to write one-sentence definitions. These questions are sometimes tests of general knowledge but they **are** always tests of the ability to think clearly and carefully and of the ability to recognize a sentence.

To give a definition of something is to say what it is. The following are examples of one-sentence definitions:

1. A vacuum flask is a container for keeping drinks hot.
2. A saw is a tool for cutting wood.
3. A motorway is a dual-carriageway multi-lane highway linking major cities but by-passing towns and villages, to which however access is provided by means of minor roads.
4. A helicopter is an aircraft which can ascend and descend vertically and can hover in mid-air as well as fly horizontally.
5. Camouflage is a means of disguising something in such a way that it cannot be easily distinguished from its background.

Have you any criticisms to make of any of these five definitions?

1. Taking care to be as precise as possible, so that there is only one thing to which each definition can apply, write one-sentence definitions of each of the following:

  1. A thermometer
  2. A colander
  3. A ballpoint pen.
  4. An electric switch
  5. A typewriter
  6. A drawing pin
  7. A press-conference
  8. A menu
  9. Sociology
  10. The Commonwealth
  11. The Common Market
  12. Socialism
  13. Patriotism
  14. Cosmetics
  15. A package tour.

2. Use all the facts in the following notes to write a *one-sentence* definition of a saw:

  implement — usually of steel — worked by hand — or

mechanically — with variously shaped blade or edge — has teeth — teeth of various forms — these are cut in or attached to it — for dividing wood, metal, stone, etc. — by reciprocating motion — or rotatory motion.

3. The following are expressions in everyday use. Choose *four* and give their meanings as precisely as you can. Write the expression and beside it the meaning, using not more than two complete sentences.

    a cartridge pen
    a dual carriageway
    an articulated lorry
    a chain store
    a picture window
    a concertina crash
    a social worker
    a general election
    a service road

(Royal Society of Arts English Language Stage I.)

Remarks and advice on definitions

1. It must be remembered that vagueness should be avoided. For example:

- A helicopter is an aircraft.
- A bicycle is a two-wheeled vehicle.
- A jumbo-jet is an aeroplane.
- A jumbo-jet is a very large aeroplane.
- Hi-jacking is a type of crime.
- A typewriter is a printing machine.

2. Definition by example is neither permissible nor possible. For example:

    Define "monarch".
    Queen Elizabeth II is a monarch.

3. Subjective language (i.e. language which indicates the attitude of the writer to the thing defined) should not be used. For example:

- A transistor-radio is a diabolical piece of equipment used by teenagers to annoy their elders. (This is not a definition in any case.)
- Oats. A grain, which in England is generally given to

17

horses, but in Scotland supports the people. (This definition found in Dr Johnson's *Dictionary of the English Language* has two faults: it is a comment rather than an adequate definition, and it is a joke.)

4. Although subjective language should not be used, certain opinions shared by most people may be implied. For example:
- Astrology is the so-called science of telling the future from the stars.
- Cosmetics are substances which are used by women with the intention of enhancing the natural attractions of their faces.

5. It will have been noted from 3 above that a dictionary definition does not form a sentence. For example:
- Cat. Small domesticated carnivorous quadruped. (*Concise Oxford Dictionary*.)

In an examination this definition would have to appear in the form:
- A cat is a small domesticated carnivorous quadruped.

But it might not get full marks!

6. The following definition is factually approximately correct but grammatically unsound:
- A monopoly is when a company has total control of the market.

A noun cannot be *when* anything. It can only be *something*. The correct form is:
- A monopoly is total control of the market by one company.

However, although the form is correct, as a full definition it is unsatisfactory.

7. All definitions are in a sense *technical*. However, there is a type of technical definition which is an exact specification. Technical definitions of this sort are often required for legal, administrative or academic reasons, especially when people have widely differing notions of the meaning of an expression Hence, some sociologists define social classes in terms of income — a dubious criterion.

In retailing, a supermarket cannot merely be defined as a large self-service store; it has been arbitrarily defined as a store which has a certain minimum floor space. In the industrial legislation of the nineteenth century a workshop was defined as an industrial establishment where fewer than fifty workers were employed while a factory was defined as a place where fifty or more workers were employed. The car ferry companies define the length of a car as the distance from the front bumper to the rear bumper to save motorists the trouble of removing their bumpers for the voyage and claiming a lower rate!

In fact it could be maintained that definitions of this sort are not statements of what things are but of what a number of people, for very good practical reasons, have agreed them to be.

8. Somewhat similarly, the writer of an essay might state his own definition of a term for the sake of clarity, e.g. "What I mean by 'working class' is those people with incomes of less than £1,600 a year."

9. A great deal of confusion and misunderstanding is caused by the failure or refusal of people to define the terms they use, particularly when these are abstract nouns, like "love", "democracy" and "fascism".

Chapter 2

Sentence improvement

A.

Few people would criticize any of the following statements if they were made in conversation but to a thoughtful reader they will seem illogical. Although the intended meaning of the sentences is clear enough, they demonstrate the fact that written language cannot be merely a written version of speech. In a sense, spoken language is incomplete; but written language must be complete in every way.

1. If you want some more cakes, there are some in the cupboard.
2. Smoking is, when you think about it, a disgusting habit.
3. If you would like to call on us to inspect our latest models, our showrooms are open from 8 a.m. until 5 p.m.
4. Oh, yes, it's raining because that man has put up his umbrella.
5. That horse is running well, when you consider she's only recently recovered from a fetlock injury.
6. If you would care to invite me to an interview, I finish work at midday on Tuesdays and Fridays.
7. I am pleased to inform you that the property is still available if you are still interested.
8. If anyone has any problems the Tourist Information Centre is just round the corner.

9. He's very rich — because he has just bought a brand-new Rolls-Royce.
10. When you consider the size of Australia, Britain is a very small country.

B.

Few people would criticize any of the following sentences if they were used in conversation, for the intended meaning is clear enough, but each sentence has a word or words missing. Write out the sentences in the full form required in writing or formal speech.

1. I don't eat Sundays.
2. Monday we went to the seaside.
3. The cheeses of England are almost as good as France.
4. You can buy a second-hand bicycle for four tankfuls of petrol.
5. Temperatures will be higher than yesterday.
6. You appear to have an IQ of 148, which is higher than 98% of the population. (From a letter sent out by the secretary of a club for intellectuals.)
7. I never have and do not want to visit him.
8. In the past and even today in some countries women were not allowed to vote.
9. He is so handsome, all the girls fall in love with him. (Put a word in place of the comma.)
10. The manageress told me that there was nothing she could do about it and I would have to refer my complaint to you. (Insert one word.)
11. The dates I am available for interview are June 9th to June 27th, any weekday.
12. The reason she resigned was she was annoyed at not being promoted.
13. After stirring well until fairly stiff, stand in a moderate oven (regulo 3) for three hours.
14. If, when clear in your opinion, you do not bother to write everything you will not develop an ability to communicate efficiently in writing and could sometimes have unfortunate results.
15. In reply to your letter of 27th November the house you were enquiring about is still available.
16. The lounge is 18 feet.

17. The accommodation is similar to the house mentioned earlier.

C.

We talk about sentence construction and sentence structure because sentences have to be planned and built so that they will carry the intended meaning. It is an essential part of this planning and building to make sure that the words in a sentence come in the best possible order and in particular to make sure that words are as close as possible to the words they "go with", e.g. adverbs should not be too far from the verbs they belong to. Readers should not be expected to sort out sentences for themselves.

Improve the organization of the following sentences:

1. Extra lessons in reading will be given to those who are slow learners from 6.00 p.m. until 7.00 p.m.
2. I was very interested in your article on country walks in the local paper.
3. He comes down on anyone breaking windows with a heavy hand.
4. The shop assistant who had served me could not understand what I meant so when the manageress appeared I explained what had happened to her.
5. After listening to my complaint, the manageress asked me to leave the shop in a not very polite way.
6. She was born and brought up in Germany but she teaches French, strangely enough.
7. I only looked at the television for five minutes.
8. I saw a man clambering over the side of the schooner through my telescope which was anchored in the bay.
9. I enclose the completed application form (Ref. AP7) together with a stamped and addressed envelope, which I trust you will consider very carefully.
10. Joseph II of Austria was as long as his mother, Maria Theresa, was alive prevented from taking any active part in government.
11. A professional is someone who does something for a living which he has been trained to do. (A student's definition of a professional.)
12. Perhaps the most important problem which we should

take into consideration in the course of this enquiry faced by school-leavers is that of deciding on a career.

13. Police have recovered a large consignment of wines and spirits recently stolen from a warehouse in Kent as a result of an announcement in this newspaper.

14. He not only represented England at football but also at cricket.

15. Slightly loosen the wheel nuts, after first making sure that the brake is on, with the spanner provided.

16. He is a very unorthodox player and has almost broken every rule in the book.

17. Packages containing perishable items such as cakes and fruit are stamped with the last date on which they may be sold by a member of the supermarket staff.

18. He lives in Switzerland half-way up a mountain in a small hotel for half the year.

19. He was not admired for his good looks but for his money. (Improve the sentence by changing the position of "not".)

20. For sale: 1975 AMC 2-litre convertible, as new, carefully cherished by lady-owner, with twin-carburettors.

D.

It is advisable to avoid inconsistency within sentences. Rewrite the following sentences, removing inconsistencies:

1. Two main causes of the Crimean War were that Great Britain wanted to protect Turkey and Napoleon III's desire for military prestige.

2. There are three qualities which every secretary should have: efficiency, courtesy and she should always be punctual.

3. The chief aim of sport is to get exercise and at the same time enjoying oneself.

4. If you are successful in your application you would find yourself in a new and exciting environment.

5. The reason he arrived late was that his car would not start and because the buses were not running on time.

6. We are in receipt of your letter dated March 9th and for your completed application form.

7. Check the level of the fluid in the batteries, and if the

fluid is not covering the plates the batteries should be topped up with distilled water.

8. After one has chosen a hotel because it is supposed to be only a few minutes' walk from the sea you often find that it is over a mile to the sea.
9. It would cost you less to avoid claiming under your policy and paying the Third Party claim yourself.
10. The Government has outlined its plans for regional devolution and they say that the proposed legislation will satisfy everyone.
11. Our prices for off-season tours range from £50 and the maximum is £75.
12. I prefer tea to coffee and beer better than wine.
13. Your starting salary will be between £2,900—£3,600.
14. I should be obliged if you will answer by return of post.
15. "Affluence" means "to be rich".
16. "Look before you leap" means "cautious inspection of the situation is advisable before action is taken".
17. He said that the three main causes of World War I were Germany's aggressive policy, "Weltpolitik" as it was called, Russo—Austrian rivalry in the Balkans; also England and Germany were rivals in naval matters.
18. The commonest revolution speeds for records are thirty-three and a third r.p.m., seventy-eight, and 45.
19. He ordered him to leave the class and that he should not attend again.
20. It is recommended that he be promoted and his salary should be raised from £4,000 per annum to £4,800 a year.

E.

The following sentences are, for various reasons, too long. Rewrite them concisely.

1. In the nineteenth century many very young babies died in infancy.
2. He was the author not only of novels but also of text-books as well.
3. The money resources will not be adequate enough to pay for the cost of reconstruction.
4. As you know, a house rarely depreciates in value.

5. Sir Alec and the Soviet Foreign Minister have had their first face-to-face confrontation since the expulsion of the hundred Russians but it is clearly obvious that neither wishes to escalate or exacerbate the situation.

6. Finally and in conclusion I should like to finish by thanking the ladies for their help in preparing the teas and by expressing my gratitude to them for performing this task.

7. One's chances of successfully passing that examination depend less on diligence, industry and hard work than on intelligence and knowledge factors.

8. There is a very real danger that food prices will in the future rise to a level higher than that prevailing at present.

9. The imminent announcement of their engagement will be made soon.

10. I shall consult with my executive committee.

11. The necessity for modernization of plant is plainly obvious and is indeed essential.

12. At this moment in time there is little to suggest any indication of a significant downturn in prices or of any appreciable fall in them.

13. We must strive to do our utmost to achieve racial harmony between ethnic groups.

14. Thank you for your letter of July 27th, which we hereby acknowledge.

15. I enclose within a photostat copy of the agreement.

16. With regard to my own personal opinion I am inclined to take the view that the effect of the accident caused his loss of confidence.

17. The amount of tax paid usually amounts in total more often than not to round about 40% of gross income.

18. Older-type houses are usually less expensive than modern-day ones.

19. It takes a very long period of time for a European to acquire a working knowledge of Chinese, for it is a language of a very difficult character.

20. At football matches differences of opinion sometimes lead to fight situations. (This sentence, like so many "situation" sentences, is of uncertain meaning. If the writer meant that arguments at football matches some-times lead to fights then the sentence is too long; if he

meant that arguments at football matches sometimes
lead to situations in which fights might occur, it is too
short.)

F.

Rewrite the following in such a way that what is presumably
the intended meaning is made clearer:

1. Kindly cane this boy.
2. Please dispose of this can thoughtfully.
3. If the baby does not thrive on fresh milk, boil it.
4. As management trainees you will be pleased to learn that
   although the course is tough the death-rate is low.
5. The herbal shampoo completely removed my greasy hair.
6. We are not certain why our product has proved unsatisfactory but if you will return the defective tea-pot to us
   we will do our best to look into it.
7. We've heard some news about Freddie Trueman's injured
   finger. Denis Compton's just come in with it. (Test
   Match Commentary.)
8. Post-mortems have revealed that the riot, which involved
   no serious injuries, was started by a difference of opinion
   between two drunken spectators.
9. He paid no attention to what I was saying as he was too
   busy looking for the football in the *News of the World*.
10. My aunt hasn't been too well lately and has been in bed
    with the doctor for a week.
11. The dent was caused when I was reversing the vehicle
    into a parking-space that was not there.
12. I shall be glad if you will replace me with a bar of
    chocolate.
13. State length of residence in Australia.
14. I am writing to complain to you about the disgusting
    state in which I received one of your products.
15. I was horrified to find that only half of the packet of tea
    had been filled.
16. The Government are not unaware of the very real need
    to improve the unemployment situation before a not too
    considerable period of time has elapsed.
17. We are not as of now currently engaged in any funda-
    mental re-thinking of our policy *vis-à-vis* the Soviets.

18. I want to suggest that losses on public undertakings can be justified, can be desirable for their own sake, and need not be synonymous with efficiency.
19. Nervously opening the cupboard, a corpse in an advanced state of decomposition fell out.
20. The population of London is the same as that of Sweden.

Chapter 3

Reported speech

Just as a character in one of Molière's plays was astonished and impressed to learn that he had been speaking prose all his life, many people might be surprised to learn that they constantly use *reported speech* — that is to say, they supply in writing or speech reported versions of what people have said. For example:

- Old Smithy says he wants to see you in his office.
- Dad said he'd be in late tonight.
- She told me she'd be arriving on the following day.
- I simply remarked that she looked rather charming in that hat.
- The President-elect declared that foreign affairs would be his first priority.

Reporting what others (or we ourselves) have said at an earlier time and perhaps in another place is in fact something which causes us no difficulty at all: although we may break some traditional grammatical rules, we are not likely to get the verb tenses wrong. Only students learning English as a foreign language would be likely to write, for example, the following:

- At eleven thirty this morning he asked me if I will marry him. He said that he has admired me for a long time.

Consequently, it is surprising that many students find difficulty with traditional Reported Speech exercises. Perhaps they are put off both by the term "Reported Speech" (or by the alternative and less suitable "Indirect Speech") and by the detailed rules unnecessarily supplied in some textbooks about changing tenses, rules which only foreigners should need to learn.

At any rate, many students when confronted by some such instruction as "Rewrite the following conversation in reported speech" seem to think that they are being called upon to do a sort of translation exercise totally divorced from anything with which they are familiar in their everyday lives. But the simple truth is that as long as they imagine themselves as reporting what someone has said they should not encounter many serious difficulties.

Examples:

Direct speech:	"I'm going out to do some shopping," said Mrs Smith.
Reported speech:	Mrs Smith said that she was going out to do some shopping.
Direct speech:	"Where are you going and why are you in such a hurry?" Mr Brown asked his son.
Reported speech:	Mr Brown asked his son where he was going and why he was in such a hurry.
Direct speech:	"When *I* use a word," Humpty Dumpty said in rather a scornful tone, "it means just what I choose it to mean — neither more nor less."
	"The question is," said Alice, "whether you *can* make words mean different things."
Reported speech:	Humpty Dumpty said in rather a scornful tone that when *he* used a word it meant just what he chose it to mean — neither more nor less.
	Alice retorted that the question was whether one *could* make words mean different things.

(Note that an interesting discussion could develop on whether the retention of "neither more nor less" in its original form and in its original position is justified.)

Even such simple examples may suggest that adjustments (apart from changes in pronouns and verb tenses, which come to us naturally) sometimes have to be made for the reported speech versions. It should be remembered moreover, that most written language, certainly the written language expected by examiners, differs from spoken language, whether it is spoken language which we hear or spoken language indicated on paper by quotation marks.

The sentence pattern used by a speaker may not be suitable for the written version; and indeed, as anyone who has read the transcript of a tape-recorded conversation will know, we often do not speak in well-organized and "complete" sentences, sometimes because we cannot be bothered or because we have insufficient time but more often because there is no need to. Consequently it may be necessary not only to exercise our skill in sentence construction to achieve a suitable written version but also to perceive that a single spoken word or short phrase may in fact represent a whole sentence. For example:

"That girl I told you about. The one I met last night. With the red hair. She was extremely attractive."

"Look, Brian! I'm not interested," replied his friend. "Whatever colour her hair was."

Brian told his friend that the girl with the red hair whom he had met on the previous evening and whom he had told his friend about was extremely attractive.

His friend replied with some impatience that whatever the colour of her hair he was not interested.

On the other hand, when one is supplying a reported speech version of a number of long rambling spoken sentences or when one is rewriting a piece of oratory in reported speech it may well be advisable, to avoid unwieldiness, to use more sentences than the speaker has used.

"We shall not flag or fail. We shall fight in France, we shall fight on the seas and oceans, we shall fight with growing confidence and growing strength in the air, we shall defend our island, whatever the cost may be, we shall fight on the beaches, we shall fight on the landing grounds, we shall fight in the fields and in the streets, we shall fight in the hills; we shall never surrender."
(Winston Churchill — June 4th, 1940.)

In a speech he made on June 4th, 1940, Winston Churchill declared that the British would not flag or fail. He said that they would fight in France and on the seas and oceans. He said that they would fight with growing confidence and strength in the air; and that they would defend their island, whatever the cost might be. They would fight on the beaches and on the landing grounds; and in the fields, in the streets and in the hills. He affirmed that Britain would never surrender.

There could be other reported speech versions accurately conveying what was said. A much shorter, though complete, version could be devised but it would not convey the tone of the original.

We may note here that the constant repetition of "said" should be avoided, and that the "stating" verb (*He declared, He went on to say*, etc.) may occasionally be missed out — though never in the first or last sentences of the reported version. Note: "They would fight . . ."

Inclusion of "that" after the leading verb

It is still a rule or at least a custom of written and carefully spoken English that the leading verb (*stated, added, said, remarked, replied*, etc.) should be followed by "that". For example:

- He said, "The project has not yet been completed but it will be by next year."
- He said *that* the project had not yet been completed but *that* it would be by the following year.

Note the use of "that" after the conjunction "but": once it has been decided to use "that" at the start of the first noun clause "that" should be used consistently. This is good style and sometimes makes for clarity. For example:

He said that she was beautiful and that he wanted to marry her.

Conversational abbreviations

Colloquial abbreviations (*couldn't, shan't, he'd've*, etc.) should be converted to the full form. One should constantly keep in mind the "completeness" of the written language. For example:

- She said, "I'd wanted to leave Saturday."
- She said that she had wanted to leave on Saturday.
- "There's no point in your doing it if you aren't interested", she told her brother.
- She told her brother that there was no point in his doing it if he was not interested.

Other colloquialisms

Even in the traditional reported speech examination question, where it is normal to follow the original spoken version closely, it may be advisable to convert slang and other language not usually found in writing to an acceptable written form. In examinations in fact this problem does not often arise — or there may be instructions which expressly state that suitable language is to be used. For example:

- "I've just about had a bellyful of this job," he exclaimed, "and I've a good mind to chuck it in!"
- He exclaimed that he was thoroughly disgusted with his job and that he was seriously thinking of resigning.

"Good Morning", "Hi!", "Ugh!", etc.

He said hello, he said goodbye are probably permissible in reported speech. *He wished me good morning*, etc., implies too much goodwill and *he bade me farewell* is old-fashioned. *Greeted* and *said goodbye*, etc., are probably the best versions. We should try to convey the force of interjections. For example, for "Ugh!" we have to write *uttered an exclamation of distaste* or *expressed his distaste*.

Using adverbs to convey a speaker's mood or manner

Adverbs can be used in the reported version to convey the mood of the speaker. For example:

- "Get out of here, you fool!" she shouted.
- She loudly, rudely and insultingly ordered him to leave.

At other times we might use *affectionately*, *kindly*, *politely*, *respectfully*, etc.

"Well — er — I'm not — er ..." suggests *hesitantly* or *nervously*. At other times we might use *emphatically*, *confidingly* or whatever.

Ambiguity of pronouns

In reported speech it is sometimes not clear who "he" or "she" is. All that can be done is to insert a name where necessary. For example:

- George told Bill that he had told Mike that he, Mike, would not be playing on the following Saturday.

When a thing is referred to by name only once in a conversation and is thereafter represented by several "it"'s it is good practice to remind the reader occasionally what "it" refers to, by using the noun instead of the pronoun.

Three other points concerning the reported speech question should be noted:

1. *All* the meaning of the original must be accounted for. For example:

"I am pleased to tell you that you have been accepted for the special course," said the Personnel Officer.

Wrong: The Personnel Officer told the applicant that he had been accepted for the special course.

2. Reported speech may be combined with other material. For example:

As she turned to go he caught her by the arm and, looking at her sternly, told her that she was not to go yet as there was something he wanted to ask her.

3. When some people give an oral account of a conversation and wish their account to be vivid, instead of using the conventional reported speech form they supply a sort of "echoed" version of the original conversation. This should *not* be done in formal writing. For example:

"So he said didn't I think the music was simply marvellous and I said no, I didn't, so he said well didn't I think I could grow to like it in time and I said no, no way."

All of the foregoing has been concerned with the traditional reported speech examination question (which appears less often than in the past), although much of the advice applies to reported speech in general. Reported speech questions are valuable exercises in written composition as they enable us to practise and test our skill in expressing meaning in an acceptable written form and at constructing sentences. The more difficult of such exercises may help us to see some of the major differences between written and spoken language, and this should help us to write more efficiently.

Yet although undoubtedly valuable, they may seem unrelated to the real world, since they usually demand that we follow the original wording as closely as possible. Sometimes of course in our everyday lives we may wish to draw attention to a speaker's actual .words but then we quote, using either a special tone of voice or quotation marks. For example:

I didn't say "You're a fool"; I said, "You're *behaving* like a fool." When charged, the accused stated: "It's a put up job. I was in Newcastle when they done the Brighton job."

But on most occasions we simply report, in any words which will do the job, what someone has said or written. We do this when summarizing passages written in the first person ("I"), when writing-up the minutes of meetings and sometimes in report-writing.

When summarizing a passage written in the first person, we use reported speech to make it clear that we are presenting the author's views and not ours. For example: "The author states that . . .", "The author maintains that . . .". As in the reported version of a long speech there is no need to remind our readers of this in every sentence.

Minute-taking

At Committee meetings the Secretary will note down the essentials of what every speaker says and note which points have been emphasized and repeated time and time again and then write-up an accurate and complete account of the discussions (The Chairman said that . . . Mr Smith suggested . . ., Miss Jones emphasized the need for . . .) in clear and correct sentences of her or his construction, free of any expressions not acceptable in formal written English and with repetitions and circumlocutory "waffle" eliminated. When they are not able to practise at real meetings and have instead a printed version of a discussion set out before them like a play, secretarial students occasionally find it difficult to pretend that they are reporting a real-life discussion and slip out of reported speech into the first person, e.g. "The Chairman strongly emphasized the need for economy and said I am hoping to save £50 this month . .". If one thinks of oneself as a reporter, no such mistakes should occur.

In report-writing statements, remarks, etc., used as evidence (e.g. *the Personnel Manager stated that . . .*) are expressed in reported speech, except when the reporter considers that the actual words used have special significance and should therefore be quoted.

Exercises

1. Rewrite the following short conversation in reported speech:
   "Where're you going for your holidays next year?" Mary asked Sue.

   "Well," replied Sue, "Henry wants to tour Scotland, but I don't much like the idea of touring. Travelling from one hotel to another in a day is not my idea of relaxation. I'd prefer to stay in one place for a fortnight — and I certainly don't want to travel as far as Scotland. Sussex would do fine."

   I must say I agree with you," replied her friend. "These husbands are always wanting to drive all over the place when all we want to do is put our feet up."

2. Give an account of the following in reported speech:
   PUBLICITY MANAGER: What about this new TV commercial? How much progress has been made with it, Mr Clarke?
   CLARKE: Well, I've stated our requirements to a couple of advertising agencies and they've promised to let me have their suggestions by Thursday week — December 2nd.
   PUBLICITY MANAGER: Well, we've got to get a move on, you know. I want the campaign to start early in the New Year.
   CLARKE: I realise that, Mr Thornton, and I'm doing all I can to hurry them up.

3. The following is a short extract from "Night Must Fall", a play by Emlyn Williams. Write an account of the conversation in reported speech, making any adjustments you consider necessary but conveying every scrap of meaning. The italicized stage directions should, in suitable form, be incorporated in your account.
   DAN: You wouldn't be bad looking without them glasses.
   OLIVIA: It doesn't interest me very much what I look like.
   DAN: Don't you believe it . . . (*Surveying the shavings in the hearth.*) Tch! . . . Clumsy . . . (*Looking round and seeing a newspaper lying on the table.*) Ah . . . (*He crosses to the table. Smiling, with the suspicion of a mock-bow.*) Excuse me . . . (*He unfolds the newspaper on the table and begins to whittle the stick over it.*)
   OLIVIA: You're very conceited, aren't you?

DAN (*reassuringly*):   Yes . . .

OLIVIA: And you *are* acting all the time, aren't you?

DAN (staring at her, as if astonished):   Actin'? Actin' what? (*Leaning over the table, on both arms*.) Look at the way I can look you in the eyes. I'll stare you out. . . .

OLIVIA (*staring into his eyes*):   I have a theory it's the criminals who *can* look you in the eyes, and the honest people who blush and look away.

DAN (*smiling*):   Oh . . .

OLIVIA (*after a pause, challenging*):   It's a very blank look, though, isn't it?

DAN (*smiling*):   Is it?

OLIVIA: You *are* acting, aren't you?

DAN (*after a pause, in a whisper, almost joyfully*):   Yes!

OLIVIA (*fascinated*):   And what are you like when you stop acting?

DAN: I dunno, it's so long since I stopped.

4. Rewrite the following dialogue in reported (indirect) speech from *The Traveller*'s point of view, using the words that he would use if he reported the whole conversation to you. Marks will be deducted if the verb "to say" is used more than once in the reported version.

TRAVELLER: On what precise powers do you base your right to interfere with our movements?

OFFICIAL: My powers are my duties as a good citizen of the republic. And you? What are you waiting for? Show me your hands. Come on.

TRAVELLER: My hands? (Holding them out.)

OFFICIAL: Proper aristocrat's hands, aren't they just? *You've* never worked for your living. A duke at least, by the look of them.

TRAVELLER: Your own hands seem to be very well-kept ones, too.

OFFICIAL: Thanks, your Grace. Very clever, aren't you? Yes, a great pianist's hands, mine are. A pity I can't play. (He laughs and turns to the porter.) Collect these people's documents.

(From a Use of English paper, Cambridge Proficiency Certificate.)

5. The following is part of a discussion which took place at a

committee meeting of a local sports club. Imagine that you were the Secretary. Write an account of the discussion as it might appear in the minutes.

CHAIRMAN: Er, turning to the next item on the agenda, what about the venue for the next End-of-Season dance? I wonder if the Social Secretary has received any suggestions about this?

SOCIAL SECRETARY: Well, Mr Chairman, two places have been suggested — the ballroom of the "Red Lion" and the Carfax Hall. I have another suggestion in mind but I'll keep that till later.

CHAIRMAN: Has anyone any comment to make on the two places Alison has mentioned?

BILL SMITH: Aren't they going to work out a bit expensive? You remember we made a loss last year? If we have to fork out fifty or sixty quid for the hire of a hall and another thirty or so for a small group — plus the cost of the catering — we'll hardly break even. Even if the tickets are put up to £2.50.

SOCIAL SECRETARY: Well, yes, that's what I was thinking of. So I wondered if it wouldn't be a good idea to hold the dance here, in the Club pavilion.

SUSAN JONES: Won't it be a bit cramped?

SOCIAL SECRETARY: Oh, I don't know. Last year nobody seemed very keen on dancing anyway, and the pavilion can easily accommodate the eighty or so who are likely to attend.

CHAIRMAN: Has anyone any comments to make on the Social Secretary's suggestion?

6. Imagine that you heard the following anecdote told by Mr Jingle. Rewrite it in complete sentences in reported speech.

"Ah! you should keep dogs — fine animals — sagacious creatures — dog of my own once — pointer — surprising instinct — out shooting one day — entering enclosure — whistled — dog stopped — whistled again — Ponto — no go; stock still — called him — Ponto, Ponto — wouldn't move — dog transfixed — staring at a board — looked up, saw an inscription — 'Gamekeeper has orders to shoot all dogs found in this enclosure' — wouldn't pass it — wonderful dog — valuable dog that — very."

(From *The Pickwick Papers* by Charles Dickens.)

7. Rewrite the following passage in indirect (reported) speech.

MR HENIG (Lancaster): Will the Prime Minister introduce legislation to create a Ministry of Leisure?

PRIME MINISTER: I have no plans to do so at present. The machinery of government is kept under constant review.

MR BOYD-CARPENTER (Kingston): Is not the Secretary of State for Employment and Productivity entitled to the title in view of the fact that she has created a great deal of unwanted leisure with the highest level of sustained unemployment since the war?

PRIME MINISTER: That was the one predictable question. I have dealt with it on many occasions.

MR MORRIS (Manchester): Now that more and more people are coming here from the Common Market — (laughter) — to spend part of their leisure time at weekends shopping in Britain, fleeing from the rigours of the value-added tax and levies on food imports — (cheers and laughter) — can we have a Minister for Leisure to help with the incoming tourists?

(Associated Examining Board G.C.E. Ordinary Level, Syll. 1 Evg.)

8. Here is part of the transcript of a tape-recorded piece of spontaneous storytelling. Using the past tense and reported speech, produce a written account of what the speaker said. Great care will be needed. Start your account: *The speaker said that . . .*

The first day at school I remember they gave us some little trays with sand in and we made figures in this sand. Both my mother and father had given me good rudiments of education before I went to school. Dad used to read to me quite a lot and spell out words to me — usually in the evenings. I think I could read before I went to school, and write a little bit too, and they were quite pleased with me when I made these figures in the sand. I think there'd be about twenty-five children in the school. I have an old photograph at home of when I was in Class 3, and there's all the village boys — some of them very poorly dressed. Most of them were quite poor, their fathers were labourers. I was quite clever — a little bit outstanding really. There were no scholarships from that school because the headmaster always said he had no time to teach us.

(From *Talkshop* — a University of London Institute of Education publication.)

9. Rewrite the following in reported speech:

Fourscore and seven years ago our fathers brought forth upon this continent a new nation, conceived in liberty and dedicated to the proposition that all men are created equal. Now we are engaged in a great civil war, testing whether that nation, or any nation so conceived and so dedicated, can long endure. We are met on a great battlefield of that war. We have come to dedicate a portion of that field as a final resting-place of those who here gave their lives that that nation might live. It is altogether fitting and proper that we should do this.

(Abraham Lincoln. From the Address at Gettysburg, 19 Nov. 1863.)

10. Write a reported speech version of the following conversation between Bertram Wooster and his valet, Jeeves.

"And that's how the matter stands, Jeeves," I said. "I think we ought to rally round a trifle and help poor old Bingo put the thing through. Tell me about old Mr Little. What sort of a chap is he?"

"A somewhat curious character, sir. Since retiring from business he has become a great recluse, and now devotes himself almost entirely to the pleasures of the table."

"Greedy hog, you mean?"

"I would not, perhaps, take the liberty of describing him in precisely those terms, sir. He is what is usually called a gourmet. Very particular about what he eats, and for that reason sets a high value on Miss Watson's services."

"The cook?"

"Yes, sir."

(From *The Inimitable Jeeves* by P. G. Wodehouse.)

Chapter 4

Punctuation

We use punctuation to help us express our meaning. It is not used as a decoration. It is not added to a piece of writing. It is part of composition and should come so naturally that it would require concentration to leave it out.

The most important two functions of punctuation are to show that one has reached the end of a sentence and to indicate pauses within the sentence so that the sentence may be properly understood.

This is another way of saying that the most important punctuation marks are the full stop and the comma.

The use of the full stop   (It is not used at the end of headings.)

The full stop is used at the end of a sentence. A sentence without a full stop is incomplete.

Use five full stops to complete the punctuation of the following:

> Thank you for your letter of January 4th I must apologize for my delay in replying the goods you require will be despatched next Wednesday I trust you will find them satisfactory Smith & Company take this opportunity of extending to you their best wishes for the New Year

Full stops should also be used, but often aren't, after initials (e.g. *W. G. Grace*), and after other abbreviations, for example, *Mr., Mrs., Ltd., dept., co., etc., e.g., i.e., c.f., c., oz., B.A.C.,*

B.B.C. (Note the dual purpose served by the last full stop.)
Note: In some modern abbreviations the full stop is never used and the initial letters have become words, e.g. *NATO, ASLEF, laser, SALT, SCUBA (self-contained underwater breathing apparatus).*

The use of commas

The most important use of commas is to mark off clauses, groups of words, or single words which have been added to the main sentence and which the writer wishes the reader to notice. Accordingly, by using commas, the writer provides pauses so that the reader may note the modifications to the main sentence. Commas may also be regarded as "separators" which indicate divisions between ideas.

There are many complicated rules for the use of commas which, expressed in grammatical terms, might seem confusing. Moreover, the question of when and where commas should be used is sometimes a matter of opinion or emphasis, and where one competent writer will use a comma another competent writer may not.

The following are examples of sentences where commas should always be used:

- Population, he claimed, would eventually outpace food production.
- Having at last arrived safely, I breathed a sigh of relief.
- Thoughtfully twirling his luxuriant moustache, he asked who she was.
- Disgusted by his failure, he stormed out.
- Impoverished by two wars, the country was beset by economic difficulties.
- Although she had done very little work, she managed to pass the examination.
- The cat, which was notorious for its dishonesty, had stolen the bone.
- If you do go, be careful.
- He ran up the stairs, dashed into the bedroom, and collapsed onto the floor.
- Mainly as a result of the war, oil prices have again rocketed.
- Despite everything, he remained optimistic.
- "I don't like this book, John," he said.

- Three qualities are needed: honesty, determination, and audacity.
- It is raining, so we can't play tennis.
- In these circumstances, is it not essential in the interests of national survival to take some sort of action, however uncomfortable it may be in its immediate consequences, to curb inflation?
- The bigger they are, the harder they fall.
- The better you become at English, the more proficient you will be at shorthand.
- Firstly, I should like to say a few words on the economic situation.
- Whatever you do, don't forget it.
- However tired you are, you must persevere.
- Well, what is your problem?
- What, then, is the problem?
- Oh, what a shame!

In most of these examples, the commas show where, if we always spoke without hesitation, we would pause in speaking. A useful practice is to read aloud what we have written to see where we pause naturally. Some people suggest that commas (and full stops) represent the pauses we logically make when talking. Unfortunately, many of the pauses in our speech are not logical and in writing would more suitably be indicated by dashes. However, the suggestion is a useful one to keep in mind.

Some advice on commas

1. Commas should always separate the words in a list. These words may be nouns, adjectives, adverbs or participles. For example:

> In my pocket there is a piece of chalk, an apple, and a banana.
> She was an exquisite, beautiful, charming creature.
> Slowly, sadly, and thoughtfully, he climbed the hill.
> Kicking, screaming, and complaining, he was dragged to the door.

Commas also punctuate a list of actions. For example:

> I woke up, dressed, had breakfast, and left the house.

Note: There is, it seems, some disagreement about whether a comma should precede the final "and". In the author's opinion,

the omission of this comma seems to imply some connection between the last two items even when none exists. For example;
> He was interested in insects, birds and sports cars.

2. Commas can be used to combine a number of short sentences. For example:
> Smith had sprained his ankle, Andrews had pulled a thigh muscle, Jones had the measles, and Carter had strained his back.

3. Commas should always be used in sentences of the following type:
> Sir Robert Walpole, the first Prime Minister of England, was born in Norfolk.
> Muhammad Ali, the former Cassius Clay, is noted for his loquacity.
> Miss Smith, the Principal's secretary, is noted for her superb typing.
> He owed £25, a sum exceeding his weekly income considerably.

4. Commas should often be used at each end of the following expressions:
> Generally speaking
> strictly speaking
> however
> on the whole
> by and large
> every now and then
> therefore
> moreover
> what is more
> furthermore
> on the other hand
> among others
> for example
> for instance
> despite this
> in spite of this
> in view of this

Note: Sometimes, for reasons of style and clarity, commas should not be used with some of the above phrases. If they were always used, a glut of commas would sometimes result, and each comma would lose some of its intended significance. For example:

> Although she was, strictly speaking, ineligible for the post, her qualifications, academic and commercial, were, all things considered, excellent.

5. Commas may be used very effectively for emphasis:

> She liked, once in a while, to play cards.
> Grey Owl claimed to be a Red Indian but was, in fact, an Englishman.

6. When simple sentences are joined by *because, as, or, but* or *for*, commas may be used or omitted. On the whole, it is probably better to use them.

7. Commas may be used to show omission (words missed out).

> John was wearing full evening dress; Michael, a shirt and jeans.

8. Consider these two sentences:

> The man who succeeded Richard Nixon as President was Gerald Ford. Mr. Ford, who was born in Michigan, was sixty-two at the time.

The underlined clause in the first sentence has no comma at either end of it as it tells the reader *which* man. It is a defining clause. The clause in the second sentence does not tell us *which* Mr. Ford. It simply tells us something about him. It is non-defining. Commas are required in such a sentence.

How, in fact, would we read these sentences aloud?

If the first sentence is read out aloud, it will be seen that one does not pause in reading it. The words "The man who succeeded Richard Nixon as President" express one idea; they would not be interrupted by pauses in speech, and should not be interrupted by commas in writing.

If the second sentence is read out aloud, it will be seen that the commas do represent pauses which would occur naturally in speech. The words "who was born in Michigan" have in fact been inserted as an added remark into an already grammatically complete sentence. ("Mr. Ford was sixty-two at the time") Before and after such added remarks in speech one would naturally pause.

Here then, we find that the rule about defining and non-defining clauses (those which add remarks) is a representation of what comes naturally in speech.

Two warnings:

Do not use a comma *before* the first item in a list.

Do not use commas every time you stop to think!

Other uses of commas

1. In quoted speech. For example:

   "What on earth," he asked, "are you doing?"

   "Well, I don't like the idea of that, Albert," he said.

Note: The name of the person addressed is split off from the rest of the sentence by a comma.

2. In numbers a thousand and over. For example:

   1,924   1,987,674

3. In addresses. For example:

   27 Monastery Walk,
   Wigan,
   Lancashire

4. In dates. For example:

   24th October, 1974.

Note: A tendency in modern business correspondence is to omit the commas from addresses and *Dear Sir, faithfully,* etc., but they should be used in written examinations.

Exercises (full stops and commas)

1. Write out the following passage with full stops added:

   The First World War broke out in August 1914 Britain declared war on Germany on August 4th France, Austria-Hungary, Russia, Italy and the United States were the other major powers involved November 11th 1918 was the date on which the Armistice was signed World War One was a disaster for mankind.

2. Write out the following passage, completing the punctuation by using full stops and commas:

   William was having a strenuous time Fate was making one

of her periodic assaults on him everything went wrong Miss Drew his form mistress at school had taken an altogether misguided and unsympathetic view of his zeal for nature study in fact when the beetle which William happened to be holding lovingly in his hand as he did his sums by her desk escaped and made its way down her neck her piercing scream boded no good to William the further discovery of a caterpillar and two woodlice in his pencil-box a frog in his satchel and earwigs in his pocket annoyed her still more and William stayed in school behind his friends to write out one hundred times "I must not bring insects into school"

(From *William the Fourth* by Richmal Crompton.)

3. Write out the following letter with the punctuation completed:

Dear Sirs

The items which I ordered from you one month ago have still not arrived I am extremely annoyed by your failure to supply them as they are urgently required by one of my customers having accepted your assurance that the goods would be delivered within a week I promised my customer an old and valued client that he would be able to collect them on the date he specified

My letter of enquiry of January 1st met with no response from you other than a formal acknowledgement and an assurance that the matter was being looked into and I have received no reply at all to my letter of January 10th

Unless I receive a firm undertaking from you that the goods will be delivered in the next three days I shall be forced to cancel the order

Yours faithfully

4. Write out the following passage with the punctuation completed:

Adam Smith saluting the dawn of the new industrial age in the "Wealth of Nations" (1776) exults in the vast accretions of wealth rendered possible under a regime in which trade is free machinery general and labour minutely subdivided in his classic treatise which is the Bible of Free

Trade the sagacious Glasgow Professor discerns the tremendous economic powers latent in the British people which a system of liberty would release the sober confidence of the Scottish economist was justified in the event Free Trade paid: industrialism was a source of accumulating material prosperity; by whatever tests national wealth may be measured its progression all through the nineteenth century was unimpeded. But ninety-one years after the publication of his "Wealth of Nations" when the British capitalistic system had reached maturity and was fast spreading through Europe Karl Marx a German Jew resident in London applied his critical intelligence to the examination of its result where Smith had seen only the sunlight Marx saw only the shadows thrown upon the human scene by the unimpeded exercise of individual liberty a subdivision of labour so minute as to stunt the intelligence and empty life of the craftsman's joy an ever-widening gulf between wealth and poverty a loss of that sense of stability and permanence which was characteristic of the older forms of society and the relentless exploitation of the proletariat by their employers the picture was overdrawn and in some important respects untrue to fact; but attention was directed to serious and undoubted blemishes which if they did not justify revolution called imperiously for reform.

(From *A History of Europe* by H. A. L. Fisher.)

Capital letters

Everyone, we hope, knows that capital letters should be used at the start of sentences and for the first letters in people's names, the days of the week, the months of the year, the names of countries, cities, regions, etc., and for nationalities and languages.

It may be useful to remind students that capital letters should also be used for:

1. All the important words in titles. Particular care is required with long titles. For example:

An Enquiry into the Sources of Inequality among Men, The Concise Oxford Dictionary of Quotations, A Midsummer Night's Dream.

2. The names of official or legal documents and the titles of qualifications. For example:

> Industrial Relations Act, Deed of Covenant, General Certificate of Education, Civil Service Commission Interpretership Certificate in Russian.

3. The names of posts in companies, nationalized industries, government departments, etc. For example:

> Secretary to the Managing Director, Assistant to the Public Relations Officer, Assistant Clerk, Medical Officer, Chief Education Officer.

Particular care should be taken to observe this rule in letters of application.

4. Official titles and bodies. For example:

> The Queen, the Prime Minister, Field-Marshal, the Ministry of Social Security, the President of the United States, the House of Commons, Greater London Council, Academic and General Studies Department.

5. Trade names. For example:

> Ford Cortina, Omo, Cinzano.

Trade names that have become ordinary words are not normally given capital letters, e.g. thermos.

It should be noted that capital letters should not be used for:

1. A king, or kings in general, a prime minister or prime ministers, a chairman or chairmen in general, a secretary or secretaries . . ., etc.

2. The seasons of the year, except in poetry.

Capital letters should certainly not be used for *dutch courage, swiss roll, french windows, german measles, or venetian blinds*!

Apostrophes

It might just be possible to get along without apostrophes. Indeed, many signwriters and some companies seem determined to do just that! (Mothers Pride, Principals Car Park.)

Other people, on the other hand, seem determined to use an

apostrophe in every word ending in s, except where it is actually needed! (tomato's 20p, babies faces'). There is no need for any confusion. Apostrophes are used to:

1. Show that a letter has been missed out. For example:

It's (= It is)	o'clock
You're, They're, We're	O'Brien
I'm	He's
There's	Will-o'-the-wisp
Would've	ne'er-do-well, etc.
I'd've, etc.	

2. Show possession.

A. Where there is one owner: Before the s

a dog's life
a woman's intuition
Britain's economic problems
a butcher's
a stone's throw
an hour's delay
John's book
Ohm's Law
Woolworth's

Of course, the stone and the hour are not, strictly speaking, owners.

B. Where there is more than one owner.

Battersea Dogs' Home
"The Old Wives' Tale" is a novel.
babies' faces
five minutes' time
six months' imprisonment

Here, as you see, the apostrophe comes after the s. The following are the most important exceptions:

men's
women's
children's
People's (But not when *peoples' = nations'*)
folk's

Don't use apostrophes with *mice, oxen, geese, deer, feet, teeth* or *fish*. It is probably better to avoid using them with *conductress, princess, actress*, etc. Use *of*, e.g. *the voice of the actress was hardly audible.*

Note well:
1.   Charles' hat *or* Charles's hat
     St. James' Park *or* St. James's Park
     Hercules' strength
     Themistocles' remarks

2.   *Its* = "belonging to it". *It's* = "It is", or "It has".

3.   Gilbert and Sullivan's, Marks and Spencer's, etc.

4.   For Pete's sake, don't use apostrophes in *ours, yours, theirs, hers*. For goodness' sake, remember that.

Exercises

Write out the following sentences, inserting apostrophes only where they are necessary.
1.   Police have discovered a hoard of witches broomsticks at a local hairdressers.
2.   Mens attitudes to the Womens Liberation Movement vary enormously.
3.   The Womens Institute is only five minutes walk from the childrens playground, isnt it?
4.   Britains economic problems will still be with her in ten years time, wont they?
5.   Its fairly certain that judges know more about criminology than magistrates do.
6.   The dog was wagging its tail.
7.   The babies faces were wreathed in smiles.
8.   Foreign holidays are, generally speaking, greatly over-rated.
9.   My sister-in-laws cats lost its tail.
10.   Its obvious, isnt it, that Charles hats too big for him?

Semi-colons

It is possible to write perfectly good English without using the semi-colon at all.

Semi-colons may usefully be employed, however, to sub-divide a long list of items which fall into distinct categories. For example:

He took with him a crate of champagne, four pints of beer,

and two bottles of gin; a set of golf clubs, two tennis racquets, swimming trunks, and a cricket bat; five sweaters, six pairs of trousers . . ., etc.

"It was the Allies especially the French who were to blame with their determination to enslave the German people; the republic with its corrupt and self-seeking politicians; the money barons, the bosses of big business, the speculators and monopolists; the Reds and the Marxists, who fostered class hatred and kept the nation divided; above all . . ."

(From *A Study in Tyranny* by Alan Bullock.)

Another use of the semi-colon is illustrated by the second passage: to provide a pause between the main parts of the sentence when to use commas would produce a confusing effect. It is also used between statements which are too closely related to be separated by a full stop.

The dash

The dash is too often used as a sort of all-purpose punctuation mark. It should be used very sparingly indeed.

The main uses of the dash are as follows:

1. After a multiple subject. For example:

Punctuality, efficiency, affability — these are the qualities a secretary should possess.

"The belief in Free Trade as the secret of our vast prosperity, the unwillingness to interfere with the world commerce on which our power and wealth seemed to stand secure, the predominance of the towns over the country in numbers and still more in intellectual and political leadership, the memories of the 'hungry forties' when the Corn Laws had made bread dear for the poor — all these circumstances prevented any effort to save the rural way of life."

(From *English Social History* by G. M. Trevelyan.)

2. To interpolate a remark into a sentence which is already grammatically complete. For example:

But the most cogent reason for the decision — and this has not hitherto been mentioned — was that the military situation demanded it.

3. To emphasize an unexpected ending. For example:
> He looked at me threateningly, pulled out a revolver — and then turned and fled.

4. To enable "which" to refer to all that has gone before and not just to the word it follows. For example:
> John paid the entrance fee — which was very kind of him.

c.f.
> He failed the examination, which was silly.

with
> He failed the examination — which was silly.

5. To indicate an unfinished sentence in dialogue. For example:
> "I don't want to interfere but —"
> "Well, don't then!" she shouted.

Colons

A colon announces something, a fact or a list which the first part of the sentence has led us to expect.
> One thing infuriated him above all else: the letter had been misspelt.

> Indo-China consists of four states: Laos, Cambodia, North Vietnam and South Vietnam.

The colon often serves to introduce a long quotation or a verbatim report.
> The Chairman's Report ran as follows:

Hyphens

Hyphens are used in:
1. Double-barrelled names. For example:
> Baden-Powell

2. Line-endings: Words should be divided at their natural break. For example, *inter-rupt*. Do not be like the student who wrote "teac-" at the end of one line and "up" at the beginning of the next!

3. Certain compound nouns. For example: *Spin-dryer, book-*

case, book-keeping, ice-cream. If you are in any doubt whether a compound noun requires a hyphen or not, you may not always find it helpful to consult a dictionary since dictionaries do not agree on this matter. For example, "ice cream", "ice-cream", and even "icecream" may be found in different dictionaries.

4. Certain adjectives which are made up of more than one word. Examples of these are:

English-speaking	do-it-yourself
brand-new	a couldn't-care-less attitude
home-made	Anglo-French
freshly-laundered	Sino-Soviet
newly-arrived	Franco-British
six-year-old	blue-black

5. Expressions which begin with *anti, pre, vice, arch, semi*, and other prefixes, where to join the two parts together would be confusing (e.g. *semiinvalid*) or produce a word which is not acceptable (e.g. *archenemy*). Examples:

Non-combustible
vice-president
semi-detached
ante-natal
pre-war
pre-paid
un-British

We may note that it is an American practice to make such expressions into single words, however awkward the result, e.g. "interunit," "coauthor."

6. Expressions beginning with *ex-* and *pro-* when they mean "former" and "in favour of". Examples:

ex-King
pro-Israeli

7. Compound numbers. For example:

Forty-one
Sixty-four

N.B. *Nevertheless, whereas*, and *nowadays* should not be broken up. For example *Now-a-days*.

An interesting question

What is the difference in meaning between *twenty-five week-old babies* and *twenty five-week-old babies*?

Brackets

Brackets can be conveniently used in technical writing to enclose brief illustrations, explanations, examples or definitions of new terms. They are also widely used in notes and in other informal writing such as letters to friends.

In all other types of writing it is advisable to avoid the use of brackets so that one is obliged not only to construct sentences properly but also to arrange one's material in the best order before starting to write. To use brackets for belated explanations or in order to save one the trouble of constructing sentences with care is a sign of laziness and is irritating to the reader. Most irritating of all is the use of brackets to force a whole sentence into the midst of another sentence.

Note: By "brackets" most people understand ( ). These, however, are called parentheses by some people, who reserve the term "brackets" for what are often called square brackets [ ]. The latter, however, are not used in handwriting. In the author's opinion it is preferable to use the terms "brackets" and "square brackets" as "parentheses" is ambiguous — for it may be applied to a pair of dashes.

Question marks

Question marks are used only after direct questions. For example:
>Who do you think you are?
>What is the time, please?
>What on earth is the use of sitting there complaining?
>What possible advantage have we derived from entering the Common Market?

They should not be used in the following types of expression:
>I asked him what he wanted. (Statement.)
>Tell me where you are going and what you intend to do. (Request.)

Perhaps you would be good enough to inform us when you have made your decision. (Request in the form of a statement.)

Exclamation marks

Exclamation marks should be used very sparingly indeed, so that when they are used they make the intended effect. They should be used:

1. After all exclamations beginning with "What" or "How". For example:

> What a ridiculous situation!
> How astonishing!

2. After statements which the writer considers surprising or striking enough to be specially emphasized. For example:

> They met on the Monday for the first time, got engaged on the Wednesday, and were married on the Saturday!

3. After emphatic commands, exhortations and wishes, and after expressions of surprise, horror, delight, or of some other strong feeling. For example:

> Whatever you do, do not make that mistake again!
> Let us not forget the contribution made by France!
> Long live the Queen!
> Ugh!
> Wonderful!

Quotation marks (inverted commas)

The former term is more suitable as it indicates their function. "Inverted commas" is only a description — and a description which is only half correct!

Quotation marks are used to show that words (or a word) are being quoted. Accordingly, they are most often used when we are punctuating speech. (See page 57.)

Other uses are as follows:

1. To enclose quotations. For example:

> Hamlet wondered, "Whether 'tis nobler in the mind to suffer the slings and arrows of outrageous fortune or to

take arms against a sea of troubles and by opposing end them."

Note how quotations within speech are dealt with:

" 'History is bunk', declared Henry Ford, but I don't think I agree with him," said the professor.

or

' "History is bunk," declared Henry Ford, but I don't think I agree with him,' said the professor.

2. To quote words which you do not consider acceptable literary English. For example:

He had a "couldn't-care-less" attitude.

Too many dismiss her work as "a load of old rubbish".

3. To quote expressions used by other people when you do not agree that those expressions are appropriate. For example:

This "striking new study" of Henry VII's reign is actually merely a collection of well-known facts with the occasional new idea thrown in.

4. To introduce a technical term which is not generally known. For example:

Almost the whole mass of the atom is contained in the nucleus, which is composed of "protons" — the carriers of the positive charge — and neutral "neutrons".

5. To quote words the meaning or use of which is being stated or discussed. For example:

"Affluent" means "well-off" or "prosperous".

In lists of several items, should a comma precede the final "and"?

What a poor style! He has started six consecutive sentences with "You".

6. To enclose titles: Although modern writers tend to use quotation marks increasingly sparingly, they should, in handwriting or typewriting at any rate, be used for titles of books, newspapers, pieces of music, paintings, films, plays and radio and television programmes. They should also, in examinations, at any rate, be used around the names of hotels, pubs, theatres, cinemas, ships and special models of commercial products. For example:

"A Textbook of Applied Physics"
"The Times"
"Bolero" by Ravel
"The Boyhood of Raleigh" by Millais
"From Russia with Love" is showing at the "Rialto".
"The Mousetrap", by Agatha Christie, has broken all records.
He was looking at "Panorama".
Having leapt from his Rolls-Royce "Silver Cloud", he dashed into the "Red Lion". Fortified by several martinis, he went into the "Odeon", where a stirring sea-epic was being shown. He was so impressed by this story of marine adventure that the very next day he booked a passage to Fiji on the "Ruritania".

7. To enclose foreign expressions, like "fait accompli" and "in camera".

Note: It is a modern practice to omit quotation marks from many of these types of name and title and from the foreign expressions, especially in printed matter, where, instead of quotation marks, italics are often used. At other times, however, these expressions get no distinguishing punctuation at all.

Examples of the punctuation of speech

(a) "Well," said Mrs. Smith, "that's only a matter of opinion."

(b) "Where are you going, my pretty maid?" he asked, twirling his luxuriant moustache.

(c) "I am not altogether sure," he remarked, "that I approve of the idea."

(d) "How often do you read 'The Times'?" she enquired.

(e) "Hey, you!" he shouted.

(f) "Yes, that's what I think," he said.

(g) "What on earth," she asked, "is the matter with John?"

(h) "Haven't I seen that person before?" Smith asked. "I seem to recognize his face."

"Yes, he was at the party last week!" exclaimed Joan.

"Oh yes, I remember now," said Smith.

N.B. A new line is required for each change of speaker.

Italics

Italics are used only in print, so when a writer wishes to emphasize an expression he should, if writing by hand or typing, underline it.

Never mind what France or America or China should do. What should *Britain* do?

On no account should you try to use *quotation marks* for emphasis.

Paragraphing

A new paragraph is needed for a new stage or point in any essay, letter, story, factual account, argument, etc.

Exercises in punctuation

We use punctuation to help us express what *we* want to say, and it is not a very realistic exercise to insert punctuation marks into a passage that has already been written by someone else! Nevertheless, punctuation exercises test our ability to recognize sentences and groups of words within sentences which should be marked off from other groups.

Moreover, punctuation exercises train us to watch out for the marks (e.g. apostrophes and question marks) which are certainly not as important as full stops and commas but whose use should nevertheless come naturally to all truly literate people.

1. Punctuate the following:

king solomons mines one of the most famous adventure tales in the english language tells how sir henry curtis allan quatermain and john good make a perilous journey into the heart of unknown africa seeking with the aid of an old map the legendary treasure of king solomon rider haggard thus described (to sir newman flower of cassells his publishers) how he came to write king solomons mines

stevensons treasure island had just been published i used to travel backwards and forwards between london and norwich in those days with my brother at week ends i told him that i had read treasure island and i didnt think much of it my brother had read the book before me and thought the world of it he said it was a masterpiece he called me a fool i bet him five shillings that i could write a book as good and he took the bet so i wrote king solomons mines on a pad on my knees during the journeys

when the book was accepted haggard urged that the map should be drawn with real blood
(From the publisher's note to the Pan edition, 1951.)

2. Complete the punctuation in the following passage:
the morning sunshine descended like an amber shower bath on blandings castle lighting up with a heartening glow its ivied walls its rolling parks its gardens outhouses and messuages and such of its inhabitants as chanced at the moment to be taking the air it fell on green lawns and wide terraces on noble trees and bright flower beds it fell on the baggy trousers seat of angus mcallister head gardener to the ninth earl of emsworth as he bent with dour scottish determination to pluck a slug from its reverie beneath the leaf of a lettuce it fell on the white flannels of the hon freddie threepwood lord emsworths second son hurrying across the water meadows it also fell on lord emsworth himself and on beach his faithful butler they were standing on the turret above the west wing the former with his eye to a powerful telescope the latter holding the hat which he had been sent to fetch.

Beach said lord emsworth
m'lord?
Ive been swindled this dashed thing doesnt work
Your lordship cannot see clearly?
I cant see at all dash it its all black
The butler was an observant man
Perhaps if I were to remove the cap at the extremity of the instrument m lord more satisfactory results might be obtained.
Eh cap is there a cap so there is take it off beach
Very good m lord
Ah there was satisfaction in lord emsworths voice he twiddled and adjusted and the satisfaction deepened yes thats better thats capital beach i can see a cow
(From *The Custody of the Pumpkin* by P. G. Wodehouse.)

3. Punctuate the following passage:
In 1955 labor was encouraged by two other developments

first the signing into some union—management contracts of a provision requiring employers to pay unemployment benefits as a supplement to the benefits administered by the states secondly the merger of two independent trade union federations into the united AFL—CIO with 15 million members evidence of corrupt practices in some unions led the afl—cio to adopt a strict ethical practices code and caused congress to pass a law requiring full public disclosure of union financial matters particularly relating to pension and welfare funds and guaranteeing union members their democratic rights other domestic problems proved less amenable to solution new advances in agricultural technology intensified the problem of large farm production in relation to national demand the eisenhower administration replaced the existing policy of guaranteeing farmers fixed price supports with a flexible scale intended to encourage farmers to grow crops which were not in surplus in addition a soil bank program encouraged the use of more land for providing forage for growing trees and for reservoirs.

(From *An Outline of American History* issued by the U.S. Information Service.)

4. Rewrite the following passage using correct punctuation.
   bizarre as the idea might seem these days there was once a time when the automobile was seen as the perfect answer to urban pollution that was back at the turn of the century when horses provided virtually all of the motive power for society and daily deposited some 2½ million pounds of manure and 60,000 gallons of urine on the streets of new york city alone small wonder that turn of the century scientists hailed the development of the auto as a clean quiet and efficient means of transportation.

   (From an article in *Newsweek*, March 1972.)

5. Rewrite the following passage using correct punctuation.
   dear sir i am writing to apply for the position of secretary to the personnel officer advertised in the daily telegraph of july 14th i received my secretarial training at the mid wessex college of further education casterbridge where i was a student from 1969 until 1971 as well as passing the london chamber of commerce private secretarys certificate

examination i gained four passes in the gce at ordinary level english language, sociology, commerce and german my shorthand and typing speeds are 100 wpm and 60 wpm for the past three years i have been employed as personal assistant to the sales manager of an engineering company based in worksop and i think i may claim that my work has given satisfaction now however that my husbands firm has transferred its head office to hampstead i am looking for a post in the north london area although i have had no direct experience of it i have always been interested in personnel work and think i could do well at it as well as performing purely secretarial duties competently i shall be available for interview on any weekday during the fortnight commencing july 19th yours faithfully.

6. Punctuate the following passage:

the chance of becoming unemployed even in the period of heavy unemployment between the wars was only about one in ten taking one year with another it was considerably higher in the exporting districts where unemployment was concentrated but it was lower in the rest of great britain but most workers are not reassured by such calculations the danger may be small but it is always there if another general world depression like that which began in the autumn of 1929 should come upon us the danger would become much greater and each says to himself it may be my turn next if the breadwinner is out of work for any length of time the standard of living of his family may be drastically lowered their plans upset their hopes destroyed true there is unemployment insurance and in the last resort national assistance but the income from these sources is less for the higher paid workers much less than what the breadwinner or breadwinners used to earn moreover a worker likes to feel he is playing his part in the community to be on the dole for long hurts his pride and saps his morale it is no wonder then that full employment has stepped out of the pages of the economic text books to become one of the most powerful political slogans of our time a certain amount of unemployment however is inevitable on any given day some workers such as builders and fishermen will not be working because the weather is too bad some will be at home through sickness some whose work is of a seasonal or intermittent nature will be temporarily unemployed some will have lost or left one job but will soon find another.

(From *Economics* by Frederic Benham.)

7. Punctuate the following:

There are perhaps two mistakes in the preceding passage it is doubtful whether what should have been used after paid workers much less than and one should probably say economics text books rather than economic text books

8. Punctuate the following passage, which contains a number of very short sentences used very effectively. "Ten o'clock" is to be treated as a complete sentence. "Quarrel" is a man's name and Bond is wondering whether the shadow belongs to him.

bond awoke lazily the feel of the sand reminded him where he was he glanced at his watch ten o clock the sun through the round thick leaves of the sea-grape was already hot a larger shadow moved across the dappled sand in front of his face quarrel bond shifted his head and peered through the fringe of leaves and grass that concealed him from the beach he stiffened his heart missed a beat and then began pounding so that he had to breathe deeply to quieten it his eyes as he stared through the blades of grass were fierce slits

(From *Dr. No* by Ian Fleming.)

9. Punctuate the following:

i suppose watson we must look upon you as a man of letters said he how do you define the word grotesque strange remarkable i suggested he shook his head at my definition there is surely something more than that said he some underlying suggestion of the tragic and the terrible if you cast your mind back to some of those narratives with which you have afflicted a long suffering public you will recognize how often the grotesque has deepened into the criminal think of that little affair of the red headed men that was grotesque enough in the outset and yet it ended in a desperate attempt at robbery or again there was that most grotesque affair of the five orange pips which led straight to a murderous conspiracy the word puts me on the alert

(From *His Last Bow* by Sir Arthur Conan Doyle.)

10. Set out the following letter in a suitable way and punctuate it.

vitaflakes ltd thornton avenue camberwick wessex j jones esq 14 manor drive barchester april 10th 1976 dear mr jones thank you for your march report which we received on april 7th i should like to congratulate you most heartily on the success of your efforts to build up sales in barset over the past five years and i am very pleased to inform you that the board of directors have decided to raise your commission from 5% to 5½% with effect from april 1st so successful have your efforts been in building up trade that we feel it would be asking too much to require you to continue to cover the whole of barset accordingly from june 1st your sales territory will be that part of the county north of a line drawn through barchester and crumberleigh your colleague in the southern part of the county will be mr henry appleton a nephew of the managing director yours sincerely a trollope regional sales manager

11. Punctuate the following:

anyone who visits the galapagos islands which are situated in the pacific ocean a few hundred miles off the coast of ecuador will almost certainly be impressed by what he sees there where else can one find penguins and albatrosses nests and fur seals breeding on the equator cactus higher than trees or cormorants that cannot fly perhaps however a visitors most striking impression is likely to be the animals extraordinary tameness

12. Punctuate the following:

well peter ive read your article and if you dont mind my saying so said john it seems rather long winded in parts you tend to go in for verbiage what do you mean by verbiage asked his brother that i use too many words yes that exactly what i mean i advise you to read sir ernest gowers complete plain words

13. Punctuate the following:

mabel he whispered as he looked into her beautiful blue eyes theres something ive been wanting to ask you for so long smiling warmly she said dont worry peter go ahead and ask i can hardly pluck up enough courage to ask you said peter and im afraid of the effect a refusal may have on me oh peter she exclaimed you know theres no need to worry very well then he said would you introduce me to your cousin sally

14. Punctuate the following:
the academie francaise which exists to preserve the purity of the french language frowns on the use by frenchmen of english words like weekend cocktail and dancing yet the english speaking world uses many french words examples of these are rendezvous detente and discotheque

15. Punctuate the following:
stainless stephen long ago in the early days of wireless hit upon the simple means of raising a laugh by peppering his speech with punctuation marks it is a device that has worn well we are still amused and at any rate it reminds us that punctuation that is pointing is a matter for writing and not for speech the inflection of the voice its rise and fall its pauses its stresses and cadences make up the punctuation of the spoken word when we say are we downhearted the voice itself asks the question which in writing we indicate by a question mark the marks of punctuation in fact merely outline the pattern and nature of the sentence for the reader who arrives at the meaning and significance through the eye and not through the ear

punctuation is then a convention practised by the writer for the convenience of the reader that and no more like language itself it has had its changes through the years we no longer punctuate like swift or johnson or hazlitt or dickens some of the differences between the punctuation of today and that of three hundred or even two hundred years ago are fundamental others are merely matters of function or degree

the basic or fundamental mark of punctuation is the full stop which marks the end of a complete sentence in formal grammar the term period is applied to both the sentence especially if it is composed of a number of dependent clauses and the stop(.) at the end of it theoretically the use of this stop should cause no difficulty at all and indeed it does not to the experienced writer who can see the pattern

of his sentence before he begins to write and therefore knows exactly where the sentence ends but the casual or inexperienced writer is not quite so sure he is apt to let his thoughts form themselves into sentence patterns to string or fit them together and to mark the periods only by inserting a few odd commas at the pauses but even he recognizes the general principle that the full stop is the sign of the end he is only uncertain where the end should be
(From *Good English* by G. H. Vallins.)

16. Punctuate the following:
vogue words are words which have become fashionable they are used particularly by some journalists and broadcasters in the hope that they will convey an impression of liveliness and modernity more often the effect is to baffle or irritate examples of vogue words in use in the nineteen seventies are traumatic confrontation and escalate in time no doubt these words will be cast aside like old toys and other trendy expressions will take their place

17. Punctuate the following:
the english language is spoken as their first language by over three hundred million people approximately two thirds of these are americans american english has a great influence on british english and many britons who pride themselves on their use of the queens english use americanisms even americanisms which are condemned by academic authorities in the united states itself an outstanding example is the use of hopefully to mean i hope it is hoped etc of course all living languages change and there are many excellent american imports like teenager and commuter which are in common use in the united kingdom today what is to be condemned however is the use by the media of expressions which are not in general use in britain many english people are not quite sure of the meaning of mugging and some may imagine that crockery is somehow involved one hears british disc jockeys use such expressions as twenty after three and this has got to be a hit one constantly hears around and presently used instead of the native british about and at present

18. Punctuate the following:

    slang should usually be avoided in written english for the effect of its use is to create an over casual tone moreover there is a chance that it will not be understood slang words and expressions are sometimes used only in one particular age group or in a particular profession some slang is restricted to a certain region or indeed to one country an american might be rather surprised if a londoner asked him if he wanted a fag if you read that someone had shot through would you know that he had in fact buzzed off

19. Write out the following with the punctuation corrected.
    (a) Barfield golf club. Captains Ball. Dance to the Montana's.
    (b) Potatoe's 11p, cucumber's 25p each.
    (c) Buy our "home made" cake's and pies'.
    (d) Principals Car Park.
    (e) Tell me where you are going and what you intend to do?
    (f) I should like to apply for the post of assistant public relations officer advertised in the sunday times.
    (g) North America consists of, Canada the United States Mexico, and a number of very small states these are sometimes referred to as "central America.
    (h) He wrote to the "International Wool Secretariat" for information about merino sheep.
    (i) The talk will be on "Dangers to Health in the Modern Urban Environment".
    (j) The French for friend is ami.
    (k) Obviously there must be some connection between the Latin mater, the German mutter and the English mother.
    (l) The lecture will be entitled american football.
    (m) It took Edward Gibbon about twenty years to write "The Decline and fall of the roman empire, it takes almost as long to read it.
    (n) have you ever read thomas hardys far from the madding crowd she asked.
    (o) oh what a beautiful morning.
    (p) The books which I ordered last week have arrived but those, which I ordered three weeks ago, have still to be delivered.
    (q) Her favourite foods were ice cream, and fish, and chips.

(r) Thank-you for your letter of August 1st, you will be hearing from us in about ten day's time.

(s) Whatever you might say its perfectly clear that your command of English leaves a great deal to be desired.

(t) Melbourne a large city in Australia was named after queen Victoria's first Prime Minister.

20. Punctuate the following sentences:

(a) in five minutes time i shall meet you outside the childrens playground

(b) talent dedication physical and mental resilience these are the qualities that a modern sportsman requires

(c) at the ordinary level of the general certificate of education i passed in the following subjects mathematics french physics chemistry and english language

(d) bright and pleasant was the sky balmy the air and beautiful the appearance of every object around as mr pickwick leaned over the balustrades of rochester bridge contemplating nature and waiting for breakfast.

(e) thank you for your letter of september 14th in which you asked for further details of our home loan scheme

Chapter 5
Correctness

". . . what we call correct grammar, correct language and recognized syntax, depends really upon usage and upon who does the using. . . .
"Usage must come first and usage must rule. The only difficulty is to *know*, whose usage? The answer is obviously the usage of the best writers; this leads to the further difficulty of knowing who are the best writers. We find them to be the writers recognized as the best by the best people."
(From *How to Write* by Stephen Leacock.)

These two quotations from an entertaining and useful book indicate a few of the many problems involved in any discussion of correct language and may even suggest to us that we should talk not about correct and incorrect English but about different *types* of English.

Some writers on the subject have come dangerously close to saying that "anything goes" while others have tried to impose on us a set of unchanging rules, even though those rules may be ignored by, or unknown to, educated people — for educated usage changes.

"But in any case," someone might ask, "what *is* educated usage? Define it!" The obvious answer is that it is the usage of people who are educated. "But who *are* . . .?" The problem is endless.

Unfortunately the problem is social as well as academic. In some circles "correct" English seems ridiculously affected. In others the breaking of a traditional rule based on Latin grammar is enough to lose one a job (e.g. "Do you mind me coming in late?").

It is certainly difficult to offer advice, for objections can be made to almost anything one says about correct language, including the following: if we know that there is a rule we should try to observe it, providing that in obeying the rule we do not write or speak awkwardly.

The following notes indicate some of the "rules", and contain some remarks and reminders which, hopefully, may prove helpful. The use of "hopefully" in the last sentence is ungrammatical. Some people would declare that it is disgracefully ungrammatical! The use of "hopefully" to mean "I hope", "One hopes", etc., has been condemned by grammarians not only in Britain but also in the United States, where it originated. But this use of the word has found its way into the 1976 *Concise Oxford Dictionary*.

1. Do not split infinitives:
    NOT   To boldly go
    BUT   To go boldly   *or*   Boldly to go
    NOT   I should like to on this special occasion say a few words.
    BUT   I should like on this special occasion to say a few words.

2. "Can" or "may":
    NOT   Can I have another cup of coffee, please?
    BUT   May I have another cup of coffee, please?

3. Double negatives:
    NOT   The local team never had no chance of winning the cup.
    BUT   The local team never had any chance of winning the cup.

We may note here that the sense of the incorrect conversational version is undeniably negative and certainly much easier to understand than those multiple negatives so dear to the hearts of some writers, e.g. "We are not unaware that there is a not inconsiderable feeling that the government's attitude in this matter has not been unbiased." Nevertheless, there "ain't no place" for colloquial double negatives in written English, not only because they are widely regarded as vulgar but also because in writing two negatives make a positive!

4. "Might" and "may":

A very long essay indeed could be written on the uses of "may" and "might", but the most important rule is exemplified by the following:

NOT   He said that I may come with you.
BUT   He said that I might come with you.
NOT   He said that I may be lucky.
BUT   He said that I might be lucky.

i.e. "may" cannot be used as a past tense.

There are, however, circumstances in which the first and third sentences would be correct.

5. The subjunctive:

Nowadays the subjunctive is in effect restricted to the verb "to be" when it refers to imagined or not yet achieved situations. For example:

- I recommend that he *be* promoted.
- He ran as if he *were* being pursued by all the devils in hell.
- If I *were* you . . .
- If she *were* more sensible, she would . . .
- I am sure that if he *were* to apply for this job . . .

6. Unwanted repetition of the past tense:

NOT   I would have liked to have gone. (Should?)
BUT   I would have liked to go. (Should?)
NOT   I wanted to try the test but I feared it would not have been successful.
BUT   I wanted to try the test but I feared it would not be successful.

7. "Kind" and "sort":

NOT   These kind and those sort.
BUT   This kind and that sort.

The fact supporting this rule is that "kind" and "sort" are singular, although many people tend to consider them collective nouns. Observance of the rule has its problems (e.g. this kind of people, this kind of persons). Perhaps the safest course is to change the construction, e.g. people of this sort.

8. Collective nouns, e.g. group, set, class, committee:

When collective nouns may be regarded as either singular or plural it is important to remember that they cannot be both singular and plural at the same time.

NOT	The committee believes that the sum they have collected will be enough.
BUT	The committee believe that the sum they have collected will be enough.
OR	The committee believes that the sum it has collected will be enough.

9. Agreement of subject and verb:

Everyone knows that a singular subject should be followed by a singular verb; but some people forget what the subject is.

NOT	A crate of bottles were in the corner.
BUT	A crate of bottles was in the corner.
NOT	John, with some of his friends, were going to the party.
BUT	John, with some of his friends, was going to the party.

10. Verbal nouns (gerunds):

NOT	Do you mind me coming in late?
BUT	Do you mind my coming in late?

This rule is sometimes criticized and indeed when pedantically obeyed results in this sort of thing: "Do you mind John's and my coming in late? In conversation at any rate the use of possessive adjectives (*my*, *your*, etc.) with verbal nouns is so rare that it is often regarded as an affectation. Nevertheless, we should for example write:

NOT	I did not like them making such a noise.
BUT	I did not like their making such a noise.

11. Comparison of adjectives:

Positive	Comparative	Superlative
bad	worse	worst
good	better	best
happy	happier	happiest
fast	faster	fastest
eccentric	more eccentric	most eccentric
beautiful	more beautiful	most beautiful

Most people know that adjectives of more than two syllables have their comparative and superlative versions formed by means of "more" and "most". It is certainly a sign of illiteracy to write "more happier", for example.

There is a rule which states that when only two things are

compared the superlative form should not be used: one can have the *best* of three but only the *better* of two. In speech at any rate this rule is frequently broken. It would certainly be unnatural to say:

May the better man win.

You must put your better foot forward.

negative comparison:

happy	less happy	least happy
successful	less successful	least successful

Some adjectives cannot be "compared". The authors of "1066 and All That" were joking when they wrote:

"Nelson was one of England's most naval officers . . ."

Nor should one write "more unique" or "less invisible". Also to be noted:

NOT   He's taller than what you are.

BUT   He's taller than you are.

NOT   He's taller than her.

BUT   He's taller than she.

Many educated people regard "than" as a preposition and to them it seems natural that "than" should be followed by "him", "her", "me", etc.

12. Adjectives and adverbs:

Do not use adjectives where adverbs should be used. Few people would write for example, "He bowled accurate" or "He did it real professional". Remember, however:

NOT   fresh-made

BUT   freshly-made

NOT   new-laid

BUT   newly-laid (pedantry?)

NOT   local grown

BUT   locally grown

NOT   drive slow

BUT   drive slowly

NOT   Kiss me quick!

BUT   Kiss me quickly!

13. Be consistent in the use of pronouns:

NOT   Before one starts on a long car journey you should check the oil level and tyre pressures.

BUT   Before one starts on a long car journey one should check the oil level and tyre pressures.

Note that in speech "They" is widely used as a convenient substitute for "he or she". For example:

> If anyone knows anything about this matter, will they please let Mr. Smith know immediately.

14. The following words:

> me   you   him   her   us   them   whom

are the objective versions of

> I   you   he   she   we   they   who

i.e. they are "on the receiving end" of verbs, for example:

> I hit him.
> We saw her.
> Whom did you see?
> Whom do you want?

or they are "on the receiving end" of prepositions, for example:

> I am not interested in him.
> He wrote to me about her.
> Give (to) them the letter from Paul.
> For whom the bell tolls . . .

Note the following correct forms:

> He saw John and me. (He did not see I!)
> She gave the apples to John and me. (Not to I!)
> Between you and me.

Many people avoid both the rule and "what comes naturally" and say, for example, "between you and I" and "She invited both Michael and I".

This seems to come from a fear of using "me" in any circumstances, the same fear which prompts people to use "myself" (e.g. He approached both John and myself) in the wrong places. "Myself" should be used only emphatically (e.g. If no-one else will do the job, I'll do it myself) or reflexively (I could have kicked myself!).

15. "Who" and "whom" pose some problems:
Such sentences as

- Whom do you believe?
- Whom did you see?
- I met the woman whom he wants to marry.

may sometimes seem unnatural or affected, for they conform to a rule which is very often disregarded, in conversation at least:

- Who do you believe?
- Who did you see?

- I met the woman who (or that) he wants to marry.

and anyone who wrote in an essay:

- "But the person who I admired most was the man who everyone else detested."

would not be likely to lose many marks for twice writing "who" instead of "whom".

However, although "Who are you talking about?" may be acceptable to many people, those who are determined not to end sentences or clauses with prepositions will probably say and certainly write:

- About whom are you talking?

Similarly:

- The person in whom I placed the greatest trust . . .
- By whom was the book written?
- To whom are you referring?

16. Relative pronouns referring to plural nouns should be followed by verbs in the plural. For example:

- He is one of the greatest footballers who have ever played for Scotland.
- He is one of those people who are always poking their noses into the affairs of others.

17. Note the following correct but unusual forms:

- It is I.
- It is he.
- It is we who must bear the responsibility.
- It is they who will want an explanation.

Even the logical French say: "C'est moi." (It's me.)

18. Everyone knows that *everyone*, *everybody* and *anyone* are singular. Thus:

- Anyone who likes a good book . . .
- Everyone likes a good book.
- Is everybody here?

However:

- Everyone has arrived and they are all enjoying themselves.

19. *Either*, *neither* and *each* should always be followed by singular verbs. Hence:

- Either one is suitable.
- Neither is suitable.
- Either John or Mary is going.

- Each of the boys was given a present.

"None" is singular by origin (not one) but usually treated as plural, e.g.

- None of the passengers were seriously injured.

20. Misrelated, unrelated and "dangling" participles:

The rule states in effect that the doer of the action expressed by the participle should be the subject of the sentence, e.g.

- Having left in a hurry, I had left my briefcase on the kitchen table.
- Kicking and screaming, the child was carried upstairs.

NOT

- Having left in a hurry, my briefcase lay on the kitchen table.
- Kicking and screaming, I carried the child upstairs.

21. Some miscellaneous points:

(a) *As* and *like*.

A lengthy essay could be written on the usage of these two words. Here we may make three points:

(i) "Like I say" may be good American English but it is bad British English.

(ii) "like he was" instead of "as if he were" is inadmissible, in Britain at least.

(iii) "like" is stronger than "as". Charles Dickens wrote in 1841 "Nobody will miss her like I shall", thereby breaking a rule still insisted upon by many people in 1977.

(b) *Between* and *among*.

Between cannot refer to only *one* of something. The following is incorrect:

- There was a distance of thirty metres between each telegraph pole.

Between refers to two. For example:

- I shared the money between my two nephews.

Note:

- I shared the cakes among the three boys.

However:

- Australia's first five batsmen scored only thirty runs between them.

(c) *Number* and *amount*, *fewer* and *less*.

Amount and *less* cannot be used with plural nouns:

NOT   Despite the larger amount of accidents less people have been injured.

BUT   Despite the larger number of accidents fewer people have been injured.

(d) *Reason* and *because*.

To use both "reason" and "because" in sentences of the following type is to be repetitive:

- The reason he failed the examination was because he did not do enough revision.

The following are correct:

- The reason he failed the examination was that he did not do enough revision.
- He failed the examination because he did not do enough revision.

(e) *Different from*.

The best preposition to use after "different" is "from", just as we say, for example, "this differs from that".

"Different to" is widely used by many writers, and in the U.S.A. the very strange "different than" is sometimes employed.

Exercises

1. Improve the following sentences in any ways you consider desirable:

(a) He never takes no notice of me.

(b) Each of the contestants were given a card on which to write their answers.

(c) Between each house there was a distance of ten feet only.

(d) Strictly between you and I, I already applied for the job.

(e) I thought I may have left my umbrella at the office, but it was'nt there.

(f) These kind of programmes are so interesting that quite literally one can never tear one's eyes away from them.

(g) I should be glad if you will send me further details.

(h) It looks like he already arrived.

(i) I don't like him staying out so late at his age.

2. Rewrite the following sentences, making any adjustments which you consider necessary.

(a) The reason why I have come here today is because

I want to protest the treatment I've been getting.
- (b) Their's is different to yours but similar to our's.
- (c) I asked him about what he was talking.
- (d) Everyone knows the important rules of their own language.
- (e) A less weaker person may have given up trying but he continued to maintain his efforts.
- (f) There is a quite unique relationship between John and myself.
- (g) There were many outbreaks of plague in medieval Europe but the one known as the Black Death was the worse.
- (h) The Government have announced plans to nationalize the textile industry and it hopes to introduce a bill in the next parliamentary session.
- (i) It's the politicians that spend the money but its us who have to in the end pay it.
- (j) If I was in your shoes I should make a point to arrive on time.

3. Rewrite the following sentences, making any adjustments which you consider necessary.
- (a) He was more happier and relaxed than when I saw him a couple of days previous.
- (b) There are far less potato's this year because of the drought and a large amount of housewifes are getting very angry about the escalating prices.
- (c) There has been many technical difficulties but hopefully the project will be fully completed by the end of next month.
- (d) The senior executive with several of his assistants were leaving the building.
- (e) He has hardly done any work but I shouldn't be surprised if he didn't pass the exam.
- (f) I prefer Mozart better than Chopin.
- (g) Having already been saddled, I mounted the steed and rode off.
- (h) When one arrives at a hotel which looks luxurious in the holiday brochure you sometimes find that it is thoroughly uncomfortable.
- (i) She gave the money to John and I.
- (j) Being a wet day, I took an umbrella.

4. Improve or correct the wording of the following sentences:
   (a) Last Christmas I saw some quite new novelties in the shops.
   (b) I would have liked to have been allowed to make the attempt but I fear it would not be successful.
   (c) Putting a man into space is one of the greatest, if not the very greatest, event that has occurred in recent times.
   (d) I resent your comment for, believing, as I know you do, in John's guilt, your words infer that I approve of his actions.
   (e) He appears to have forgotten — though he cannot possibly be oblivious to the fact — that its me he owes the money to.
   (Royal Society of Arts III). Note, however, that the R.S.A. have not set sentence-correction questions in recent years.

5. Rewrite the following sentences, making any corrections you consider necessary.
   (a) The typists became involved in an argument as to who had made the mistake on the invoice, but neither the one or other of them would admit their error.
   (b) He said that the firm has offered him an absolutely unique opportunity of buying the car cheaply. I know that he is in debt so I think he wants to economize and I do'nt agree with him spending so much money.
   (From a Shorthand-Typist's Certificate examination of the early 1960s.)

Chapter 6
Plain language

Language is used to communicate and we should therefore choose and arrange our words for the sole purpose of conveying meaning.

Some inexperienced writers, as well as making elementary errors of spelling and punctuation and writing in badly organized sentences, pad out their sentences with unnecessarily long or unnecessarily formal expressions. Dimly perceiving that what is expected in written language is in some way different from everyday speech and possibly from what they usually read, they try to achieve dignity by avoiding the use of short, convenient and common words. Hence the practice of using "therefore" instead of "so" — and using it improperly. They are particularly fond of the unnecessary use of "with regard to", "in relation to", "in the region of", "in respect of", "prior to" and "with reference to". Few go so far as to call a spade "an entrenching tool" but many prefer "commence" to "start" and "financial resources" to "money". When this sort of thing is combined with the use of traditional clichés like "in this day and age" and brand-new and even sillier ones like "at this moment in time", and when vogue words like "charisma", "escalate", "syndrome" and "area" (as a metaphor) are dragged in for decorative purposes, the resultant piece of writing, no doubt peppered with so-called mechanical errors, is usually a shambles. To them, we should say: "Use plain English: it is what your readers want!"

This is not to say that good writers always use the obvious

word or phrase. They may, for example, employ euphemisms (pleasant ways of stating unpleasant facts) to soften the harshness of a blunt statement; they may use abstract nouns and impersonal constructions (e.g. "It is strongly felt that unanimity is essential") for the sake of tact or politeness. They may, on other occasions, prefer one word to another to avoid a clash of sound, or choose certain expressions for stylistic purposes. They may even on occasion use words and expressions which are not strictly necessary to convey meaning but which help the "balance" of the sentence.

There are, however, other educated people who concentrate less on conveying meaning and achieving the right tone than on showing off, who seem to put more effort into searching for impressive language than into searching for words which will best do the job of communicating. One can picture them saying to their readers: "Look how knowledgeable and intelligent I am! Look at the size of my vocabulary! Look how ingeniously and intricately I can express this idea!" or perhaps "Look how fashionable I am!" This is a foolish and irresponsible attitude: foolish, because some readers will see what such writers are up to and lose respect for them and their views; irresponsible, because other readers might say to themselves: "I cannot understand this, but it seems very learned and intellectual and 'with it' and it was written by an educated and important person and it must be my fault that I cannot make head nor tail of it." Some readers, then, will become irritated and scornful — even when the writer has something worthwhile to say; others will become needlessly depressed. A writer who is striving more to impress than to communicate is not playing fair — to his readers or to himself.

This is not of course to say that we should assume that any piece of writing which we find difficult to understand must be badly expressed: we should all realize that we may not be sufficiently knowledgeable or intelligent to grasp the meaning of everything we read. However, we should never rule out the possibility that when we cannot puzzle out the meaning of a piece of writing it may not be our fault but the writer's.

The author of this book keeps firmly in mind the former possibility and this, together perhaps with professional courtesy, has deterred him from quoting examples of academic and bureaucratic writing which he finds both puzzling and dispiriting.

For authoritative and heartening denunciations of baffling and even meaningless writing by learned people the reader is advised to consult Sir Ernest Gowers' *The Complete Plain Words* and Mr G. H. Vallins' *Good English*. An exhaustive treatment of redundancy, circumlocution, jargon, verbiage and other hindrances to communication will be found in Mr Peter Little's *Communication in Business*.

Exercises

Note that although the sentences in the following six questions may be criticized, the meaning of most of them is clear or at least can be worked out.

1. Write out *three* of the following in simpler and clearer English:

(a) In the event of a breakdown in the negotiations between management and shop floor, industrial action by the latter appears inevitable. (Company Report.)

(b) In this sub-standard match, Everton clawed their way into a victory position by their aggressive approach, although Ipswich had every chance to pocket the points before half-time. (Football Report.)

(c) David Cassidy's latest disc, released this week, will have sufficient appeal to the teenyboppers to make it another chartbuster. (Pop Report.)

(d) He is an extrovert who shines in extra-curricular activities but tends to be a disruptive influence in the classroom situation. (School Report.)

(From the Joint Matriculation Board G.C.E. Ordinary Level English Language Examination, Paper B.)

2. Express the meaning of the following sentences in simpler language:

(a) You will no doubt as part of the Yuletide festivities be permitting our young charges to bring along some seasonable comestibles so that they may partake of them in the course of the matutinal break in their academic pursuits.

(b) He is to be for six months a guest of Her Majesty and is consequently about to enjoy a period of somewhat restricted liberty.

    (c) Pecuniarily embarrassed, she was perforce obliged to take in paying guests.

    (d) What measures shall we take with regard to the inebriated member of the nautical profession?

    (e) There is nothing inherently wrong with this plan, *per se*.

3. Express the meaning of the following in plain English:

    (a) It is regretted that the Minister does not feel at this moment in time that he is in a position to consider your request for planning permission favourably.

    (b) Quite clearly, the British boxer is now finding himself in a tiredness situation.

    (c) We are in grateful receipt of your esteemed communication of the first instant and would respectfully beg to acknowledge same.

    (d) Care should be taken to capitalize the initial letters of praenomens and cognomens.

    (e) City's tactics became increasingly physical and in the course of a confrontation between their chief striker, Smith, and Jones, United's keeper, the latter sustained a cracked fibula — an experience which he most certainly must have found traumatic.

4. Correct and clarify the following sentences, all of which are taken from a student's essay:

    (a) School holidays with regard to pupils attending state run schools have about the same amount of holidays as each other with the exception of a day or two here and there.

    (b) The period in total usually amounts to about thirteen weeks this comprising of six in the summer three each at Christmas and easter and a week for one of the half terms plus odd days here and there.

    (c) Holidays given by private schools are usually a longer period of time.

    (d) With the question of whether holidays are too long one must take into account the differences in the types of home environments with regard to pupils.

5. (a) Convert the following pompous piece of writing into simpler English:

    Having availed himself of this sumptuous repast he further fortified himself with some Bacchic refreshment from

Portugal and, having sunk into a chaise longue, commenced perusal of an equestrian contest on the flickering kaleidoscopic screen. After a not very protracted period of time had elapsed, however, he was in the arms of Morpheus.

(b) Is there anything to be said in favour of this type of language?

6. Wherever possible, express the sense of the following in plain English:

(a) We at J. Argon & Co. Ltd. have an ongoing dialogue between Board Room and shop floor so that there is optimal flexibility relative to the latter's holiday entitlements.

(b) In terms of remuneration adult males are still significantly better placed than the great majority of adult females.

(c) As the area under consideration is an area of low population density it is in my opinion to be doubted whether a more frequent bus service would prove economically viable.

(d) He failed to satisfy the examiners not so much as a consequence of being inhibited by the nervousness syndrome as of an unfamiliarity with the factual background of the subject in which he was being examined.

(e) The two main areas of written communication as used in business reports cover graphical and technical representation. (From an examination in Communications.)

(f) Temperatures will be around yesterday's levels.

(g) Although he was maintaining a low profile, the latecomer was apprehended by the headmaster.

(h) As far as subject options and attendance are concerned choice is not a factor as far as students are concerned.

(i) It was with a certain amount of *angst* that I realized that I would have to give my informant a *quid pro quo* for telling me the whereabouts of her *pied à terre*.

(j) Prior to my return to my place of employment I have to prepare and serve my husband's midday meal.

(k) The American Revolution may be said to have had its inception at Lexington.

(m) This piece of music really communicates; I can relate to it.

Chapter 7

Essay-writing

An essay is a prose composition in which the writer, either for an examiner or for a large number of readers, tells a story or writes a description or sets out to prove or demonstrate something or "conducts a discussion" or (more rarely) writes on a given subject with no aim except his own and his readers' entertainment. Very often the writer's own ideas, impressions, suggestions, views and opinions will be expressed even when they are not specifically requested, for an essay is very much a *personal* composition. An essay is a personal composition even if the word "I" is not used and even if no personal views are expressed, for it will convey to anyone who reads it some impression of the personality of the writer.

A point made by some people is that no-one, except journalists and that very small number of professional writers who specialize in essay-writing, ever has to write an essay once his school or college days are over, and they ask why it is that essay questions, usually carrying a third or more of the total marks, appear in most English Language examinations. This question may be answered as follows: English Language examinations are (or should be!) tests of a candidate's command of the English Language and the Essay question gives him a unique opportunity to demonstrate that command in his own way and at some length — unique because he is afforded more freedom than he enjoys in any other question; much more freedom for example than in a Precis or Comprehension question. He is free, within wide limits, to choose his subject; he is free to decide what he is going to say and how he is going to say it. The Essay question, dreaded by so many examinees, is not only the most important part of an English examination but also the most inviting!

Even if there were no essay question in English examinations, essay-writing would still be a valuable activity, because:

1. It is creative. All forms of creative activity are satisfying and beneficial and are a means of self-expression.
2. The planning and organization required in essay-writing is excellent mental exercise.
3. Practice in planning, organizing, and writing clearly what one wishes to say has practical value in everyday life, e.g. in letter-writing.
4. Essay-writing is useful preparation for all those examinations which consist partly or entirely of essay questions! How often one has heard, "They know the facts but they won't organize their answers or express themselves clearly."!

Yet here it should be stated that students will profit from essay-writing only if they plan and write their essays with care. It is sometimes assumed that in essay-writing there is no great need to express oneself clearly, that anything which may appear from a casual reading to carry approximately the intended meaning will do; that providing that a sentence of uncertain meaning sounds vaguely "interesting" the uncertainty does not matter; that the throwing down of words and ideas haphazardly onto the paper — a sort of literary action-painting — will somehow create an interesting effect; that it is permissible to stray from the subject or deliberately misinterpret the title of the essay; that organization, sentence construction, grammar and spelling are of no consequence if the views expressed are likely to please the reader. Recently, one university lecturer went so far as to suggest that the low standard of literacy of some of his students was the result of their having had to write too many essays at school! Probably it was the result of their having written too many *bad* essays.

Most students, of course, understand the need for a high standard of written composition and strive to say clearly and correctly what they want to say. Yet many often fail to produce satisfactory essays. There are various reasons for this. Some students are pessimistic and over-cautious in their approach to essay-writing; others have little idea of the possibilities of the essay subjects they choose; sometimes students are not sure what sort of material may be legitimately included in an essay; very often their method of planning, if such exists, is in some way unsound.

It is primarily for such students that the advice in this section of the book is intended.

The approach to essay-writing

We have already noted that an essay is very much a *personal* composition. Although the views, feelings and ideas expressed may not be unusual, they should be written about in an individual and personal way. Consequently although the essay-writer should keep in mind the need for a high standard of grammar and sentence construction, his approach should be imaginative and adventurous. If he adopts such a lively approach, he will be unlikely to run out of ideas. Moreover, he will avoid that dull anonymity which characterizes so many so-called essays.

The essay-writer's approach should above all be optimistic. Thrusting aside any visions of spiteful examiners ready to pounce on errors or on views they do not agree with, he should decide that he has something interesting to say and confidently resolve to say it clearly. This approach will in itself help the essay-writer to achieve a high standard of written composition.

Reading and understanding essay questions

Essay questions must be carefully read and thoroughly understood. This may seem a very obvious statement!

However, it is unfortunately true that many examinees do not read essay questions with sufficient care and consequently write the "wrong" essays. Consider, for example, the following question:

- What might be the causes of the increase in the number of violent crimes in recent years?

A careful reader will realize that he is being invited to suggest what the causes might be or perhaps to discuss the opinions expressed by other people on this matter. He will understand that he is to suggest and discuss *possible* causes of the increase in violent crimes, and he should realize that he is perfectly at liberty to say what, in his opinion, the main causes are.

A careless reader, on the other hand, may not notice the words "might be" and will leap to the conclusion that he is being asked to say what the causes definitely *are*, in the way that a person might be asked for example to state the cause of lunar eclipses or to explain why hot air rises. This careless reader will then write the wrong sort of essay, or, having decided that he does not *know* the causes of the growth of violent crime, he may decide to rule out that question. Thus his choice of questions will be unnecessarily restricted simply as a result of his own carelessness. Careless reading of essay questions is the cause of many examination failures.

Sometimes, however, the wrong essay is produced not as a result of careless reading but through a failure of understanding. This is particularly common with essay titles consisting of a single word or phrase, such as "Holidays Abroad" or "Cats" or "Patriotism". As every foreigner learning English is taught, plural nouns (e.g. "cats") and abstract nouns (e.g. "patriotism", "solitude", "jealousy") on their own have a general connotation, i.e. they mean these things in general. The title "Cats" requires an essay on cats in general, "Holidays Abroad" an essay on holidays abroad in general (e.g. Are they worth the trouble? Do they broaden the mind?), and "Patriotism" an essay on the feeling of patriotism (e.g. What is patriotism? Is it a noble feeling or an unworthy one?). Accounts, for example, of the irritating habits of the cat next door or of one's adventures on a particular holiday abroad or of an act of patriotic bravery would *not* be essays on the prescribed subjects, though such material might well be drawn on to illustrate the general themes.

It is essential to read essay questions carefully and make sure that they are understood.

Possibilities of essay topics

One often hears the complaints: "I couldn't think of anything to write about" and "I ran out of ideas half-way through". When someone makes these complaints it is often a sign that through inexperience they do not realize how very large is the amount of relevant material which they can make use of in any essay. Most examiners (and teachers of English) take great care to choose essay topics which could be written about for hours — literally for hours!

Consider, for example, the following essay question:

"Was it right, in your opinion, to raise the school-leaving age from fifteen to sixteen?"

Now in answering this question there are a great many points which could be made and a great many things which could be discussed but let us suppose that the essay writer can think of only three points:

1. The work done in the extra year should be useful.
   [Who is to decide what is useful?]
2. Teenagers kept on at school against their will are nuisances.
3. Before the leaving age was raised some parents forced their sons and daughters to leave at 15 when they wanted to stay on.

The question in the square brackets after point 1. shows that what appears to be a simple point may itself lead to a discussion. But here we are not talking about development of the main points. Nor, incidentally, are we talking about the planning of an essay. We are noting how simple points may be exemplified and perhaps proved. Our imaginary essay-writer might, quite properly decide to do this as follows:

1. We should study things which are going to help us get jobs. Should learn about career possibilities. Spent too much time reading rubbishy poetry last year. Also spent one afternoon a week doing algebra. No use at all. Who cares about quadratic equations? The talks on industrial relations bored me stiff.
2. Bill Brown absolute pest. Time he kicked up that row during Commerce. Broken windows. And Sally Robertson — desk more like the cosmetics dept. of Selfridges than anything else, etc.
3. Jane wanted to take some "O" Levels — talked into leaving by her father — wanted her to work in his betting-shop. (This some years ago.)

The main points may, then, be illustrated and enlarged upon and to the essayist's satisfaction proved with examples. These examples may sometimes take the form of anecdotes. These examples can themselves be expanded with descriptive and narrative and explanatory matter, e.g. what sort of a person Bill

Brown is, what the circumstances were in which he "kicked up a row", why Jane particularly wanted to take "O" Levels, and so on. Just imagine the wealth of relevant material which could be used! And all this in a discussion essay too! Few people run out of material in a descriptive or story essay, even if they provide no introductory or explanatory matter such as how they came to see what they are describing or why they think their story is worth telling. The fact is that whatever the type of subject only three or four main points properly supported and illustrated will probably provide enough material for an hour-long essay. Few people should ever have any problems in finding enough to say.

But another reason why we so often hear the two complaints quoted at the start of this section and the related complaints that the essay subjects in an examination paper are boring or childish is that many students are insufficiently experienced to see the various ways in which essay topics may be legitimately interpreted and treated. Consider the following essay titles:

(a) Photography
(b) Describe a great occasion in sport.
(c) Can nuclear war be prevented?
(d) Pets

The reactions of many a student to this selection might well be something along these lines:

(a) I don't know anything about photography.
(b) I've never been present at a great occasion in sport. I suppose I could make it up but I'd probably run out of ideas.
(c) I've no idea and I've never thought about it, thank goodness.
(d) How childish!

Then despair would follow. Yet this despair would be unjustified.

Photography? Most people could write a perfectly good essay on photography without knowing a thing about cameras, film speeds, shutter speeds, light meters, etc. Most people have taken photographs. Most people have had their photographs taken and perhaps been pleased or horrified at the result. Many have been bored by having to look at other people's holiday slides. Most people have seen tourists festooned with cameras, light meters, filters and all the rest of the paraphernalia. Some have been shocked or pleased that the telephoto lens has destroyed the privacy of famous people. Everyone has seen films and a few have perhaps been impressed by an effective piece of camera work. Many have noted the interest that photographs add to books and newspapers. Some may have found to their fury that the camera *can* lie, e.g. with photographs of "spacious" hotel rooms not big enough to swing a cat in. All these points, here randomly made, could, properly organized, be used in an essay on photography. A title, then, which at first sight may seem to demand a technical treatise can be followed by a non-technical essay. This is not, however, to say that a student who *has* the technical knowledge is prohibited from demonstrating it; but it must be demonstrated in an interesting way, e.g. by explaining the advantages of different apertures.

A great sporting occasion? This could quite legitimately be interpreted humorously. For example: "I little realized on that misty morning in February when I reluctantly offered to carry my girl-friend's golf clubs that this was to be the day when she would achieve her life-long ambition, a round of under 200 — and, incredibly, with only twelve balls lost!"

Can nuclear war be prevented? As with most discussion essays there is only one possible interpretation of this question. A discussion of whether pollution or over-population was a greater danger than nuclear war would not be permissible. Having never thought about this topic, our student would almost certainly be right to reject it.

Pets? It would be quite wrong of him to denounce this as a childish subject, as something left over from primary school. Why do people keep pets? For companionship? To add interest to their lives? Why do some people seem to prefer pets to children? Why on earth did that man in the Midlands want to keep a lion as a pet? Are animals capable of affection? Can cats really tell the difference between various makes of cat-food, as the television commercials would have us believe? What tolerance some dog-owners have of the activities of their pets! (It's all right. He's only a puppy!) What loyalty animals can show! These are just some of the points which could be considered and written about in an essay on pets — and written about in a mature way.

Here we may note an important fact: the intellectual level of an essay and its sophistication depend not so much on the topic as on how the topic is interpreted and treated. An essay on pets could in fact be a great deal more "advanced" than an essay on a more serious subject.

It is hoped that the foregoing remarks have shown that titles may often be interpreted in more than one way.

Here we may briefly note that a discussion of the meaning of a title can sometimes form part of the essay itself. Very rarely, some examiners fail to perceive the ambiguity of an essay question which they have set. More often, questions are set which require some definition and discussion before they can be answered. For example:

"A good education is more important for a boy than for a girl." Discuss.

Before anyone attempted this essay-question he would have to decide exactly what "a good education" is. Even if he did not discuss the vagueness of the expression he would surely have to state what *he* meant or understood by it. In fact a definition of a good education as one appropriate to the abilities, needs and hopes of someone could provide almost all the material for the entire essay.

Treatment

This rather vague heading means here the vein or mood in which an essay is written — sombre, serious, light-hearted or whatever. Some essays, for example a discussion of euthanasia, demand a serious treatment. It would be in bad taste to drag in the joke about people you think would make good candidates for mercy-killing. But as indicated above it is quite wrong to think that essays can never be written in a light-hearted way. The essay question "Discuss the advantages and disadvantages of being an only child" requires a sensible discussion, but one could nevertheless make the minor point that one advantage of being an only child is that you never have the expense of buying birthday and Christmas presents for hordes of nephews and nieces.

Choosing the essay topic

It is astonishing that a few students, quite capable of understanding essay questions and of realizing how they must or may be treated, decide that they are not going to write on any of the prescribed subjects! They prefer to write on subjects slightly different from those prescribed by the examiners or in academic examinations decide to write essays they have already prepared but which do not "fit" the questions. One sixth-form student, at the time of the nationalization of the Anglo-Iranian Oil Company in the 1950s, after being asked to write an essay entitled "The Persian Problem" perversely wrote about the cats which were keeping him awake at nights. More recently, another student, having chosen to answer the question "Why is there so much gambling in Britain?", wrote an essay on illegitimate children! Then there are those examinees who, regardless of the topic, turn every essay into a description or a story.

This wilful misinterpretation of essay questions is inexcusable and in examinations disastrous. Those guilty of it do not realize how lucky they are. In the entrance examination for one Cambridge college candidates were confronted with this request: "Write a three-hour essay on Red Indians." There was no choice.

In most English Language papers of course the problem is quite different. The essay question usually has a good selection of topics. Having carefully read the questions, made sure that he thoroughly understands them, thought of the ways in which each question could legitimately be interpreted and of how much he could say on each, an imaginative student might indeed have a problem — that of deciding which of a number of inviting questions he should choose. Students will of course always be on the look-out for subjects which particularly interest them, but it is to be hoped that by the time they take their examination they will have had enough experience to know which *type* of essay best suits them.

Types of essay

Before considering the main types of essay we should note that in English Language examinations almost every essay is in a sense a mixture of types: a story may include descriptions, a description some narrative, a discussion essay an anecdote to illustrate a particular point, and so on. Some essays may be very mixed indeed. An essay entitled "The Seashore" may be almost purely descriptive or it may, for example, consist of a description of a certain stretch of unspoilt seashore on a particular occasion perhaps followed by reminiscences of bucket-and-spade days and then a discussion of ways to prevent the pollution of the seashore by litter and oil slicks.

Usually, however, an essay is, in the main, one of the following types:

1. *"Argumentative" and discussion essays*

In an "argumentative" essay a writer sets out to prove a point. For example, he may argue (seek to prove conclusively) that a certain point of view is the right one, that a certain decision was a mistaken one, that something was caused in a certain way, or that a certain attitude is justified. Organizing his material to the best of his ability and backing up his statements with evidence, he seeks to arrive at a conclusion with which his reader cannot possibly disagree.

An essay of this type may well be *argumentative* in the usual sense of the word since the writer will probably spend some of his time attacking and attempting to refute the points likely to be made against him.

A *discussion* essay may be defined as an argumentative essay in which the writer seeks to show to his own satisfaction and to his reader's that no definite conclusion is possible. In a discussion essay the writer will discuss ideas which occur to him and the ideas of other people. He will state his views on these ideas, supporting these views with evidence. He will compare and contrast; he will comment and judge. It must be remembered that the meaning of "discuss" is "examine by argument, debate" (*Concise Oxford Dictionary*). It is not enough to state a point of view or merely mention suggestions or describe attitudes — merely to make a list of what people say.

Here is a selection of essay titles each of which might prompt an examinee either to argue or to discuss:

- It has been suggested that all issues of national importance should be decided by referenda and not by votes in Parliament. Discuss your attitude to this suggestion.
- Euthanasia
- "Honesty is the best policy" Is this always true?
- "Monarchy is an anachronism." Discuss.
- How free is the Press?
- Advertising
- How much say should students have in the running of their college?

- "It is not women who need to be liberated but men" — R. J. Alexander.
- What were the main causes of the War of American Independence?

Only a very few essay questions *demand* (e.g. *Illustrate the truth of the statement that all power corrupts*) that the writer should prove a point. Usually, the essay-writer himself decides whether he wishes to argue a point or merely conduct a discussion. If, for example, he believes that euthanasia is wicked he will write an argumentative essay on that subject; if he has not yet decided what his attitude to euthanasia is he will discuss the views for and against. If he has strong views on, say, the British Monarchy he will want to express them: if he has no strong views or if he is torn between his intellectual convictions and his emotions he will carry on a discussion.

Two points may be made here about the above titles: (1) a serious and controversial subject like euthanasia almost certainly calls for an argumentative or discussion essay, but advertising, though many people might choose to attack it or praise it, could be written about discursively. (2) Questions which ask *What? Which? How? How far? To what extent?* etc. do not require mathematically precise answers. In their answers to such questions writers will use expressions like "probably", "possibly", "hardly at all", "to a very great extent" and so on. They will of course make it plain why they use them.

The Essay Question in OND, ONC and other post-"O" Level examinations usually consists entirely of questions calling for argument or discussion, but questions of this sort also appear in Ordinary Level papers and in others of similar standard.

The inclusion of a history question in the above selection of essay titles reminds us that most academic essays, apart from those concerned with exact sciences, are of the argument or discussion type. Here, it will be salutary to read the following extracts from a recent (1976) article in *The Times*. These were some of the remarks of its author, an "A" Level examiner in English Literature:

"Very few candidates can assemble an argument: most move erratically from observation to observation and then try to wrap it all up with a 'Thus we see . . .' conclusion."

". . . instead of *answering* a question on the paper they will respond to it by writing an essay they have prepared already, making one or two token alterations.

Connected with this is the fact that candidates very often misapprehend questions, not usually from a lack of intelligence or misunderstanding, but because they have not been trained to see that some intellectual application is needed for a full appreciation of the meaning of questions posed at this academic level."

"Technical errors are legion. The possessive apostrophe as in 'Milton's' is shunned as though it carried rabies. Many candidates start a line with a comma. Most use pronouns without any regard to their referents. . . . Sentences are commonly linked with commas and not with conjunctions. Many sentences have no verb. Prepositions are misused all the time: bored *of*, compared *to*, fed up *of*, contrast *on*. Spelling is regaining a freedom it has not known since the Middle Ages. . . ."

Take care, then! We may, incidentally, note here how ridiculous is the frequently heard assertion that examinations test nothing more than the ability to regurgitate facts. A well-designed examination question may indeed test this ability but it will also determine whether the candidate has a real understanding of the subject. This understanding can be achieved only by careful study, not by "swotting up" on the night before the examination.

2. Discursive or "rambling" essays

Essays of this type, often written in response to a title consisting of a single word or phrase like "Cats", or "Holidays Abroad" or "Patriotism" or "Photography" or "Advertising", *appear* to ramble from point to point. The essay-writer will appear to use anything that comes into his head on the subject — idle thoughts, unusual ideas, jokes, interesting facts, commonplace facts, anecdotes — but each point will lead naturally to the next. Even an apparently unplanned ramble follows a route.

Essays of this rambling or discursive type rarely deal with serious subjects and perhaps never should. They are light-hearted essays. Outside the examination room and, it may be hoped, inside they entertain the writer and the reader.

There is an opportunity to write essays of this type in the Ordinary Level examination but such essays are often frowned on and not invited in more advanced examinations. This seems a pity since they are just as good tests of a candidate's command of English as any other type of essay and require careful planning. Few things require more planning than an apparently relaxed and carefree progression from point to point.

This sort of essay is not a common literary form nowadays and the following extract is taken from a discursive essay written by Robert Lynd in the 1920s:

> Having decided to write about Easter, I took out a volume of the "Encyclopaedia Britannica" in order to look up the subject of eggs, and the first entry under "Egg" that met my eyes was:
>
> "Egg, Augustus Leopold (1816—63), English painter, was born on the second of May, 1816, in London, where his father carried on business as gun-maker."
>
> Even so, Augustus was not the only Egg. He was certainly not the egg in search of which I opened the Encyclopaedia. The egg I was looking for was the Easter Egg, and it seemed to be the only egg that was not mentioned. There were birds' eggs, and reptiles' eggs, and fishes' eggs, and molluscs' eggs, and crustaceans' eggs, and insects' eggs, and frogs' eggs, and Augustus Egg, and the eggs of the duck-billed platypus, which is the only mammal (except the spiny ant-eater) whose eggs are provided with a large store of yolk, enclosed within a shell, and extruded to undergo development apart from the maternal tissues."

The author then goes on to express his wonder at the number of eggs there are and asks himself how long it would take to count the 14,311,000 eggs laid by the turbot. Later in the essay he remarks on the prettiness of ducks' eggs (a cricketer would not agree!), complains that he never gets the sort of egg with a beautiful sunburnt look but consoles himself with the thought that he may get it sometimes but not recognize it because it is fried. And so on.

The following is an example of a recently written discursive essay:

Holidays Abroad

> "Oh, you went to Blackpool this year, did you?" said the woman in the supermarket queue. "We went to the Costa Blanca. It was absolutely marvellous!"
>
> In fact she had spent two weeks risking sunstroke and

living on food and drink she would never have put up with in an English hotel.

It is certainly true that many people seem to derive most of their enjoyment of foreign holidays by boasting about them when they are safely back in Britain. Others enjoy or console themselves by telling all their friends what a dreadfully uncomfortable or expensive time they had.

One sometimes wonders in fact why some people go abroad at all, for it would be cheaper for them to stay in Britain at some secret hideout and think up stories of starry nights in Tahiti or exciting passport difficulties on the Bulgarian frontier.

But obviously people go abroad for their holidays for good reasons. Some are in search of warmer climates, others of adventure, others of knowledge. But perhaps the reason that most people go abroad is that they feel a need for a complete change of environment.

Their chances of success in finding a new environment depend on where they go. Alassio can be very like Southend, Rome like London — only hotter and more expensive. It is hardly worth paying a fortune to see a sign which says "Buvez Coca Cola" instead of "Drink Coca Cola", etc., etc.

3. Descriptive essays

In a descriptive essay the writer describes something. Yet "describe" is a word used rather freely, as the following requests may suggest:

(a) Describe a hacksaw.
(b) Describe a visit to the dentist's.
(c) Describe your reactions to the proposals to give Scotland and Wales more autonomy.

(a) calls for an objective technical description, not for an essay. (b) seems to be asking for an essay in which there is a large amount of narrative, although there is of course ample scope for description. (c) would be better worded "State your reactions . . ." or "What are your reactions . . .?"

Yet what most people rightly understand by descriptive essays are essays in which the writer describes a scene or a person.

97

Descriptions should be as full as possible.

Descriptions of scenes and places might deal, according to the subject and the writer's inclinations, not only with sights but with sounds and smells, taste and touch. How inadequate, for example, would be the descriptions of a hospital ward, a ladies' hairdresser's, a Chinese restaurant or a garden in June if the odours, aromas and fragrance were not mentioned! A writer might also describe his feelings when he looks at a certain scene, might describe the effect a place has on him. He will perhaps describe the "atmosphere" of a place — dreary, commonplace, magical, exciting, ominous, depressing, exhilarating, or whatever.

A description of a person should not be just an account of his or her career (hardly a description at all!), nor just a description of his or her appearance. It should be a description of a whole personality — appearance, character, habits, talents, idiosyncrasies, interests, and so on. Such an essay might well start with a description of the subject's most striking feature, physical or mental.

In descriptive essays, as in all essays, careful planning and a high standard of written composition are essential. Believing that descriptive essays are easy to write, students often set out to write them without a plan. Often they make no attempt to write properly: they use dashes as all-purpose punctuation marks, they change tenses — e.g. past to present to past again — and very often they write in non-sentences, e.g. "Rain pattering on the windows. Gusts of wind buffeting the trees. Leaves being blown from the branches. People hurrying home. To their warm firesides." The occasional non-sentence is permissible. What is not permissible is an entire essay or a large part of it written in bits of sentences.

4. Narrative essays

A narrative essay narrates; that is to say, it tells a story. As anyone who has ever tried to tell a story "off the cuff" knows, organization is essential. Accordingly, an essay which is to tell even a simple story must be thoroughly planned in note-form first. Writers of humorous fiction may say something like, "Hang on, you don't know what all this is about, do you?", but this should not be done in an essay. The story must be introduced in some way and then clearly told in such a manner that it can be easily followed. The use of explanatory material in brackets is a sure sign that the story-teller has not planned the telling of his story; it is the equivalent in writing of "Oh, I forgot to say . . ." in speech.

Care should be taken to ensure that the important parts of the story are adequately dealt with in the essay, and in particular that the introduction does not go on too long. There are still many students who, if asked to write an account of an interesting day, are likely to spend a third or more of their essay describing their breakfast. Be warned, too, by the example of the student who, having decided to write a 5,000-word extended essay on the history of shipbuilding, had after 4,000 words taken his story to 600 BC!

As we have noted earlier, descriptive material should probably be included in narrative essays. One might also include incidental remarks and even discussion material, providing that these do not obscure the line of the story.

5. *Essays which merely state facts, without comment or discussion*

It is doubtful whether the mere statement of facts should be regarded as essay-writing at all. An essay like "Dangers to Health in the Modern Urban Environment" may seem to invite a list (e.g. industrial pollution, fast-moving traffic, stress induced by noise and overcrowding) but a list of facts, however interesting and well-presented, is not much of an essay. Here is the start of another essay which is basically a list of facts:

> The nearest planet to the sun is Mercury. It is far too hot for any living thing to survive. Then comes Venus, which appears to be wreathed in vapour of some sort and is probably too hot for life. The nearest planet to Earth is Mars, which is sometimes called the Red Planet and was named after the Roman god of war. Many people used to think that it was covered by a network of canals and H. G. Wells wrote a story about a Martian invasion of Earth. However, the Viking space-vehicles have revealed that . . .

In an English examination, at any rate, such a bald recitation of facts is not likely to be wanted or welcomed by examiners. Unfortunately, many students who have, as part of their course, to write extended essays joyfully seize the chance of choosing their own subjects for once and then content themselves with a list of facts, especially when they are writing the history of a company or of an industry or describing a geographical region or giving an account of a technical process, e.g. the production of plastics.

Planning the essay

As we have already noted several times, essays should be planned.

A writer who realizes that essay-writing presents an opportunity to show that he has something to say and that he can say it clearly and effectively and who has carefully decided on his subject and considered its possibilities has in fact to some extent planned his essay. It only remains for him to finalize his plan. Having done this, he can then write the essay, secure in the knowledge that each part of the essay will lead naturally on to the part that follows; that the essay will have continuity so that the reader, who may be an examiner, will easily follow his line of thought.

On the other hand, the writer who regards essay-writing as a matter of writing a minimum number of words or of covering paper with words and who has not considered his subject carefully may be aware that an essay should be planned but he will have no plan in mind and the "plan" he notes down will be a useless formality — just a list of unconnected facts leading nowhere, rather like a blueprint for a machine which has no purpose. The resulting "essay" will hardly be worth the name.

Really, then, instead of saying that all essays should be planned we should say that all true essays *are* planned: if a writer has a genuine essay in mind he will already have a plan in mind; if he has no essay in mind he will never have a plan — at any rate, not one worth the name.

The plan on paper

This is developed from the plan the essayist already has in his mind. It is the framework of the essay and — to change the metaphor — will mark out the route for the essayist to follow.

100

A few people, very few, are capable of developing and remembering their plan without writing it down; but it is always advisable to put the plan down on paper and to put it down in as much detail as time and the need for legibility permit.

A written plan has several advantages

1. It gives the essay-writer a general picture of his essay; it enables him to see the essay as a whole. Keeping in mind the amount of time he has at his disposal and the number of words he may reasonably hope to produce in that time, he can work out how long he should spend on the various parts of the essay, according to their importance.
2. It enables the writer to sort his main points into the *most* suitable order. He may have second thoughts on the order of his material and he can adjust the order by means of arrows and numbering.
3. It saves him the trouble of remembering supporting material such as examples and illustrations. These can be noted down on the plan under the main points. Moreover, when he is writing one part of the essay the writer will often think of material which he can add to later parts of the essay. Thus the plan can sometimes be filled out throughout the time he is writing the essay. Essay-writers who, despite all their efforts, have difficulty in "lasting out" should bear this possibility in mind.

It is worth spending about one-sixth of the total time allowed on planning the essay, for a good and fairly detailed plan (as opposed to a very rough draft) is half the battle, perhaps more than half. With no problems about what to say or in what order to say it, the writer can concentrate on conveying his meaning clearly, on choosing the best words, on getting the sentence construction and grammar right, on producing an essay of which he can be proud.

A suggested method of planning

1. Note down the points you have thought of, and any others as they occur to you, allowing plenty of space on the paper for additions.

The most important points will tend to come first, especially if you have strong views on what you are going to write about, but supporting material (e.g. explanations and examples), qualifying material (e.g. objections and exceptions), and linking material and even major points may occur to you at any time and should be noted without delay, lest such material is forgotten. Often supporting material will be noted down immediately beneath the appropriate main point.

2. Make it clear in your mind which are your *main* points. Then, using any numbering system you like, sort out the main points in the order that seems to you most suitable. This order will partly be determined by the relative importance of the main points — you may for example decide to deal with the most important point first or to lead up to it via less important main points — but you should constantly bear in mind that in the essay one point should lead on naturally and logically to the point that follows it.

Make sure that supporting or qualifying material is physically linked (by arrows or loops, for example) to the main points which it supports or qualifies.

Example:

Imagine that an examination candidate had chosen to answer the following question: "Should the smoking of cigarettes be made illegal?"

His final plan might be as shown opposite.

Remarks on this plan

    (a)   The plan may be open to criticism but it is certainly better than many plans which have been used in examinations.

    (b)   The student has decided to arrange the points in favour of banning on the left and those against on the right. (3a), although it stems from (3), has strayed towards the left as it is a point in favour of banning cigarette smoking. The speed limit example has suggested itself to the student (3b). He has used the exclamation mark to remind himself to stress (3b) pretty vigorously.

    (c)   Each point leads naturally to the next, thus ensuring that the essay will have continuity. No doubt after stressing the need to limit people's freedom to kill (3b), the student will admit that restrictions on people's freedom

Causes disease (1)

Would interfere with people's
(3) <u>liberty.</u>

Cancer
Bronchitis
Heart trouble (1a)

Old Brown smoked 60 a day-
lived to 97.
(1c)   (just an exception)

<u>Couldn't be enforced.</u> cf. drug
problem and Prohibition in U.S.
(5)

Number of deaths increasing.
Think so, anyway (1d)

But other beneficial laws
limit people's liberty, e.g.
speed limits for motorists.
(3a)
Liberty to kill, even yourself,
ought to be limited!
(3b)

Does smoking really cause
disease? Yes, statistics
show this. (1b)

Money got from cigarette tax
would have to be got from other
taxes. Possible? Don't know.   (4)

Smoking annoys people who
don't smoke.
Not important.

Banning of cigarette
smoking would have very
beneficial results.   (2)

Even if it can't be made
illegal, should be more
strongly discouraged (not
(6) rubbish about not wanting
to kiss girls with smoky breath)
More restrictions, alarming
publicity wanted.

are regrettable and cause resentment. The transition
from (3) to objections (4) and (5) might seem awkward,
but after discussing objection (3), a matter of principle,
the student might continue in some such way: "There
are, however, two very strong practical objections to any
proposal to ban cigarette smoking. The first is that . . ."
and then go on to deal with (4) and (5). These objections
seem so powerful to him that he has decided on the
conclusion noted in (6): strong discouragement.

(d) The conclusion (6) is relevant. Although the question is whether cigarette smoking should be *banned*, it would be legitimate to conclude that it would be a good thing if it were banned but that as banning is probably impracticable it should be strongly discouraged instead.

(e) The point about Brown's long life was originally put down on the right as evidence that there was no need to ban smoking. The student's second thoughts have led him to conclude that exceptional cases do not disprove statistics.

(f) One point, originally put down as a major point in favour of banning cigarette smoking, has after consideration been dismissed as unimportant. It has not been numbered. It would probably be excluded from the essay or mentioned only briefly.

(g) Only a few main points have been listed but these would be enough for a long essay. Our imaginary student has recalled a television anti-smoking campaign; no doubt other material will come to mind as he writes the essay, for example, the incredible assertion that it is just a coincidence that people who smoke suffer from disease.

(h) It should be noted that the type of continuity secured by the above plan is a genuine, logical and natural continuity very different from that illusion of continuity which disc-jockeys offer!

There is little doubt about this student's views: he is not against a ban on cigarette smoking; he is not neutral; he would like it to be possible to ban it. Consequently it is natural for him to put forward first the strong reason for smoking to be banned. He could, on the other hand, have decided to deal with the objections to the suggestion first.

Example of a plan for a discursive or "rambling" essay

Title of the essay: "Smoking". We will imagine that the essayist has no strong views on smoking: having no point to prove, he decides to write neutrally and interestingly about smoking, but he is at great pains to secure continuity. Accordingly he will note down all the points that occur to him and then number them so that each point leads to the next. His plan might look something like the one opposite.

My first cigarette (1)   a drug   social ice-breaker

regarded by many children as a sign of adulthood (2)

Famous smokers — Sherlock Holmes, Churchill,
Red Indians, Raleigh (14) They've a
soothes the nerves (5)   lot to answer for — costing me a fortune.

effect of advertising, tactics of advertisers (4)

helps one concentrate? (6)   Are health hazards proved?
Don't know. (8)

Addictive (10)

expensive (11)

Regarded by some adults as a
sign of sophistication (3)

Types of smoker — cigarettes, pipes, cigars — do these indicate
character?

Unpleasant habit, say some people.   Big source of revenue to
Government. (13)

High tax on tobacco (12)   Health hazards? (7)

Sponsorship of golf and cricket
by tobacco companies (9)   Smoking relieves boredom.

An essay based on this plan might start something like this:

Smoking

I smoked my first cigarette on Guy Fawkes' Day three
years ago, when I was thirteen. I cannot say that I enjoyed
it very much, but I certainly felt very grown up.

It is certainly true that many young teenagers regard
smoking as a sign of adulthood and that thousands of
young children have the same idea. One frequently sees
ten-year-olds sharing a "fag" in the belief that it is the
thing to do. Many children have been known to spend
their school-dinner money on cigarettes.

They can hardly be blamed for concluding that to
smoke is to be grown-up, for millions of adults smoke
continually, despite publicity designed to discourage them.
Adult smokers of course obviously enjoy smoking or they
would not smoke, but perhaps they too, because of the
advertisements of tobacco companies, regard smoking as

a sign of sophistication. "The international passport to smoking pleasure" is one company's description of its product. The man in the poster smoking a Rothmans King-Size as he drives his Jaguar is obviously, from the rings on his sleeve, an airline pilot. . . .

Remarks on this start to an essay:
(a) The English is open to some slight criticism but the essay has the great merit of continuity.
(b) Not all the points have been numbered. Those that have been numbered are ample for a long essay. Already 170 words have been used and the fourth point is not yet finished. One might imagine a final total of 700 or 800 words.
(c) The essay could of course have been started from a different point, for example,
"Have a cigarette?"
Most people know that Red Indians used to pass round a pipe of peace and today we sometimes offer people cigarettes in the hope of establishing a friendly atmosphere. . . .

We have used as examples an argumentative essay and a discursive essay, but planning by noting down and sorting out is applicable to all types of essay – to narrative essays, for example. In narrative essays a note will be made of the main stages of the story or the history.

An introduction, a middle and an end?

We are often told that an essay should have an introduction, a middle and a conclusion, "conclusion" here meaning not an inference or deduction but a tidy and appropriate ending. This is true, but too often examination candidates with the above advice in mind write an introduction which serves no useful purpose and a dull conclusion which repeats something which has already been said more effectively earlier in the essay.

The fact is that intelligent and careful planning should bring to mind a suitable introduction and conclusion.

Introductions
The writer of a discursive essay might start with any remark he finds interesting; the writer of a story might start by describing

the situation in which the events he is to recount took place or by introducing the characters or by saying why he thinks the story worth telling, or perhaps by bringing forward an exciting part of the narrative in order to grip his reader's attention — in the manner of adventure-story writers and many newspaper reports. A descriptive essay could begin with a description of the main or central feature of a scene or with a short account of how the essayist came upon a scene, or first got to know the person he is describing. Some discussion essays might start as follows: *My reactions to this suggestion are mixed. On the one hand I* . . . or the writer could decide to make his first main point the introduction: *Perhaps the greatest advantage of being an only child is that* . . .

The writer who sets out to present an argument, to prove a point could well start with the point he intends to prove: *The smoking of cigarettes should be made illegal without delay*, or he could start by stating his main reason for holding the view he does: *Every year thousands of people die prematurely and in great distress because they have been unable to give up smoking.*

Some of these suggested introductions may seem rather abrupt yet an abrupt but useful introduction is a great deal better than this sort of thing: *There are many points for and against this question. First I am going to deal with* . . . or *There were several causes of the War of American Independence. The first cause* . . . (i.e. in the writer's history notebook!) or *This is a very complicated question. People have argued about it a great deal. It is doubtful whether it will ever be decided one way or the other.* . . . (Get on with it!)

Conclusions

A discursive essay might finish with some suitable general remark. For example, the writer of an essay on "Solitude" might conclude by saying that whatever its blessings or disadvantages, solitude is becoming in Britain increasingly hard to find. A narrative essay will of course often end with the end of the story, but it could end with a comment: "This was an experience which he was never to forget." A writer might decide to conclude a descriptive essay by telling of his final impressions of the subject or perhaps by describing how a scene changed as night fell or people departed. An argumentative essay will no doubt end with some forceful summing-up. If the subject of the essay merits it, the writer might even conclude with a demand or a challenge: "What needs to be done is clear. How long must we wait for someone to do it?" A discussion essay will probably end with a neutral conclusion: "There is simply not enough evidence for us to decide one way or the other. We shall have to wait for the results of future research."

Language and style

Both "language" and "style" are ambiguous words but together they make a convenient heading for the following advice:

Essays should be written in good continuous prose — in grammatically correct, well-constructed and suitably punctuated sentences which communicate the writer's meaning to the reader perfectly.

Conversational abbreviations like "can't", "won't", "shouldn't", etc., should usually be avoided, as should an extremely conversational style (e.g. Well, I mean, it's all right to *say* that, but how on earth do you prove it?). That sort of style is hardly ever suitable and it requires a great deal of punctuation.

Slang should be avoided, unless a special effect is aimed at, as with the use of "fag" on page 105. In the following sentence the writer has used a popular abbreviation to express his contempt:

"By the beginning of this century her grand-daughter lived on bread and scrape, bran-filled sausages, scraps of bad meat, sanded sugar, aniline jams, dirty milk, sodden stale vegetables, chips and marge."

What an impact that last word has! However, even if you feel you could achieve a similarly striking effect by the use for example of "up the bingo" or "nosh-up", take care. The use of slang and other colloquialisms too often produces a casual effect. Moreover, such expressions may not be familiar to the reader. If you cannot think of an acceptable alternative, make sure that slang is enclosed in quotation marks.

The following advice on style is often given. Use linking expressions like "however", "in view of these facts", "despite this", "consequently", "therefore" to enhance the impression of continuity. Vary the length of paragraphs and the length and type of sentences, using short sentences for dramatic effect, for example. Use exclamations and questions sparingly. Employ vivid and suitable metaphors and similes. Use repetition only for emphasis. Choose the most suitable words and do not be content with approximate equivalents. Write in a style to suit the subject.

All of this is very good advice but to those who, through much reading, have developed an understanding of what is required in written English it will appear obvious: and for those who never read or read nothing but the words in comic strips it will be useless. They might indeed vary the length of sentences and drag in the odd simile, but this will be done simply for the sake of doing it. The only way to achieve an understanding of what sort of language is required in essay-writing and to develop a sense of style is to read well-written books, newspapers and magazines. Indeed it is the only way to improve most types of written communication. However conscientiously a student's work is marked and however constructively it is criticized, he will never be able to write well unless he has read well.

Some miscellaneous "don'ts"

1. Don't announce your plan, for example, "I will deal first with . . ." If the essay is well planned, the reader will be able to follow its course for himself.

2. Don't use *e.g.*, *i.e.*, *etc.*, etc. *Etc.* too often means in effect "I can't think of anything else." It should mean "and the other things of this type", so its use after the names of things which have nothing obviously in common is inexcusable: "he was interested in golf, astronomy, etc."

3. Don't use the sort of "punctuation" used in the balloons in comic strips (*!!!!**! Grrh!! Eh??!*) or any underlining unless it represents italics, and don't use unnecessary capital letters. If you do any of these things you are admitting that the words you have used are inadequate.

4. Don't use words in their colloquial sense when this is different from their literary sense. Some examples are: *fabulous fantastic, lousy, decent, aggravate, lovely, putrid, livid, great.* Perhaps the main meaning of "nice" is now "pleasant", but the word is best avoided. It is too often used in speech to mean *fine, sunny, exhilarating, delicious, tasty, friendly, attractive, respectable. . . .*

5. Don't use cliches — worn-out unoriginal expressions like "in this day and age" and "from nine to ninety" or ridiculous expressions like "at this moment in time".

6. Don't drag in unusual words or apparently impressive words and expressions to show off your knowledge. Use the words that do the job, regardless of whether they are well-known or uncommon. The remark that an essay provides to examinees an opportunity to show off their knowledge of words has often led to some most unfortunate results, for example, "Having consumed with alacrity these sumptuous comestibles, I sank into a fauteuil in front of the flickering kaleidoscopic screen but within the space of a few minutes was in the arms of Morpheus."

Technical points

1. Always write the title of your essay, unless you are asked not to.

2. Indent the start of new paragraphs. Do *not* use the block paragraphing found in some business letters.

3. When you have finished with your plan, cross it out. Your reader is interested only in the finished product, the essay itself.

4. Having finished the essay, read through it carefully so that you may correct avoidable mistakes. We all make them. Dot your i's and cross your t's, literally and metaphorically.

Two unsatisfactory essays

We will conclude this lengthy section on essays by criticizing two essays, the first on "Boats", the second on a subject of which the reader of this book is perhaps getting rather tired!

Boats

Nothing, according to the Water Rat in "The Wind in the Willows" is so marvellous as "messing about in boats". I certainly agree with him.

The "QE 2", although smaller than the "Queen Mary" and the "Queen Elizabeth", is a very fine ship. It is extensively used for cruises as well as for the regular transatlantic trips. For luxury liners have to be used as often as possible if they are to pay their way. This is because of competition from airliners.

My cousin has a catamaran which he keeps at Weymouth. He takes us for trips which I find most enjoyable, although I am not a good sailor.

At one time water transport was cheaper than land transport. In the early eighteenth century most roads were so bad that heavy goods had to be transported by sea. Coal was brought to London from Newcastle by sea. Well into the nineteenth century most industrial goods were transported in barges.

Probably the first boat was a hollowed-out tree trunk. Later a number of logs were bound together to form a raft. Then some imaginative person thought of using windpower to propel a craft, and so masts and sails were invented.

Boats have a fascination for most people. . . .

We need read no more. What are we to think of this "essay"? The spelling, punctuation and sentence-construction are faultless; the writer has useful general knowledge at his command; the opening paragraph is very effective; there is a new paragraph for each change of topic. But it is a poor essay: it has no continuity; it is a collection of unconnected remarks. Obviously, the essay has not been planned.

Should smoking be banned?

This question raises many besides. It is in fact a question as to whether or not the desires or freedom of the individual can be infringed upon by a minority.

Smoking itself is always a contreversial subject Some say
5 it encourages ill health, others say it doesn't but one thing it does do is cost money. For this reason alone people could wish smoking to be banned but surely the individual has the right to decide on what he spends his money.

A great deal of research continues to find out whether
10 or not smoking causes cancer but no definite answer has yet been found. It is true that smoking can cause shortness of breath and a general lowering of the standard of health particularly in the lungs but there is, as yet, no definite link with cancer. Despite the health hazards millions of
15 people smoke, the numbers increasing annually and few of these would stop even if it were banned.

Although it is wrong to ban smoking much more could

be done to show smokers, particularly the young, the hazards, so that fewer would start smoking. People now
20 start to smoke at a younger age despite the age limit for buying cigarettes being 16.

In a supposedly "free" society nothing should be banned that does not affect others. It is left to the individual if he smokes. He is the one harming himself not
25 others. No group of people should be able to decide what others should do in their private lives, it should be left to them.

If, however, smoking was banned important minorities might take it upon themselves to ban other things thought
30 harmful, drink for instance. If it did happen a black market would spring up as it did in the war, and where supplies of tobacco ran out other materials would be used, possibly dangerous. This can be confirmed when one look's at the result of prohibition in America. "Boot-leg"
35 whiskey was made, killing many because of the harmful content.

Another possibility is that people would change to some other form of addiction — drugs or drink, drugs being far more dangerous than any cigarette. Drugs are banned, but
40 the number of addicts continues to increase. This shows that if people want something badly enough nothing will stop them.

Smoking should not be banned as it is the right of everyone to decide what they do with their time and money but
45 restrictions on where smoking is allowed could be made, and also a tighter watch should be kept on the age of those buying cigarettes.

It would take several hundred words to point out *everything* which is wrong with this essay. Here, in order of occurrence, are some of the points which would be raised:

Line 1   What are these many other questions?

    3   "Infringed" — the right word?

    3   Who is the minority referred to?

    4   Misspelling of "Controversial".

    4   Full stop forgotten.

 5—6   Unjustified ending to a sentence — it has nothing to do with the first two parts.

 6—8   One point (cost) incorrectly linked with the rights of the individual.

9	Research cannot "find out". Researchers can try to.
12—13	"Standard of health in the lungs."
15—16	No evidence produced to support this statement.
17	Here we have a conclusion but it is in the middle of the essay.
20	A *lower* age? An *earlier* age?
22	The use of the quotation marks is unjustified and confusing.
23	Inconsistency of using "is" after "should be".
24—5	Confused sentence.
25—7	Repetition of individual choice argument.
26	The comma should be replaced by a full stop, and a new sentence should be started.
28	Who *are* the minorities the writer keeps talking about? Two points hopelessly confused.
34	Apostrophe wrongly used in a verb.
43—4	A return to the theme of individual rights.
43—7	A good conclusion.
43— 4	Commas omitted.

What a mix-up! Though the errors in punctuation and spelling are regrettable, they are not of tremendous importance. What makes this a bad essay is the lack of organization. This is a pity, as the student's ideas are good and we can guess what has led to her final conclusion.

Her arguments for and against the proposal to ban smoking are as follows:

For
It would save people's money. (A minor personal point.)
Smoking is damaging to health.

Against
It would be an encroachment on people's freedom, perhaps to be followed by other encroachments. It does not affect other people. (True?)
A ban difficult to enforce.
Something worse might take the place of smoking.

Conclusions
It shouldn't be banned. But people should be discouraged.

Essay questions from examinations

Notes: (1) The order in which these examination questions appear does not necessarily always indicate the level of the examination. Nor should it be taken as an indication of the standard of essay-writing required. For example, the Royal Society of Arts, Stage I, is officially designated as elementary but essays of a very advanced standard could be written in response to many of the essay questions set in R.S.A. I examinations.

(2) Some sets of questions may include a question asking for something other than an essay.

(3) Ideas for "starters" do not often appear in advanced examinations.

1. Write a composition on ONE of the following subjects. You are advised to spend about 50 minutes on this question.

(a) Give an account of your favourite entertainment. It may be a sport, the cinema, television, music, reading, dancing — or something else. State why it appeals to you more than other forms of entertainment.

(b) The roads of this country become more congested as the volume of traffic on them increases every year. Suggest ways of overcoming the problems caused by this congestion.

(c) Write something interesting about animals. Here are a few ideas to help you; but if you wish you may ignore them completely.

Cruelty to animals. Animals as pets. Zoos and "safari parks". Strange animals. Animals as food. Your favourite animal.

(d) People today often speak of the "generation gap". By this they mean that older people and teenagers do not understand one another and that this leads to all kinds of problems, difficulties and misunderstandings. Do you, personally, find that the "generation gap" exists? If so, give some examples of how it has shown itself in your life, and suggest, if you can, how it might be overcome.

(e) It has been said that schooldays are the happiest days of our lives. Say whether you agree or disagree with this statement and give reasons for your answer.

(f) Describe your favourite holiday district, whether it be

country, seaside or town. Then say why this particular area is your favourite.

(R.S.A. English Language I, June 1973.)

2. The following comments were made by young people on the subject of the raising of the school-leaving age to sixteen:

"It makes you think a bit more about doing O-levels and C.S.E.'s, instead of leaving school, as I did, with no qualifications at all. Also, pupils whose parents would have made them leave at fifteen now have the chance to gain some qualifications."

"It gives you a better chance of choosing the right job, and being a year older when you leave makes you better able to cope."

"There's a hard core of people who absolutely hate school and just can't wait to get out. They are never going to appreciate that there's anything good about school, and I reckon that it's a waste keeping them there. If they had been allowed to leave, the rest of us could have prepared for our examinations in peace."

"Anyone who wants to stay at school can anyway. It's silly forcing people to stay."

"I want to do a proper job, and earn some money. They treat us like kids, make us do bookwork that'll be no use to us, and then wonder why we play up."

"If you've got the sort of parents who just want you to get out and earn some money, then I reckon the year's a waste of time."

"It's probably a good thing, but the extra year shouldn't be just a continuation of the things you've learned before. You need a much more practical approach that bears some relation to the work or the environment you will be entering when you leave school."

Considering some or all or none of the above comments, write 2—2¼ pages of average handwriting on ONE of the following:

(i)   Is, in your opinion, the raising of the school-leaving age a good thing or a bad?

(ii) You are a headmaster. Write a report for submission to the governors describing how the extra year is being spent in your school, and with what success.

(iii) Write an account of your last year at school, saying

how valuable you found it and how it might have been improved.
(Joint Matriculation Board English Language Ordinary Level, Paper, C, June 1975.)

3. Write for about 50 minutes on ONE of the following topics (about two pages of average handwriting):
  (a) World Government: is it possible? is it desirable?
  (b) Charities: today there are many local, national and international charitable organizations, e.g., Oxfam, Save the Children, St. Dunstan's, Help the Aged. What are your views about them?
  (c) The Wedding.
  (d) Flying Saucers or Unidentified Flying Objects (UFOs)! Many people claim to have seen them, even spoken to people from them. What do you think about such reports?
  (e) "Women's Lib!" What does it mean to you and what are your reasons for supporting or opposing it?
  (f) The pleasures and thrills of any of the following: sailing, canoeing, climbing, motor-racing, pot-holing, hunting or fishing.
  (g) My earliest childhood memories.
  (R.S.A. English Language II, November 1974.)

4. Write for about 50 minutes on ONE of the following topics:
  (a) The future of space travel.
  (b) The office of the future.
  (c) The welfare of old people.
  (d) Holidays.
  (e) It is said that modern Britain is a "permissive society". What do you understand by that expression? How far do you approve or disapprove of the "permissive society"?
  (R.S.A. English Language II, March 1970.)

5. Write from two to three pages on ONE of the following subjects. If, however, your handwriting is unusually large or unusually small, you should make some adjustment in the number of pages you fill.
  (a) Describe an occasion when you panicked.
  (b) Each form in a school tends to develop its own special characteristics: it also tends to have its own characters, two or three people well known both to the staff and to

the rest of the school. Write your impressions of your form and its characters.

(c) Write your views on advertising and advertisements, referring, if you wish, to the following extracts from "The British Code of Advertising Practice":

All advertising should be legal, clean, honest and truthful.

Advertisements should not contain any description which is misleading about the product advertised.

Medical advertisements should not contain copy which is exaggerated, for example, the use of the words "magic", "miraculous".

(d) Experiences of a Saturday job.

(e) Write a short story to illustrate ONE of the following sayings.

(i) The best things in life are free.

(ii) Don't count your chickens before they are hatched.

(iii) If a thing's worth doing, it's worth doing well.

(f) Describe an occasion when you have been part of a large crowd at a public event. Concentrate on the crowd, its behaviour and reactions, the variety of individuals in it, rather than on the event itself.

(g) "You can't tell the boys from the girls. They all look scruffy." "There's no quality in the clothes. They won't last." "Ridiculous! Why don't they wear something sensible?" Write your views on the clothes young people wear today, commenting, if you wish, on the above criticisms.

(J.M.B. English Language Ordinary Level, Paper A, Part I, Section B, June 1974.)

Note: The eighth question has been omitted here since it was based on cartoons supplied to candidates. The numbering of the topics has been altered for simplicity. Candidates were advised to spend no more than 50 minutes on this question.

6. Write a short essay of about 450 words on ONE of the following:

(a) The countryside in Autumn or Winter.

(b) The best film or play you have seen or the best book you have read in the past six months.

(c) A national hero or heroine.

(d) Keeping up with fashion.

    (e)   "Convention kills". Discuss.

    (f)   The influence of the past.

OR

    (g)   A story beginning with the words "Could I possibly face up to the challenge which was being offered me?"
(R.S.A. English Language III, June 1972.)

7. Write between 400 and 450 words on ONE of the following:

    (a)   The advantages and disadvantages of working in a small branch or for a small firm.

    (b)   My rights and my responsibilities.

    (c)   A disaster relief force. (Write an essay about the formation, finance, supplies and operations of an organization which provides help anywhere in the world.)

    (d)   "Call a tiger master, it will still eat you." Discuss this saying.

    (e)   Popularity.

    (f)   Phone-ins. (Radio or television programmes in which the public is invited to telephone the studio to express views, air difficulties or put certain points to experts.)

    (g)   Overmanning. (The problem of having too many employees for the work available.)
(The Institute of Bankers, Part 1, English, April 1976.)

Candidates were advised to allow one hour for this question. The following request was made: Please note that essays are always preferred to stories.

8. Write a short essay of about 450 words on ONE of the following:

    (a)   A justification of "pop" art *or* "pop" music.

    (b)   "Advertising is no longer as influential as it was." Discuss.

    (c)   A critical account of any book you have read which deals with the past.

    (d)   A short story based either on a proverbial saying *or* a local legend *or* on fantasy.

    (e)   A practical undertaking.

    (f)   Dining out.

    (g)   Demonstrations.
(R.S.A. III.)

9. Write an essay on ONE of the following:

    (a)   Some spectacular cases of child neglect have been

brought to light in recent months. Is the State meeting its responsibilities in this respect?
- (b) "If your work is interesting, you do not need a hobby." Discuss.
- (c) Why do you think many young people reject the acquisitive society in which we live?
- (d) The importance of the theatre.
- (e) Loneliness.

(Association of Medical Secretaries Diploma Examination, June 1976.) This question carried 30 per cent of the marks.

10. The following are a selection of essay subjects which, at one examining centre, have appeared in the English papers of the ONC and OND in Business Studies examinations.
- (a) Do you agree that most of Britain's economic ills are of our own making?
- (b) In a recent television play one of the characters fired a double-barrelled shot-gun at a television set given to him by a friend. What, in your opinion, might have been the reasons for such drastic action?
- (c) What, in your view, constitutes a successful career?
- (d) "For all practical purposes the Commonwealth has ceased to exist." Discuss.
- (e) "The function of Members of Parliament is to lead public opinion, not to follow it." Discuss.
- (f) What criticisms have you of the presentation of news on radio *or* on television *or* in popular newspapers? What changes would you make?
- (g) Are you optimistic or pessimistic about the world's future? Give your reasons.
- (h) In what circumstances, if any, is a person justified in taking the life of another?
- (i) What changes would you make in our system of taxation?
- (j) "Undoubtedly, part of the decline of the Christian Church in general arises from the increasing disposition by the public to regard Christian belief not so much as incredible but rather as simply irrelevant to their day-to-day concerns." (*New Society*, Dec. 5 1974.) State your views on this matter.
- (k) How free is the Press?

(l) Democracy is government by the people. How far, in your opinion, does our parliamentary system live up to this definition?

(m) There has been criticism of examinations recently. Write a defence or condemnation of examinations. If you wish, suggest ways in which the present system of examinations could be improved.

A further selection of essay questions

1. The problems of being old in Great Britain today.
2. The world population explosion.
3. "All men have equality of rights but all do not have equality of ability, potential or achievement; therefore a classless society is impossible.
   (These first three questions are from the English paper of the Association of Medical Secretaries Diploma Examination, 1968.)
4. "What you say is more important than how you say it." Discuss.
5. "Differences of accent are of no importance." Discuss.
6. There is strong medical evidence that the smoking of cigarettes causes many premature deaths. Should the smoking of cigarettes be made illegal?
7. Write two descriptions of a scene: as it is now and as it is likely to be in six months' time.
8. "What's the point of writing good English? No-one would understand it." Comment on this remark by a student.
9. An ideal husband.
10. "Why bother to write? All communication will be oral soon and tapes and cassettes will be used instead of books and written records." Discuss.
11. "For most of the day I had travelled across a singularly dreary tract of countryside, without seeing another living soul. At last, as night was falling, I came to the lonely old house." Continue the story.
12. What is a good education?
13. Bores.
14. Discuss what you hope to be doing five years from now.
15. It has been strongly urged that the death penalty should

be re-introduced for terrorist crimes resulting in death. Do you agree?

16. "Religion has no relevance to modern life." Discuss.
17. Describe an autumn walk.
18. Saturday night — and Sunday morning.
19. Napoleon called England a nation of shopkeepers; now we are a nation of spectators.
20. What law would you most like to see passed by Parliament? State your reasons.
21. In a magazine article the years from 1950 to 1975 were described as easily the best in the history of the world. Discuss this contention.
22. Do you agree that the best way to secure peace is to prepare for war?
23. Cats.
24. Is it in your opinion right that leading sportsmen and entertainers should be able to make so much money?
25. Should euthanasia be legalized?
26. Your favourite or least favourite television personality.
27. An old man looks back on his life.
28. "Examinations divide people into categories and therefore all examinations should be abolished." Do you agree?
29. "Bad laws should be broken." Do you agree?
30. "There's the banjo serenader and the others of his race,
    And the piano-organist. I've got him on the list.
    And people who eat peppermint and puff it in your face
    — They never would be missed.
    Then the idiot who praises with enthusiastic tone
    All centuries but this and every country but his own."
    The Lord High Executioner in Sir Arthur Sullivan's and W. S. Gilbert's *The Mikado* is enumerating the people he would like to remove from society permanently. Who would you put on *your* list? State your reasons.

Chapter 8

Short compositions

In some examinations candidates are required to write short compositions. The time to be spent on one of these is usually not more than thirty-five minutes and may well be considerably less. The following are *some* of the main types:

1. **Reviews of books, plays, films, television and radio programmes, etc.**
When writing a review or a criticism (which is not necessarily hostile!) you should not merely recount the story of the film or book or play. Indeed the story or plot should be dealt with very briefly, possibly in the opening sentence. Those who have read reviews in newspapers and magazines will know that they should ask themselves the following sorts of question: Is the story easy to follow? Is the story interesting? Is the dialogue interesting, boring, unconvincing, natural, etc.? Is the theme usual or unusual? Has this play got a "message"? Are the actors suited to their roles? Is the photography good? Do the characters seem real or merely cardboard cut-outs? Is the incidental music suitable? Does the fact that the scenery is impressive compensate for the poor acting? Are the publicity claims justified ("This gripping tale", "Not for the nervous!" "A magnificent evocation of Renaissance Italy", etc., etc.)? Is the book readable (as opposed to "legible")? Is the language easy or difficult to understand? Is the style clear or involved, affected or natural?
Sometimes candidates are asked to write a critical (not necessarily disparaging) description of a newspaper. Here, one might

discuss the proportion of news to articles and features and of printed matter to illustrations and what one thinks of the prominence given to serious news, sports reports, gossip and scandal, and so on. One might even deal with such questions as: Is the newspaper too big to read in the train? Are the photographs clear? Does the ink come off on your fingers? Why are there so many misprints in such a well-written newspaper?

2. Describing processes (e.g. preparing your favourite meal, changing a car wheel)
It is a good practice to start by listing, in a properly constructed sentence, all that is required — equipment, ingredients, or whatever. All stages of the process should then be dealt with in a logical order. Very often one is asked to describe a process to someone who knows nothing about it and here it is essential to include explanations of unusual terms. (Attach the whang-bar to the differential distributor and re-align the outer flange!)

One type of sentence should predominate: if you start with an instruction you should continue with instructions and not, for example, drop into the boring passive; but in order to avoid having a large number of short imperative sentences you should exercise your skill in varying sentence patterns, e.g. "Having checked that the tea-pot is empty and clean, put three tea-spoonfuls of tea . . .".

It is not permissible to adopt a cookery-book style, e.g. "Loosen wheel-nuts with spanner, then jack up car."; "Stir until thoroughly mixed up then stand in oven for three hours."

3. Letters
These may be either business letters or letters to friends or relatives. Business letters are dealt with elsewhere in this book.

In examinations, letters to acquaintances should in style be somewhere between those carelessly phrased and extremely slangy letters which most people often do write to people they know well and those artificially formal letters sometimes recommended in textbooks, e.g. "My Dear Aunt, How elated I was to learn that . . . Your affectionate nephew". No extra marks are awarded for ingeniously humorous addresses and names!

Sometimes an advertising letter to be sent out as a circular is asked for. Here, it is advisable to devise an opening sentence which grips the reader's attention. Subheadings may be sparingly used.

4. Reports (e.g. on visits and courses)

The principles of good report-writing apply. A full and appropriate title should be followed by an introductory paragraph and then headed sections. The report will of course be signed and dated.

5. Newspaper articles or reports

These require headlines, but headlines in ordinary handwriting. A report or article should probably start with a sentence which states the most startling or interesting fact or which summarizes the theme of the article. The remainder of the passage will follow, logically arranged. All relevant details should be included. The use of very short sentences and parts of sentences in very short "paragraphs", as found in certain popular newspapers, is not recommended.

6. Descriptions of objects (e.g. a lampshade, a lawn-mower, a vacuum flask)

The following suggested plan may be helpful, though clearly it will not always be suitable:

(a) a one-sentence definition
(b) a description of the essential parts with, where appropriate, some account of how the object works.
(c) a description of the less-important parts.
(d) minor details such as colour: This last section could be used to mention variations in type. For example, after describing a conventional thermometer one could mention the bellows type.

It is extremely advisable to think carefully before tackling such a question and to decide what are the central or essential parts of the object to be described. People have been known to start descriptions of a lawn-mower by dealing first with the handle and then working along to the other end of the machine!

7. Descriptions of rooms and buildings (e.g. a dental surgery, a railway station waiting-room)

Such descriptions may be technical, dealing precisely with such matters as size, shape, furnishing, equipment and so on, or they may provide a picture of one particular place at one particular time. The latter sort should start with a brief introduction which tells how the writer came to be there. The former type will be an objective description, the latter a subjective one; that is to say, the writer will tend to give prominence to those features which he finds most noticeable, e.g. dirty cups and saucers not yet cleared away from restaurant tables.

8. "Mini-essays"

Often one is asked to write a very short essay, to write a limited number of words on a subject on which a full-length essay could be written. If a word limit is not specified by the examiners they will nevertheless give a clear indication that they expect answers to be fairly brief.

Good organization and a high standard of written composition are required. Jumbled notes are certainly not! Examinees should briefly plan their answers and then get down to the subject in the very first sentence, resolving to make every word and every sentence count — as in all good written composition.

Exercises

1. Choose ONE of the following and write very clear and concise instructions which can be carried out by a person who has not done the job previously. Assume, however, that the person is familiar with the items or ingredients involved. Use about three-quarters of a page for your answer.
  - (a) preparing, cooking and serving of a hot snack.
  - (b) preparing, dressing and serving of a vegetable salad that contains at least five items.
  - (c) selecting and packing the clothing and articles needed for a stay of two or three days away from home. State whether you are staying in a town or in the country.
  - (d) fitting of a plug (three-pin) to the flex of a new piece of electrical equipment.
  - (e) checking battery and oil level in a modern car; giving instructions for any necessary action, assuming each item needs attention.
  - (f) the washing, rinsing and spin-drying of a "single" load of washing at a launderette.

  (R.S.A. I)

2. A friend intends to spend a fortnight's summer holiday in a district very well-known to you. He has written to ask your advice about accommodation, places of interest in the neighbourhood, and any special problems that might occur. Write a letter in reply, giving the necessary information. (R.S.A. I)

3. Explain ONE of the following processes to somebody who knows nothing about it. (Write between 150—200 words)
   (a) How to operate a tape or cassette recorder.
   (b) How to look after a typewriter.
   (c) How to mend a bicycle puncture.
   (d) How to change a wheel on a car.
   (e) How to operate a washing machine.
   (f) How to weed a piece of land.
       (R.S.A. I)

4. Imagine that you are ONE of the people listed below. Write an account of your feelings as you look back on previous experiences and forward to what lies ahead. Answer in about 24—30 lines.
   (a) A pupil on his/her last day at school.
   (b) An emigrant standing on the quayside or at an airport, waiting to embark.
   (c) A shepherd *or* farmer seeing the last of the winter snows melting on his pastures.
   (d) A person who particularly enjoys summer sports (e.g. cricket, tennis, sailing), on seeing the first signs of spring and warmer weather.
   (e) A young person on his/her eighteenth or twenty-first birthday.
       (English Language Ordinary Level Joint Matriculation Board.)

5. *Either*
   (a) You are putting yourself forward for election to a school council, student union executive, local council, or similar body.
       Compose an election leaflet about yourself, your beliefs and aims, for distribution among the voters. Credit will be given for an effective layout of the leaflet.
Or
   (b) You have been invited to take part in a television or radio discussion programme on the subject of "Youth and Authority". The programme chairman is expecting to select from topics such as parents, drugs, an extended

school-leaving age, dress, hair, music, but participants in the programme may introduce their own subjects.

Write out, in dialogue form, some central part of the programme.

You should write about one page.

(Royal Society of Arts, Stage II)

6. Write not more than 200 words on ONE of these subjects:
   (a) Outline the principal difficulties facing immigrants to your country.
   (b) Can young people usefully take an active part in the government and administration of their school or college?
   (c) Do television or radio programmes really influence the behaviour of young people?
   (d) Are we justified in keeping alive people who are incurably sick and in pain?
   (e) Do you favour the censorship of books, plays and films?
   (The London Chamber of Commerce Junior Secretary's Certificate.)

7. Write not more than 200 words on ONE of these subjects:
   (a) With the prospect of a shorter working week and earlier retirement before the end of this century, what provisions would you like to see made for people to spend their increased leisure time profitably and enjoyably?
   (b) To what extent is it appropriate to describe the advertising industry as "The Persuasion Industry"?
   (c) My country, seen through the eyes of a foreign tourist.
   (d) What might future historians find particularly good or bad in present-day society?
   (e) Would you support or reject the allegation that all "pop" music lacks seriousness and is trivial and irrelevant?
   (The L.C.C. Junior Secretary's Certificate, to be renamed the Secretarial Studies Certificate with effect from 1977.)

8. Describe carefully one of the following. Do not spend more than half an hour on this question:
   (a) The waiting room of a doctor's surgery.
   (b) A swimming pool on a chilly day in early September.
   (c) A church hall.
   (d) A discotheque.
   (e) The interior of a cathedral.

9. Write a review of a film or play which you have recently seen. Do not use more than 250 words.

10. Answer ONE of the following. About half an hour should be spent on this question.
  (a) Write a letter to a friend tactfully putting off a pre-arranged weekend visit to him.
  (b) Explain the game of cricket to someone who has never seen it played.
  (c) Give a full description of a vacuum flask *or* a domestic refrigerator *or* a typewriter.
  (d) Describe your ideal house.
  (e) Write a letter to your local paper in which you protest against the closing of a road which has been used by many motorists as a short cut. You suspect that it has been closed as the result of pressure from influential local citizens.

11. Write, *either* a critical account of the newspaper which you read regularly *or* an appreciation of a book which you have recently read.

12. Either
  (a) Draw a word-picture in about 200—250 words (not more) of ONE of the following:
      (i)   A producer or director.
      (ii) A ward orderly in a hospital.
      (iii) A racing-driver.
Or
  (b) Write a paragraph of 200—250 words (not more) on ONE of the following:
      (i)   The balance of payments.
      (ii) A film which has improved your knowledge of a particular subject.
      (iii) A disappointing occasion.

13. Write a short essay of about 450 words on ONE of the following:
  (a) The contribution of television to education.
  (b) "This is the age of the assassin." Discuss with regard to events in the last few years.
  (c) On being alone.
      (Questions 12 and 13 are from an R.S.A. III paper of 1969.)

14. In not more than 200 words try to convey the "atmosphere" of ONE of the following:
- (a) The promenade of a seaside resort in winter.
- (b) The streets of a town in late afternoon on Christmas Day.
- (c) An Underground station late at night just before the last train.
- (d) The interior of a house which has not been lived in for several years.

15. State your opinion of a recent television serial or series. Do not spend more than 35 minutes on this question.

16. Spend about half an hour on *either* (a) *or* (b).
- (a) Imagine you are a reporter working for a national daily newspaper.
  Write an account of an important sporting event.
- (b) Write for publication in your local paper an article in which you draw readers' attention to the lack of entertainment facilities for young people in your home town or village and suggest what facilities could be created.

17. In not more than 200 words write a description of a typical gymnasium *or* supermarket *or* launderette *or* fish and chip shop.

18. Describe carefully, in about 200 words, ONE of the following:
- (a) a vacuum cleaner
- (b) a bicycle
- (c) a gas or electric cooker
- (d) a crash-helmet
- (e) a lawn-mower
- (f) a washing-machine

19. Write a letter to a relative thanking him or her for a cheque sent to you as a present and explaining how you intend to spend it.

20. Write BRIEFLY (approximately 125 words) on each of TWO subjects from the following:
- (a) Seeking a job
- (b) Britain in Europe

    (c) Pollution
    (d) Being entertained
    (e) Spectator or Player?
    (f) Advertising in our lives
    (g) The right to strike
    (h) Forming opinions
         (The London Chamber of Commerce Private Secretary's
         Certificate Examination, 1972.)

21. Write an account of ONE of the following as it might appear in a national newspaper. You should not spend more than 35 minutes on this.
    (a) A great natural disaster
    (b) A serious industrial accident
    (c) A robbery
    (d) A speech by a leading politician
    (e) The settling of an industrial dispute

22. Write a report on ONE of the following as it might appear in your local paper. Spend about thirty minutes on this question.
    (a) A school prize-giving
    (b) An exhibition held by the local Chamber of Commerce
    (c) An amateur drama production
    (d) A football or cricket match
    (e) A flower show

23. Write an article of about 250 words for your local newspaper on ONE of the following:
    (a) A nearby stretch of countryside suitable for an enjoyable walk
    (b) A round-the-world tour made by a group of local people
    (c) Plans to create a traffic-free precinct
    (d) A new sports centre
    (e) Local facilities for adult education.

Chapter 9

Precis and summary

To make a precis or summary of a passage is to convey all or most of its meaning in a much smaller number of words.

The main purpose of this section is to suggest to students various ways of making a precis or summary (two words for the same thing) and to provide practice in the sorts of exercise which still appear in many English Language examinations.

It has been objected, especially in recent years, that the examination precis is very much an artificial exercise not very similar to the summarizing one may be asked to do in business or which may be required elsewhere outside the examination room. In business one might be asked for a summary but it is unlikely that anyone will stipulate a rigid limit to the number of words, and not very likely that they will insist that the summary be written in continuous prose. And the sort of summarizing we all do in our everyday lives — for example, giving the gist of a conversation or newspaper article or lecture to a friend or telling someone what a play or radio programme was about or what points it was making — is likely to be done orally and very briefly.

Possibly for these reasons, some examining boards, although they may (in the Comprehension question) ask candidates to summarize an author's views or remarks on a certain matter, no longer set the traditional precis question.

However, a precis/summary question of the conventional type is still found in many examination papers. Moreover, whether or not one is going to be confronted with such a question in an examination, exercises of this type are, for the following reasons, very valuable:

1. Practice in the techniques they involve helps us to do efficiently the sort of summarizing we may do in business, e.g. summarizing correspondence or articles in trade journals, or extracting relevant material from a report.

2. The concentration we have to employ to write a summary adequately, clearly and grammatically in a limited number of words is good for our brains and increases our ability to communicate clearly and concisely, both in speech and writing.

The precis question

1. *Reading the instructions*

It is essential to read the instructions carefully. Here is a typical set of instructions:

Write a summary of the following passage in good continuous prose, using not more than 120 words. State at the end of your summary the number of words you have used.

(a) Prose is the ordinary form of written language; that is to say it is any piece of writing (except poetry) written in complete sentences. The important point here is that the summary must certainly not be made in note form.

(b) "Not more than 120 words" means what it says. 121 words would be too many.

(c) Make sure that at the end of your summary you state correctly the number of words used. Some students are sometimes guilty of poor arithmetic — though not of course of untruthfulness!

Here is another very typical set of instructions:

Write a precis of the following passage, which contains 390 words, in about a third of its length. The precis should be written in your own words. Supply a title.

(a) "About a third of its length" here probably means between 120 and 140 words. If you were to use fewer than 120 words or more than 140 you would probably lose marks, for the precis would almost certainly be unsatisfactory.

(b) "in your own words". This means in sentences of your own construction (i.e. which you have to put together yourself) and in words which come naturally to you. The "lifting" of whole sentences or groups of words from the original passage will probably be heavily penalized. On the other hand this does not mean that none of the words used in the passage may be used!

This advice applies to all examination summary-writing.

(c) The title should be specific and not vague. It should be, as it were, a sort of summary of the passage.

2. *Method*

(A) Reading the passage and noting the theme

All methods of summary must begin in the same way — with a very careful reading of the passage. This must be followed by an even more careful reading of the passage and possibly by a third or fourth reading, until the examination candidate is sure that he or she understands it as fully as possible.

There is no denying that, however much care is taken, the extent to which anyone understands a piece of writing largely depends on his ability and on his command of English; and luck may also play a part. However, a candidate's approach to this reading stage should be optimistic as well as cautious: he should not be discouraged or demoralized if the passage is about an unusual or uninteresting subject, or be thrown into a panic if it contains unfamiliar words. The meaning of words may perhaps be deduced from the context, and sometimes such words form part of an unimportant section of the passage.

Having made sure that he understands the passage as fully as possible, the student should then mentally or on paper note the theme: what exactly the passage is about, what the author is "putting across", what the main idea is — according to the nature of the passage. Whatever method of doing the summary is then employed, the theme should be kept constantly in mind.

(B) Doing the precis

When the student has carefully read and re-read the passage for summary and noted the theme and resolved to keep the theme constantly in mind, he or she is ready to start the summarizing

process. This process may be carried out by one of the following methods:

1. (a) Note down the main points on rough paper, leaving
       plenty of space between them.
   (b) Read the passage again and add important modifying,
       supporting and connecting material to the main points.
   (c) Write out a summary of approximately the right length
       from the resulting notes.
   (d) Trim it down with as little loss of meaning as possible to
       the right number of words.
   (e) Neatly write out the final version.
2. (a) Mark off the passage into sections, using perhaps a
       pencil.
   (b) Write a summary of each section, using at every oppor-
       tunity every possible means of reducing the number of
       words.
   (c) Make sure that the maximum number of words has not
       been exceeded.
   (d) Neatly write out the final version.
3. (a) Giving yourself plenty of space, write down a summary
       of what you can remember from your readings of the
       passage.
   (b) Read the passage again and add any important points
       which you may have left out.
   (c) Turn the resulting version into continuous prose.
   (d) Check the number of words and make any necessary
       adjustments.
   (e) Neatly write out the final version.
4. (a) Work through the passage, writing down the summary as
       you go along, constantly looking for ways of reducing
       the number of words.
   (b) Check the number of words, make adjustments, and
       neatly write the final version.

Other methods may suggest themselves to students according
to their personal preferences and the nature of the passage. One
could for example, decide to underline the main points in the
passage and then use method 4. Or one could decide, especially
if summarizing a long passage, to use different methods for
various parts of the original passage.

Whatever method is employed, it is essential for the student
to keep in mind the theme of the passage and to remember that

his task is to express in his answer as much as possible of the meaning of the original passage in his summary — but within the prescribed word limit. He has then, while expressing the essential points, to be constantly on the look-out for ways of cutting down the number of words.

He must also bear in mind that anything mentioned in the finished summary will appear important, even if it is not.

It is therefore essential to:

1. Omit material which is irrelevant to the theme, or which is unimportant.
2. Wherever possible, save words by combining sentences, reducing some sentences to clauses, and clauses to phrases or single words. (Cf. Exercises in Ch. 1.) These ways of saving words may be applied to the original passage and to the student's own version. If any words in the passage serve no purpose they may be missed out altogether.
3. Summarize related items, ideas, feelings, etc., in a word or short phrase.
4. Cut out examples and other illustrative material. Examples may be single words, but also complete sentences.
5. Cut out figurative language (metaphors, similes, etc.) unless the comparison expressed by a metaphor or simile forms a major part of what the author has to say.
6. Express circumlocutions and indirect allusions in their simplest form. For example:
   "that substance which does not grow on trees and is supposed to be the root of all evil but which we all like" — money.
7. Where particular terms are used to represent a whole class, use a general term. For example:
   "He preferred Mozart and Bach to the Stones and the Osmonds" — He preferred classical music to "pop".
8. Avoid repetition of any sort, but remember that repetition by the author may well be designed to emphasize a point. Such emphasis must be reflected in the summary.

The following advice should be borne in mind:

Structure

1. The number of words used to summarize any part of the original passage should be roughly proportional to the importance of that part. A very important part may have

to be summarized in almost the same number of words. On the other hand, a long but unimportant part, like an illustrative anecdote for example, could perhaps be dealt with in a few words or ignored altogether.

2. The precis should be given continuity by the use, where appropriate, of such linking words as *consequently*, *accordingly*, *however*, *despite*, etc.

3. Usually a summary should be written in a single paragraph but if the passage is a very long one or there is a distinct change of subject, it may be advisable to use more than one paragraph. It is usually a bad idea to have as many paragraphs in the summary as there are in the original passage, especially if this contains several paragraphs.

4. The material in the original passage may be presented in a different order in the summary, but it is usually advisable to keep to the order of the original.

Language

1. The summary must be written in complete and grammatically correct sentences. Slang should be avoided, and no abbreviations (for example *hadn't, shouldn't, wasn't, e.g., etc.*) of any sort should be used.

2. A good flowing style should be aimed at but it is better to have a couple of sentences which are awkward (though grammatically correct) in a precis of the right length than a pleasant-sounding but overlong precis.

3. It is not necessary to use reported speech (*The writer said that . . .; The author remarks that . . .*) unless you are asked to in the instructions, or the passage for summary is written in the first person (e.g. I noticed . . .; this was my most interesting experience). The authorship of the passage may be indicated in the heading.

4. Questions and their answers, rhetorical questions (e.g. What's the use of worrying?), and exclamations should be turned into statements. Quotations should, in general, be ignored or their purport very briefly summarized.

Some general comments

1. As with all language exercises, the more reading you have done and the more words you know, the greater chance of success you will have.

2. As well as being optimistic and cautious in your approach to summary-writing, you may, with advantage, sometimes be ruthless — and even a little angry! Above all you should be alert. How, for example, would you summarize "at the very start of the twentieth century"?

3. If there are imperfections or awkward parts in your summary it could be that these merely reflect faults in the original passage.

4. In a sense there is no such thing as a perfect summary. Altered wording and a reduction in the number of words inevitably alters the meaning, to some extent. Moreover, no two people ever agree completely on the "best" summary — for opinions vary on what should be emphasized, included or omitted, especially in advanced work. The aim then is a good competent summary, sensibly but not *too* fastidiously produced.

Concluding advice

1. Do not add comments, however much you agree with or disagree with what the author has to say. Do not introduce metaphors of your own, or any other extra material. The rash use of a single word can add a new and unwanted idea!

2. Concentrate at every stage of the summarizing process. Students have been known to submit for inspection summaries stating that America was discovered in 1943, that the gramophone was invented in the 9th century, and that the autobahn from Munich runs through Australia!

3. Be sure to check the final version for avoidable mistakes of spelling and punctuation. Everyone makes mistakes.

4. Before you hand in an examination precis make sure that everything except the final version of the precis has been crossed out. If you fail to do this you may be marked on your rough version!

A worked example

This example may, it is hoped, be of some help to those who are inexperienced in tackling summaries of the traditional type.

It is an account of how someone *might* decide to summarize one particular passage, rather than a description of how all summaries ought to be done. Summary-writing is a matter for personal judgement: different people have different ideas as to what is or what is not important; and different people prefer different methods. Moreover, the various examining authorities do not set the same types of question. It should also be noted that the instructions accompanying examination questions sometimes dictate the type of summarizing which is to be employed.

Summarize the following passage in good continuous prose. Do not use more than 120 words. State at the end of your summary the number of words you have used.

> English food was not originally among the worst in the world — on the contrary, two centuries or less ago it was quite probably among the best, if not the actual best. From about 1720 onwards the standard of living rose steadily, and by 1750 the English were eating better than any other people in Europe. "They live well, eat and drink well, clothe warm, and lodge soft; they spend more of their money on their backs and bellies than in any other country," wrote Defoe in 1726. Even beyond the end of the eighteenth century there was no subject more liked by cartoonists and their audiences than the half-starved Frenchman, German or Spaniard with his "meagre soup" and skinny scrap of meat, contrasted with the huge and jolly English countryman or townsman blowing himself out with vast meat puddings, roasted and frizzling joints, thick hot soups rich with herbs, pies, cheeses and superb bread. Right up to the time when Dickens was a young man the tradition was continued; there are splendid meals in all his earlier books.
>
> But English food — both the cooking and the raw material — during the nineteenth century became not only infinitely worse than French, but lower than even the modest standards of Germany, Italy and Spain. This was the result of the enclosure acts and the industrial revolution. The English farm-worker lost his livelihood during the half-century that began roughly in the 1770s. The common land on which his goose fed and his cows were pastured was taken from him and he and his family were forced to seek work in the great new mill towns. In the

slums his wife no doubt remembered the traditional country recipes and had her old skill in dressing meat and making pastry; but she could rarely use it. Her daughter had a dimmer memory, and almost never used it. Her grand-daughter knew nothing, and by the beginning of this century lived in the world of bread and scrape, bran-filled sausages, scraps of bad meat, sanded sugar, aniline jams, dirty milk, sodden stale vegetables, chips and marge.
(From *The Good Food Guide* by Raymond Postgate.)

Having carefully read the passage two or three times, a student might note the theme and main points as follows:
Theme:
The decline in the quality of English food, to 1900.
Main points:
English food once perhaps the best.
Living standards rose from about 1720.
High food standards continued after end of 18th cent.
Decline:
Became some of worst in western Europe.
Result of enclosures and industrialization.
Women could no longer use culinary skills.
Descendants forgot them.
Situation in 1900.

Having once more read the passage, the student might decide that some words and phrases could be omitted and that the meaning of others could be expressed more briefly. He might well be pleased at the amount of supporting and illustrative material which could be summarized or only briefly mentioned. He might note with pleasure how dates could be used to save words.

The student might write out the summary as follows:
Two centuries ago English food was perhaps the best in the world. After about 1720 living standards rose steadily and by 1750 the English were the best-fed Europeans. Defoe remarked on their high living-standards in 1726. Even after 1800 a favourite cartoonists' subject was the half-starved Continental contrasted with the Englishman with his rich, filling food. Even during Dickens' youth the tradition continued.

In the nineteenth century, however, English food became some of the worst in western Europe, as a result of the enclosures and industrialization. Between the 1770s and the 1820s the English farm-worker lost the common land on which his livestock fed and he had to find work in the new factory towns, where his wife could not use her country cooking skills. Her descendants in time forgot them and by 1900 lived on poor, low-quality food.

(Some readers might criticize that summary. Someone might ask: "Doesn't the first sentence of the passage imply that English food is among the worst in the world *now*? Is it necessary to mention Defoe, or Dickens? Surely the mention of cartoonists is merely an example, which may be omitted? Isn't 'best-fed Europeans' rather an awkward expression?", etc. One answer to these queries is that the student has used his personal judgement.)

The student would then discover that he had used 140 words and then he would look for ways of reducing the number of words by 20. Having reduced his answer to a maximum of 120, he would then write out neatly his final answer — which might run as follows:

Two centuries ago English food was perhaps the best. After 1720 living standards rose steadily and by 1750 the English were the best-fed Europeans. Even after 1800 a favourite cartoonists' subject was the hungry foreigner contrasted with the well-fed Englishman. Even during Dickens' youth the tradition of good food persisted.

In the nineteenth century, however, English food greatly deteriorated, as a result of enclosures and industrialization. Between the 1770s and the 1820s the English farm-worker lost the common land on which his livestock fed and he had to find work in the new factory towns, where his wife could not use her cooking skills. Her descendants gradually forgot them and by 1900 lived on very poor food. (118 words.)

Exercises

Section A consists of single sentences to be summarized, section B of short passages, and section C of full-length examination passages.

A.

Summarize each of the following sentences in the number of words indicated in the brackets.

1. John's wife spent too much on chairs, tables, cupboards, three-piece suites, sideboards, deck-chairs and other such items. (7)

2. The ideas of many people are derived solely from films, television, radio, newspapers and magazines. (9 or 10)

3. People are influenced less by their reason than by their fears, anxieties, jealousies, affections and desires. (11)

4. Cricket, football, tennis, golf — these and other activities of that nature were all that interested him; although, as a matter of fact, he was not very good at any of them. (6)

5. Brakes screeching, horns sounding, engines roaring, gears crashing, tyres screaming, the thunder of giant tankers and other juggernauts — all these sounds and others of the same sort frequently assault the ears of anyone living in London, New York, Tokyo, Los Angeles, Paris or any similar place. (About 8)

6. In that part of the world whose inhabitants according to some people exist on a diet of haggis and whisky and have an undeserved reputation for meanness there are large areas where one can travel for miles without seeing another living soul. (About 8)

7. She is acutely aware of the existence of class distinctions and tends to despise people who, in her opinion, come from a poor background or have had an inferior education. (4)

8. He wanted to be able to afford a new sports car every year, holidays on the Riviera, and a private aircraft. (5)

9. She shows more interest in the latest shade of lipstick and the most glamorously advertised eye-shadow than in such a mundane matter as getting to work on time or arriving on time for "dates". (About 9)

10. Even if they have moral qualms, most people dream of "winning the pools" or of gaining a fortune by means of some ingenious equestrian speculation and of exchanging a bicycle and semi-detached for a Rolls-Royce and a large house with a gravel drive and spreading lawns. (About 11)

11. That huge expanse of territory between Poland and Japan, bounded in the north by a frozen ocean and

arctic tundra and in the south by a dozen states, has amongst its inhabitants not only Russians but Turks, Armenians, Mongols, Jews and representatives of many other ethnic groups, even including Germans. (6)

12. What do the Government know about the problems encountered by a young man and woman, newly married, looking for a house they can afford and hoping that they will be able to keep up with the mortgage repayments, searching for furniture, choosing curtains and wallpaper and wondering whether they can afford a refrigerator? Nothing! (Maximum 15)

13. Anyone who owns a motor-cycle is well aware of the need to change the gear oil regularly, to check the tyres for signs of wear, to check the steering, to make sure that the front and rear lights are in working order, to check that the exhaust system is not obstructed in any way and generally to ensure that the machine is road-worthy. (About 10)

14. Eight out of ten cases of housebreaking with intent to rob occur between dusk and dawn. (6)

15. Deposits of this mineral are found in Alaska, Canada, Texas, Oklahoma, Florida and Louisiana and in that area of Mexico around Acapulco. (11, then 7)

16. After the earthquake, the inhabitants of the ruined city had no homes to go to, nothing to eat, and hardly a drop of water to refresh their parched tongues, and they anxiously wondered if there was any danger of another serious earth tremor. (About 15)

17. Although they were extremely tired — almost exhausted in fact — they went on working until the task which had been set them was accomplished. (11)

18. One Sunday morning in November, the 17th actually, they were just about to attack an early lunch of roast shoulder of lamb when Bill burst in and, wide-eyed and looking as if he had been pulled through a hedge backwards, exclaimed, "I'm engaged to be married!" (About 8)

19. England's prospects in the next World Cup and Yorkshire's chances of becoming County Champions interested him a great deal more than French irregular verbs, quadratic equations or technical drawing. (9)

20. By the end of the nineteenth century Great Britain's

commercial supremacy had been challenged by the United States of America and the German Empire. (11, then 8)

B.

Summarize the following passages in the number of words indicated in the brackets.

1. The policeman was proceeding on foot at a moderate pace along a thoroughfare in the principal shopping locality of the town, when he saw an adult male person seeking to effect an illegal entry into a commercial enterprise devoted to the sale of periodicals. The policeman ceased his perambulations in order to maintain surveillance of the malefactor's nefarious activities. (About 20) (G.C.E. Passage for simplification)

2. "What is the point of scanning the skies with telescopes, optical or radio?" he asked. "What is the point of searching for signals from outer space? What possible reason is there to send a spacecraft to Mars? What is the point of a space-probe to Mercury? Or to Saturn or Jupiter? Why send men to walk on the Moon, for that matter?" (The speaker said that +9)

3. Angela worshipped the very ground her husband walked upon, could hardly wait for him to come home from work, and in fact completely idolized him. She irritated him considerably, however, by spending so much money on expensive dresses, jewellery, hi-fi equipment and champagne. (15)

4. Certain types of advertising are misleading. "Britain's best selling cigarette at only 34½ pence for twenty!" The glib voice pauses after "cigarette". "Britain's best selling cigarette!" we gasp, suitably impressed. Then a split second later we hear that it only costs 34½ pence for twenty. The fact is that it is the *only* cigarette selling at 34½ pence for twenty.

   "Contains sodium chloride!" screams a label, trying to convince us that this is some wonder ingredient, perfected no doubt by a Viennese scientist. We should not be impressed, for sodium chloride is salt.

   An offer of a free car wash with every ten gallons of

petrol may materialize as a sachet of car shampoo, worth perhaps three pence. We should be on our guard against this sort of thing. (As few words as possible)

5. Many criticisms, some of them perhaps justified, are made of advertising but it certainly cannot be denied that advertising makes people aware of the existence of new products and, because it increases sales and thereby engenders economies of scale, makes a substantial contribution to a process whereby a downward trend in wholesale prices is established and costs to the consumer significantly lowered. (11)

6. That there has been such a swift advance in consumer research during the past few years argues one of two things. Either the development has been prompted by growing dissatisfaction with consumer products in general; or it has been derived from the greater multiplicity of similar products. The second is surely the right one. The problem of the shopper who knows what to buy is immediately which to buy. We cannot all have expert knowledge of the technical properties to be sought in a satisfactory motor car, a bar of soap or a mattress. (Express the main statement in not more than 30 words.)

7. At that time of the year when "a livelier iris changes on the burnish'd dove and a young man's fancy lightly turns to thoughts of love", at the time when fresh green buds and leaves begin to appear and early blossom is white against an azure sky, when Nature seems to have finally cast off her drab winter garments, everyone, young and old, male and female, tends, despite rising prices and rumours of wars, despite news of violence and disaster, to feel a little more optimistic, to feel that things are not perhaps quite as bad as they seem. (7)

8. Despite the regrettable attenuation of the Commonwealth, my friends, despite the parlous state of the economy, despite the proddings of the United States, despite all the plausible persuasions of economists — despite all these factors, there was no earthly reason for our island race to distort its administrative and legal practices to fit the caprices of Continentals, to abandon its pounds and miles for kilograms and kilometres or to submit itself to the whims of a pack of foreign bureau-

crats in Brussels. (The speaker said that +11 or fewer)

9. The expression "shooting stars" is a misnomer. Shooting stars are not stars at all. They are meteors. Meteors are small masses of matter from outer space rendered luminous by collision with the earth's atmosphere. They appear as moving points of light against the dark backcloth of the night sky because they are travelling so fast that the friction produced by their headlong rush through the atmosphere causes such intense heat that they become white-hot. (About 20)

10. If we sought the beginnings of the decline of the Roman Empire — that great political entity which extended from Britain in the West to Mesopotamia in the East, from the forests of Germany to the sun-scorched lands of North Africa — we should find that the process of deterioration started at some time between AD 200 and 300. (10)

11. Those people who are so slavish in their adulation of man's best friend might do well to bear certain facts in mind. Dogs are carriers of disease. They foul pavements and grass verges. Alsatians and other large breeds of dog have been known to attack strangers and even their owners and to kill young children. The highly capricious behaviour of dogs is a contributory factor in many road accidents. The loss of sleep and the stress caused by the uncontrolled barking of dogs in the early morning must be added to the list of charges against these troublesome pets. (About 24)

12. There was a story in France in the 1950s that a man went into a newsagent's and asked if the newsagent had a list of the names of the members of the government. The shopkeeper was supposed to have replied that unfortunately he didn't sell periodicals.

This little story certainly reminds us how rapidly French governments of the 1940s and 1950s were formed and fell, though of course the lives of most governments were not quite as brief as we might imagine from this no doubt apocryphal anecdote. But there certainly was — until 1958 at any rate — a great deal of political instability.

Until 1958 the President had performed purely decorative and formal functions — much like those of a constitutional monarch — but once he was firmly established as the leader of France in 1958, Charles de Gaulle created a constitution in which the President wielded most power and appointed and dismissed the Prime Minister, who became, according to some people, a sort of glorified office-boy. Criticisms were made for example, that the constitution was dictatorial, that it was unresponsive to public opinion, that it was antediluvian. There was no denying one thing, however: governments now were certainly stable. After all, between 1958 and 1974 there were really only three of them. (Maximum 30)

C. Exercises from examinations

1. Summarize the following in not more than 100 words:

There are many factors and aspects that must be taken into consideration when considering the driving test as it is today. The only possible reason for anyone's thinking we ought to make it tougher is that the basic car manoeuvres demanded by the test have remained virtually unchanged over the years. The fact that the test has been made progressively more difficult by the increase in traffic and the growing road congestion is an aspect of the problem which is often ignored or overlooked: if changes in connection with testing are needed (and the point is debatable) possible improvements would concern the overall standard of tuition, and the standards of both car-control and road-sense reached immediately prior to testing — the elimination of obviously unsuitable candidates at this stage would undoubtedly seem to be a step in the right direction.

If proof is required in support of the assertion that the driving test is sufficiently difficult, the test failure rate should be noted: the latest figures show that the pass-rate among L-drivers taking the test for the first time is only 44 per cent, and the overall pass-rate is only slightly over 50 per cent.

It is a recognized fact that it is especially easy for L-drivers to acquire bad driving habits if they are taught by amateurs, particularly if those amateurs are relatives. It is equally true that there are some very bad professional driving instructors who, in effect, are earning a living by false pretences. The recently introduced register of driving instructors seeks to remedy this state of affairs; on a voluntary basis at present, it could easily be made compulsory if necessary. The co-operation of learner drivers must be sought — they must be persuaded not to submit to instruction from unqualified persons, but to seek tuition only from trained instructors who have gained official approval. (R.S.A. Shorthand-Typist's Certificate II, 1965. Note that the present R.S.A. Shorthand-Typewriting Certificate Examination does not contain a summary question.)

2. Summarize the following passage using *not more than 100 words*. The use of additional words will be penalized.

The conditions favourable to property investment are, essentially, freedom to borrow and a low and, if possible, falling rate of interest. The conditions we have to endure, and are likely to have to endure for a long while, are precisely the opposite. These factors led us to the view that the time had come when we should realize a substantial part of our United Kingdom holdings and re-invest the proceeds where they could be employed in conditions more favourable to our type of business, and at the same time provide a desirable spread in both the character and the location of our capital security.

The Canadian company provides the means. Through it we now own a large fund in Canadian dollars (securely invested in land and Government bonds) available for our participation in the immense possibilities of that great country. The Dominion of Canada, as the whole world knows, is possessed of natural resources of quite exceptional richness, the development of which has only just begun.

It is upon the future in Canada, rather than the immediate present, that we should found our anticipation of profitable return. Canada needs very large sums of capital to develop her vast potential wealth: she is in equal need of men — of population. Only by the building up of these two essential elements can she attain to that high degree of commercial prosperity to which she is destined by virtue of her mineral and other wealth.

Such a building up is not accomplished in just a year or two. It is a much more lengthy process, and, in the meantime, caution must be the watchword where investment is concerned; but, given this element of caution and careful judgment, we are confident that your Canadian subsidiary will in the years to come prove itself to be a valuable and rewarding investment.

(R.S.A. Shorthand-Typist's Certificate II, 1960.)

3. Write a summary of the following passage in good continuous prose, using *not more than 120 words*. State at the end of your summary the number of words you have used. The passage contains 347 words.

Looking beyond our lifetimes at modes of transport should be an interesting exercise. Predictions tend to be based on known technology and current fashion. The Victorians thought that the skies of the twentieth century would be darkened by steam-driven balloons manned by gentlemen in top hats. The Thirties idea of the airliner of the future was an enormous aeroplane powered by a score or more propellers. Only the immediate future can be viewed with a reasonable certainty of what will happen.

A look backwards demonstrates how rapid are the changes. A hundred years ago there were no motor cars, no aircraft, no electrically-powered trains and trams; but it seemed then a wondrous era. Thanks to steam, man could roam the seas at will, or reach the furthermost corner of the country from London in a matter of hours. Someone aged fifty in 1872 was born three years before the first railway, in an age when man was still dependent on animal and wind-power. But if that same Victorian had lived on for another fifty years he would have seen changes that would have made 1872 look like the Dark Ages. By 1922 the whole of Greater London was covered by a network of tramways and motor bus routes. Underground electric trains carried commuters to distant suburbs. Private cars had superseded the horse. It was possible to fly to Paris, but most overseas travellers voyaged on ocean liners in unexcelled comfort. Those people of 1922 would have found it hard to believe that those same liners would be made obsolete by jet airliners. They would have regarded it as incomprehensible that the efficient British trams would become as extinct as dinosaurs, and they certainly would have had difficulty in accepting that men actually would go to the Moon.

So there are no holds barred when it comes to looking a hundred years ahead. In the intervening time there are many discoveries to be made, new technologies to be applied, new energy sources to replace those that are running out or are too damaging environmentally to be further exploited.

George Perry

(Associated Examining Board English Language Ordinary Level, Paper 2.)

4. In sentences of your own construction, and using *not more than 140 words*, write a precis of the following passage. State at the end the number of words you have used.

"What are leavers' hopes for jobs in the 1970s? How are they helped — or hindered — in their search for employment by their schooling, the youth employment service, and employers themselves? Do these really contribute to job choice, or do parents, relatives and peers on the one hand, and advertising on the other, play major roles?

Employers were quite effective in attracting leavers to various jobs through advertising and also by taking account of applicants' wishes. For example, some offer further education not only because it produces a more fully trained work force, but also because there is a generally favourable attitude — even with those of lower educational achievement — towards jobs which involve further education. In the current study, about half in each ability group said they would be more interested in jobs which offered further education, the most popular method being day release.

Many leavers claim to have looked at careers literature at school. The proportion making this claim increased from 40 per cent among fourth year leavers, to 85 per cent among the two or more A level group. In the second group 34 per cent said they had looked up information on specific professions, and 43 per cent of the first group used careers libraries to read up about *specific* skilled trades. In contrast careers conventions seem to be attended by relatively few of the better qualified.

However, the careers literature issued by employers was criticized by careers teachers. It was seen as being too glossy and not conveying sufficient hard information about the organization and the job itself. The major criticism was that most literature was aimed at attracting the more highly qualified leavers. There was little intended for fourth year leavers and which could be understood by them.

The study showed very large variations between schools in the provision made for careers advice. The schools which allocated most resources to 'careers' tended to be those with large numbers of fourth year leavers, and no sixth forms. Sixth form leavers seemed to be encouraged to set their sights on higher education and were often not thought to need organized careers advice.

Though this employment end of education may not be the primary concern of schools, they should be *committed* to making the *transition* from school to work as smooth as possible. There are many schools with this *orientation*, but they are not always helped by the policies of the local education authorities. For example, some Local Education Authorities do not allow trial employment to be part of a school's careers programme."

(*Extract from New Society.*)

(London Chamber of Commerce Junior Secretary's Certificate.)

5. *In not more than 140 words* write a precis of the following passage. State at the end the number of words you have used and supply a title.

Although its application to business documentation is fairly novel, microfilm does not really involve using techniques that are particularly new. Rather the contrary: it is fundamentally based on ideas that are long-established and familiar in everyday life. For example, think back to when you were on holiday. Every time you took a snapshot, you were recording what the camera could see in highly miniaturized form on the film, and later you will have had the negative re-enlarged to make a positive print that you could look at. Microfilm in business works the same way. Subject matter, of course, is limited to documents, but the principles don't change.

The great advantage of microfilm is the space saving potential. The sheet of paper is replaced by a photographic image smaller than a postage stamp. Indeed the idea of using microfilm essentially as a compact means of sending information from one place to another has a long and distinguished pedigree. More than 100 years ago — during the siege of Paris in 1870 to be precise — microfilm was used as a long-distance communication medium, small packages of films being sent by carrier pigeon.

If microfilm is such a boon of a space saver, why is it not now commonplace in every office? What has held it back are the problems associated with information retrieval. An unfortunate limiting factor is that business microfilm developed as an alternative use for industrial photography, rather than as a better way of filing office documents. The upshot is that the methods devised — at least in the early days — reflect an emphasis on following photographic principles. In other words, the people trying to sell microfilm had given insufficient thought to how it fitted in with established document control disciplines.

Microfilm in its basic form destroyed ease of access. Every paper that went through the camera was there on the 100 ft. long film reels. Somewhere, But where? Disenchantment naturally resulted. The reason was that the microfilm didn't fit the filing system. The long strips of images were just about as useful as huge bundles of paper (but let it be admitted that this sort of roll microfilm is often used with great success as a replacement for huge paper bundles in archival storage situations).

Given enough money, it is of course possible to make roll microfilm work as a substitute for conventional filing systems. Sophisticated indexing procedures can be devised and computers can be brought in to assist rapid location of one film frame among tens of thousands. But it becomes a doubtful virtue. For if the principal purpose in contemplating microfilm was to save money by saving space, how do you justify spending more than the saving just to make the new regime as satisfactory as the old? (470 words)

(*Adapted from an article in Office Skills, published by Pitman Periodicals Limited.*)

(London Chamber of Commerce Junior Secretary's Certificate.)

6. The following passage has been taken from an article dealing

with equal pay for men and women. *Using only the information given in the passage*, write a report, consisting of *two* paragraphs, summarizing:

(a) the arguments for giving men and women equal pay for equal work, and

(b) the arguments against giving men and women equal pay for equal work.

Your report should not exceed 150 words altogether. Select the arguments required, arrange them in a sensible order within the appropriate paragraph, *and write in clear and concise English.* Some words or expressions cannot be accurately or economically replaced, but do not copy out long expressions or whole sentences; *use your own words as far as possible. State at the end the number of words you have used.*

Governments in recent years have been in favour of the principle of "Equal pay for equal work". This support for what is an obvious and undeniable human right has come about because the nation cannot afford to waste a large proportion of its potential labour force by discouraging women from working through unjust treatment in wages and salaries. If girls are rewarded equally with boys they will be similarly encouraged to look upon their jobs as careers and to study for the necessary qualifications. Some argue, however, that if women are lured to go out to work they will neglect their families and there will be an increase in marriage-breakdowns and delinquency in children, who really do need their mothers at home with them.

Our society still imposes more responsibilities on men than on women in financial matters; it is the men who are expected to be the bread-winners, provide the family house, and pay the hundred and one bills which fall through the letter-box. Yet some women have responsibilities equal to those of some men and require just as much money to support and bring up children or to look after aged parents; it is not fair that they should be penalized merely because of their sex. Single women, too, have expenses similar to those of single men — they have to pay for flats, buy clothes, find fares to go to work, and save up for holidays; there is no justification for automatically paying them less than their male counterparts. In any case, some women are better than men in some jobs but nobody suggests that they should receive more;

"unequal" pay never acts to the advantage of women.

Prejudice still maintains that women cannot expect equal pay, because they are suited in some way to the less demanding and more repetitive jobs, and because they cannot tolerate the physical and mental strains which accompany the better-paid posts usually occupied by men. Such discrimination against women in what they can earn denies them any dignity in work and adds to their frustration. The exclusion of women from the "top" jobs by denying them equal pay has resulted in women being in fierce competition with one another, and with some men in the lower posts, so that employers have been able to keep wages low and resist any claims for the improvement of pay scales. In some cases, employing women has meant that some men have lost their jobs because firms have preferred to employ women at lower rates than they would have had to pay to unskilled men. Equal pay for equal work would stop or discourage the continuation of depressed wages and the exploitation of those who work in unskilled jobs.

It is a fact, however, that women are reluctant to accept shift work, which involves periods of night work, and if they are not prepared to accept equal conditions of work with men they can hardly expect equal pay. Women seem to lose more time from work than men owing to sickness or family problems; some regard their jobs only as stopgaps until they marry and leave. Employers cannot be expected to provide equal opportunities for both boys and girls to learn a trade when experience shows that women often leave a year or two after training in order to marry and set up home; they prefer to devote their training opportunities and financial incentives to young men from whom they can expect about forty years of continuous service. The introduction of equal pay, therefore, may well result in women finding it difficult to secure jobs in competition with men.

(University of London — English Language Ordinary Level, Paper 1.)

7. Write a precis of the following passage *in not more than 190 words*. The passage contains about 550 words.

But the greatest single event of the 'seventies, fraught with immeasurable consequences for the future, was the sudden collapse of English agriculture.

From 1875 onwards the catastrophe set in. A series of bad seasons aggravated its initial stages, but the cause was the development of the American prairies as grain lands within reach of the English market. The new agricultural machinery enabled the farmers of the Middle-West to skim the cream off virgin soils of unlimited expanse; the new railway system carried the produce to the ports; the new steamers bore it across the Atlantic. English agriculture was more scientific and more highly capitalized than American, but under these conditions the odds were too great. Mass production of crops by a simpler and cheaper process undercut the elaborate and expensive methods of farming which had been built up on well-managed English estates during the previous two hundred years. The over-throw of the British landed aristocracy by the far-distant democracy of American farmers was one outcome of this change of economic circumstance. An even more important consequence has been the general divorce of Englishmen from life in contact with nature, which in all previous ages had helped to form the mind and the imagination of the island race.

The other States of Europe, which still had peasantry and valued them as a stabilizing element in the social fabric, warded off the influx of American food by tariffs. But in England no such policy was adopted or even seriously considered. The belief in Free Trade as the secret of our vast prosperity, the unwillingness to interfere with the world-commerce on which our power and wealth seemed to stand secure, the predominance of the towns over the country in numbers and still more in intellectual and political leadership, the memories of the "hungry 'forties" when the Corn Laws had made bread dear for the poor — all these circumstances prevented any effort to save the rural way of life. Least of all did the late Victorians see any need to grow food in the island to provide for the necessities of future wars. After two generations of the safety won at Waterloo, real national danger seemed to have passed away for ever, like a dream of

"Old unhappy far-off things
And battles long ago".

In 1846 Disraeli had prophesied the ruin of agriculture as an inevitable result of Free Trade in corn. For thirty years he had been wrong. Now he was suddenly right — and now he was Prime Minister. Yet he did nothing about it, and allowed the "curse of Cobden" to blight the English corn-fields. Immersed in oriental policies, the old man made no attempt to oppose the spirit of the age at home, to which in fact he had become a convert.

Statesmen regarded the fate of agriculture with all the more indifference because it involved no acute problem of unemployment. The farm labourer did not remain on the land when his occupation there was gone, as unemployed miners hang around a closed mine. When "Hodge" lost his job, or when his wages fell, he slipped away to the towns and found work there. Or else he migrated overseas, for the Colonies and the United States were still receiving the overplus of our still rapidly rising population.

(G. M. Trevelyan *English Social History*.)

8. The following passage is part of a radio discussion on the organization of pop-festivals in Britain. *Using only the information in the passage*, make a summary consisting of two paragraphs as follows:

   (a) the measures taken by the organizers of pop-festivals to ensure that they are properly run; and

   (b) the objections made to pop-festivals.

Select the material you need and arrange it in a sensible order within the appropriate paragraph. *Write in clear and correct English.* Some words and expressions cannot be accurately or economically replaced, but do not copy out long expressions or whole sentences; *use your own words as far as possible.*

Your whole summary *should not exceed 150 words* altogether; at the end of your work you must state the exact number of words you have used.

CHAIRMAN: It is agreed that here in Britain the days of pop-festivals are over and yet they still appear every year. There are certainly some who would be glad if they were to vanish altogether.

SPEAKER A: I can see that; but from my experience of helping to organize a number of these festivals I am sure that they help to meet the need of young people to enjoy themselves.

SPEAKER B: If we are going to speak from experience, as a local councillor from Whitely which had to put up with the last one, I can say what a nuisance such events are. They interrupt the daily life of the village community, on whom the mobs of pop-fans descend like a plague of locusts. Livestock is threatened; shopkeepers have to endure the petty pilfering of their goods; and householders lose the milk off their front doorsteps.

SPEAKER A: As organizers, we take great care to reduce any possible annoyance to the local people. We make sure that there are enough buses and trains to carry the crowds quickly to and from the pop-festival site and we provide plenty of space there for the parking of cars, motor-cycles, and caravans. Moreover, we go to great pains to arrange for the rubbish to be cleared up once the event has finished.

SPEAKER B: Yes, at the expense of the already over-burdened local rate-payer! He's the one who has to pay for additional refuse-collection and the restoration of local amenities which your crowds have destroyed!

CHAIRMAN: There are clearly very real problems here; but surely considerable planning goes into the preparations for a pop-festival?

SPEAKER A: Of course. Public-health inspectors are consulted and they see that we keep the food stalls and snack bars clean and they insist on the provision of toilet facilities for the crowds that are expected. These are just a few examples to show the care we take.

CHAIRMAN: Can you provide *adequate* toilet facilities for thirty thousand people in a field? I should have thought that these pop-festivals endanger the health of the local people.

SPEAKER B: They do. My fundamental objection, however, is to the enormous noise thrown out by loudspeakers night and day. It is a pity that the manipulation of the young by those wanting to make quick, easy money and by those who use the occasion for active political campaigning should inflict such a din on innocent people.

SPEAKER A: I really must make a few points clear. By providing enough staff, we go out of our way to ensure that the festivals are properly organized. This provision costs large amounts of money. We have to see that numbers are properly controlled and so we take steps to stop gate-crashers. We employ security organizations to eliminate violence and we consult experts in crowd-control to make certain that stands and barriers are safe so that no accidents occur.

SPEAKER B: You appear to provide adequate first-aid and medical treatment in case an emergency does arise. I must admit it. Mind you, the drunkenness and the drug-taking that I saw at the Whitely pop-festival kept the medical staff at full stretch for the three days the jamboree lasted! Some young people also decided to light fires under trees and so created an enormous fire hazard; and I've no doubt that, in this permissive age, promiscuity was the order of the day!

SPEAKER A: There are always those who will abuse a gathering of any kind. I really can't see that there was much risk of Whitely's burning down as it rained steadily for twenty-four hours during the festival. In fact, one of the things we try to do when we make our arrangements is to provide some shelter from the English weather and the young people appreciate it. We have our problems, however, when both the weather and the local councillors band together to defeat us.

(University of London — English Language, Ordinary Level, Paper 1.)

9. Write a summary in continuous prose of the following passage. *Do not use more than 180 words.* State at the end of your summary the number of words you have used.

Few defenders of capitalism have tried to justify the system in terms of the nobility of its motives. But what prodigies of material achievement we enjoy as we travel the motorways; what miracles of engineering we command to wash our clothes and dishes, tell the time to the nearest tenth of a second, detect our incipient cancers, converse with friends in distant cities! Are we not only healthier and longer-lived than our forefathers, but better-informed, better-entertained — in short, "better-off" in nearly every measurable dimension?

But does this recital reveal what has not been gained? Are we better citizens as well as richer than our antecedents? Are we more at peace with our children, our parents, ourselves? Are we wiser as well as more informed; happier as well as more pampered; sturdier and more self-reliant as well as better fed, housed, clothed transported? To ask these questions, rhetorical though they be, is, I think, to imply a hollowness at the centre of a business civilization — a hollowness from which the pursuit of material goods diverts our attention for a time, but that in the end insistently asserts itself. What is the nature of this hollowness? I would trace it primarily to two aspects of the business civilization that undermine the gains that material advancement undoubtedly confers. The first is the tendency of a business civilization to substitute impersonal pecuniary values for personal nonpecuniary ones. Consider, for example the conversion of sport — one of the oldest and most stirring rituals of mankind — into a commercial enterprise, in which athletes are no longer heroes but money-makers, games no longer contests for glory but for cash, and the mercenary qualities of participants, which would have been a source of shame in a Greek or medieval festival, are trumpeted aloud as an admirable character trait.

Or consider advertising, perhaps the single most value-destroying activity of a business civilization. How strong, deep, or sustaining can be the values generated by a civilization that encourages a ceaseless flow of half-truths and careful deceptions, in which it is common knowledge that only a fool is taken in by the charades and messages that supposedly tell us "the facts"?

There is, I think, a second reason why the material achievements of a business civilization fail to generate the satisfactions we expect of it. This is the disregard of business for the value of work. A business civilization regards work as a means to an end, not as an end in itself. The end is profit, income, consumption, economic growth, or whatever; but the act of labour itself is regarded as nothing more than an unfortunate necessity to which we must submit to obtain this end.

The market mechanism contains profound weaknesses that have been overlooked during the period of uninhibited capitalist expansion. One of these is its tendency to create extremely uneven distributions of income and property, a tendency that a straitjacketed economy will no longer accept with the forbearance of an expanding one. Another weakness is the failure of the market to protect us against the socially deleterious side-effects of production, such as pollution, an aspect that becomes intolerable in a threatened environment. And a third weakness is the exclusive focus of the market on economic activity conceived and measured in quantities of material output, not in qualities of human input. The market celebrates private consumption and ignores private production. This indifference to the experience of work corrodes and corrupts much of the way of life in a business civilization.

(*From an article in* The Observer *(28 Dec. 1975) by Robert L. Heilbroner.*)

(Passage set for summary in OND examination at one examining centre.)

10. Your employer does not have any fireproof cabinets for his important documents. You have read the following extract and decide to prepare a brief summary of the hazards of fire and how they can be overcome. Draft a suitable summary, giving it a title and taking *not more than 150 words*.

Do you keep thousands of pounds in your office? No, you probably don't. Like most offices, yours is likely to be full of correspondence files, order books, stock lists, financial records and so on. Nothing of interest to a thief.

Why is it, then, that leading firms of safe manufacturers supply so many security cabinets to offices? The answer is a single word: fire. No burglar could carry away tons of documents, even if he wanted to. But fire can completely destroy such documents within hours and often within minutes.

Businessmen often don't realize that, with their records destroyed, their entire business could be ruined overnight. Even if it is possible to compile a fresh set of records, the long delay can be disastrous. However, those who do realize their vulnerability to fire are wise enough to install security cabinets in which the most vital documents can be stored.

You may say, "But surely most filing cabinets and sets of drawers are made of steel nowadays, and won't burn?" This is true, of course, but remember that steel is a good conductor of heat. In an office fire the furniture (if made of steel) will quickly become red-hot, and anything inside it will simply become roasted to ashes.

Some firms produce specially toughened and insulated equipment that can withstand very high temperatures for some hours. Naturally, any security cabinet would *eventually* get very hot inside if it were in a fire, but in normal circumstances an office fire will be detected fairly quickly and be put out in a few hours. During that time the precious documents inside the security cabinet will remain safe and unscorched.

There are other hazards associated with an office fire which these cabinets must withstand. Suppose the office is on an upper floor. If the building catches fire the floors (if made of wood) may burn through, causing the furniture to fall heavily for some distance. If the cabinets were to burst open, the documents inside then would immediately spill out into the flames. A similar danger may arise if firemen direct their water hoses on to the cabinet, which is liable to split open just as a hot glass bottle can be cracked by being plunged into cold water. And then the documents would once again be exposed to the fire and flames.

The solution to these problems is to install proper security cabinets which will withstand fire safely, including heavy blows, falls, sudden cooling and so on. The cost is not low; but how much more expensive it is to have all one's vital records destroyed because of one careless match or dropped cigarette!

If a businessman does take the trouble to equip his office in this way, he might as well spend a little more on providing good fire extinguishers too. Then the dreaded fire might never happen. (About 500 words)
(London Chamber of Commerce Private Secretary's Certificate.)

11. Read the following passage carefully and then answer the questions printed below it.

Among the hundreds of such fortifications which survive in a *reasonable* state of preservation a rigid uniformity of design could not be expected to prevail, although the main features of the type are in fact reproduced with general
5   consistency, amid the most diverse of local conditions. It is in regard to the number and disposition of the baileys, and in their relation to the castle mound, that variations were commonly made upon the simple type. Where more than

10 one bailey occurs in a single castle, the second *bailey* will generally extend beyond the first on the face remote from the mound, as at Ongar, Essex; less frequently, both baileys, with a ditch between them, will *abut* upon the mound, as at Newtown, Montgomery, and in a small group of castles, to which Nottingham, Arundel, and Windsor
15 belong, the mound occupies the centre of the whole fortification. In the latter case, however, it is a *reasonable* inference that one or more of the baileys represents later addition to the original fortress since the normal position of the mound on the outer edge of the defences was un-
20 doubtedly felt to be of value in giving to its defenders, in the last resort, a means of *egress* to the open country. In regard to the more important English castles, it is generally possible to establish a rough *correspondence* between the several parts of the fortress as they have descended to the
25 present day and the statements in chronicles or records relating to the progress of building operations on the site; and the result, save in the rarest instances, is to leave the mound with its external bailey as the nucleus around which defensive works of greater elaboration have been
30 grouped by later designers.

The nature of the sites on which these early castles were planted varied indefinitely in different cases. Many a site which would be recommended by its inaccessibility would be held unsuitable for lack of water, while, on the other
35 hand, in the days before gunpowder, it was immaterial that a castle should be overlooked by higher ground near it so long as that ground lay beyond missile shot. In general, there is a strong tendency for an early castle to stand immediately against some river or stream, one side of the
40 defences thus being impregnable from the *outset*. When a castle was built in order to command a town, it will nearly always be found to stand on the borough walls, or just out-side them; and as most towns are built on rivers, the castle will commonly stand at the point where the wall and river
45 defences of the town *coincide*. This is the case at Oxford, Cambridge, Wallingford, Bedford, Chester, York, Warwick, Stamford, Hereford, Leicester, and Shrewsbury, to name a few examples. Stafford and Lincoln are exceptions; result-ing, in the latter case, from the fact that the town wall
50 itself was drawn along the face of the hill at a considerable

161

distance from the river below, in the former case, apparently, from the wish to command the important road which led from Shrewsbury to the Midlands. The motive which planted the castle on the edge of the borough
55 defences was evidently the wish to facilitate communication, in case of siege, with a relieving army, combined with a recognition of the danger which would follow from the firing of adjacent houses by an enemy. (563 words)

Reproduced with permission from *Social Life in Early England*, "The Development of the Castle in England and Wales" by Sir Frank Stenton (Routledge & Kegan Paul Ltd).

(a) Write a connected summary of the above passage, *as far as possible in your own words*, in about one-third of the length.

(b) Replace each of the following words used in the passage by a synonym *or* phrase which could be substituted without change of meaning:
   (i)   bailey (line 9);
   (ii)   abut (line 12);
   (iii) egress (line 21);
   (iv)   correspondence (line 23);
   (v)   outset (line 40);
   (vi)   coincide (line 45).

(c) Explain clearly what is meant by:
   (i)   in order to command a town (line 41);
   (ii)   drawn along the face of the hill (line 50);
   (iii) the firing of adjacent houses (lines 57—8).

(d) The word *reasonable* is used twice in the passage. Indicate clearly the shade of meaning conveyed on each occasion.

(Royal Society of Arts, English Language III.)

12. Write a precis of the passage given below. You must use your own words as far as possible and reduce the passage to about one-third of its original length. Give a title.

Today, when English is one of the major languages of the world, it requires an effort of the imagination to realize that this is a relatively recent thing — that Shakespeare, for example, wrote for a speech community of only a few millions, whose language was not thought to be of much account by the other nations of Europe, and was unknown to the rest of the world. Shakespeare's language was confined to England and southern Scotland, not having yet penetrated very much into Ireland or even into Wales, let alone into the world beyond. In the first place, the great expansion in the number of English speakers was due to the growth of population in England itself. At the Norman Conquest, the population of England was perhaps a million and a half. During the Middle Ages it grew to perhaps four or five million, but then was held down by recurrent plagues, and was still under five million in 1600. It was approaching six million in 1700, and nine million in 1800, and then expanded rapidly to seventeen million in 1850 and over thirty million in 1900. At the same time, English penetrated more and more into the rest of the British Isles at the expense of the Celtic languages. But the populations of other European countries were expanding too, and even in the eighteenth century, when England was beginning to be powerful and influential in the world, the English language still lacked the prestige in Europe of French and Italian; and it was not until the nineteenth century that it became widely respected as a language of culture, commerce, and international communication.

However, English has become a world language because of its establishment as a mother tongue *outside* England, in all the continents of the world. This carrying of English to other parts of the world began in the seventeenth century, with the first settlements in North America, and continued with increasing impetus through the eighteenth and nineteenth centuries. Above all, it is the great growth of population in the United States, assisted by massive immigration in the nineteenth and twentieth centuries, that has given the English language its present standing in the world. In 1788, when the first American census was held, there were about four million people in the United States, most of them of British origin. By 1830, the population was nearly thirteen million; by 1850 it was twenty-three million, and had overtaken that of England; and then it shot ahead — to fifty million by 1880, seventy-six million by 1900, and a hundred and fifty million by 1950. At the same time there was a less grandiose but nevertheless important expansion of native speakers of English elsewhere in the world, so that today there are some twelve million in Canada, ten million in

Australia, two and a half million in New Zealand, and over a million in South Africa.

There are very few native speakers of English in South America or in Asia, but English is an important medium of communication in many parts of the world where it is not a native language. In India, with its three hundred and fifty million people and its two hundred and twenty-five different languages, English is still the main medium of communication between educated speakers from different parts of the country, and is widely used as a language of administration and commerce. As could be expected, the Indian schools have changed over to teaching in the regional languages since Independence, but English is still used as the medium of instruction in most Indian universities, and university students rely to a very large extent on textbooks written in English. A similar situation is found in other countries, especially former British colonies: in Nigeria, for example, where there are three main regions with different languages, English is still an essential language for internal communication, and the universities carry out their teaching in English. This situation cannot continue for ever: such countries will ultimately change over to teaching and administering and publishing textbooks in one or more of their own languages, and nobody will want to quarrel with them for that. But it is clear that for a long time ahead English will be an important language for them, playing a role somewhat like that of Latin in medieval Europe.

Moreover, the use of English as a medium of international communication is not confined to such countries. In the past few hundred years the English-speaking peoples have played a large part in seafaring and international trade, and English has become one of the essential commercial languages of the world. So that if a Norwegian or Dutch business firm wants to write to a firm in Japan or Brazil or Ceylon, it will probably do so in English, and will expect to receive a reply in English. In science, too, the English-speaking peoples have played a large part, and in recent years there has been an increasing tendency for scientists in other countries to publish in English, which in this field has gained at the expense of German. Of course, English is not the only important international language.

Arabic, French, German, Malay, and Spanish all play an important part in certain areas. Russian has become of greater international importance than ever before, and will undoubtedly continue to go up; and we can confidently expect that Chinese will soon follow. But at the moment it does seem that English is the most important of the international languages. (913 words)

C. L. Barber

(Associated Examining Board — English, Advanced Level, Paper 1, 1973.)

13. Reproduce the substance of the following passage, which contains about 680 words, in *note form*, using between 170 and 180 words. Divide your answer into sections, each with an appropriate heading: your layout should help the reader to grasp the meaning quickly. The material should be presented in roughly the same order as that used in the original, but you may make minor changes in the order if you think it advisable. State at the end the number of words you have used, including headings but excluding any letters or figures you may have used to indicate sections and sub-sections. You will lose marks if you do not use note form.

It is essential to avoid questions in your notes.

How to recognize a good employer.

It is easier to judge one firm against another once you have studied the evidence they provide in their literature, attended your first interview and particularly (if you get one) your second interview which will be at their own premises.

What training do they offer? The key to this is how much early responsibility and how much opportunity to learn by doing, rather than by trailing round looking at other people, are given.

How soon do they expect you to earn your keep? Some firms offer specific responsibility the first day. Six to twelve months would be a long time to wait for it.

How much opportunity is given to have responsibility in a number of *different* specialist functions in your early years, so that you can help decide which suits you best? Do people move round in their early and middle years in the company, as part of an organized plan to create versatile managers?

Many companies will tell you that they do all these things. The more cautious applicants will, in the nicest possible way, be persistent in asking for examples of how such company policies have been applied to particular individuals. The best test of all is to ask employees who have joined in the last two or three years. Award high marks to the companies which go out of their way to let you talk to previous employees on their own. You can also keep your eyes and ears open when you visit. You can seldom judge how up-to-date the equipment and operations are. But are you received and passed from A to B politely and unfussily? Does the whole interview procedure appear to have been pre-planned? When you pass through commercial and manufacturing areas do people at work look up with a smile or as if they regard you as an unwelcome intruder? When someone explains to you what he is doing, does he seem to take an interest, and possibly some pride, in it? When moving from A to B, how does the person with whom you are in tow greet other people — is he welcome, or a nuisance? More particularly, does he really seem to *know* them? In a production shop, is the industrial housekeeping good or dirty and/or untidy (but make allowances for the nature of the process)? Do the people in general seem purposefully engaged in what they are doing in offices and factory? If your answers to these rather general questions are favourable, the odds are that it's a well-run and therefore happy organization.

What makes for early success in industry?

Obviously enough, most important is the ability to make sound business judgments and decisions, and to see that things happen. Initially, however, you may not have many decisions to make and your success will depend very much on how you get on with other people, and whether you can exist in a department and then make things happen in it without too much friction. Taking the initiative is important — making suggestions and acting without waiting to be told. So also will be taking private steps to become proficient in some skill which is, or could be, of use to the firm, such as learning a language. Most important of all you have to make your own training effective. Do not rely on the company. If you are bored, don't just complain, but suggest where you should go and what you should do. Features which have gone with lack of success in early industrial careers are unwillingness to accept responsibility and unpreparedness to get down to detail.

Two frustration periods often occur. Firstly, in the middle of your second year, when you have learned a good deal, and have arrived at a stage when routine obscures the interest of the next stage. Secondly, usually at the "next stage", you may feel that the "assistant" job that you are doing satisfactorily at the moment holds no clear prospect of promotion. In some instances this diagnosis may be right, but it may often be influenced by temporary factors outside the firm's control.

Based on *University of London Careers Advisory Service Information Paper*.

(The Institute of Bankers, Part 1.)

14. Reproduce the substance of the following passage, which contains about 670 words, in *note form*, using between 180 and 190 words. Divide your answer into sections each with an appropriate heading; your layout should help the reader to grasp the meaning quickly. The material should be presented in roughly the same order as that used in the original, but you may make minor changes in the order if you think it advisable. State at the end the number of words you have used, including headings but excluding any letters or figures you may have used to indicate sections and sub-sections.

Britain 1975

In the last decade average earnings have risen more than prices. Women's earnings have risen in Britain rather less than men's. The principle of equal pay for equal work applies in many occupations and is being extended under legislation to come fully into force in December 1975; the average earnings of women are a little over half the average earnings of men. The real incomes of manual workers, especially unskilled workers and young people under 18 years old, have risen both in absolute terms and in relation to the incomes of non-manual workers. The weakest groups economically are retired people wholly or mainly dependent on pensions, households in which the father is dead or absent, and low-wage earners with a number of young children.

Illustrative of the widening opportunities for education

and training is the increase in the proportion of young people benefiting from non-compulsory education. In 1971, for instance, over 43 per cent of 16-year-olds were in some form of full-time education, compared with 33 per cent in 1964. The proportion of 18-year-olds continuing full-time education in universities, colleges of education and technical colleges is also steadily increasing. A large number of undergraduates are, moreover, "first generation" students, neither of whose parents had a university education. Although the children of professional parents are still more likely to go on to higher education than the children of manual workers, a higher proportion of the children of manual workers receive higher education than in most other European countries.

Over the last decade social differences between manual and other workers have become less pronounced. Increased prosperity and modern production and marketing methods have allowed many workers to acquire household goods and personal possessions previously beyond their means. The increased diversity of market products and greater spending power have permitted a much freer expression of individual taste for everyone. Styles in clothes, for example, vary more according to age group than according to income group or occupation.

The general level of nutrition is high. The movement towards a greater use of convenience foods, and imported foods in the 1960s, has been partly offset by a reversion to a slightly less expensive diet. Increases in meat and fish prices have resulted in greater demand for poultry. Cheese and vegetables other than potatoes, are among the foodstuffs consumed in greater quantities than a decade ago while the consumption of bread and flour has declined. Tea remains the most popular beverage, but many more people are drinking coffee, including "instant" coffee, than before. The consumption of considerable quantities of sweets and chocolate (some 8 oz — 226.8 gr — per person a week) remains a notable feature of British eating habits. Many more people are now interested in "good food", both traditional English and exotic dishes. Restaurants providing the national dishes of other countries are to be found throughout Britain; Chinese restaurants predominate but there are also many which

specialize in Indian and Italian food. Interest in cooking
has also widened and menus have become more imaginative, helped by cookery journalism, including television
demonstrations, and a great variety of recipe books.
Increased affluence and tastes acquired abroad have like-
wise increased the demand for wines, spirits and liqueurs —
during the 1960s, sales of wines nearly doubled and consumption increased by nearly 44 per cent between 1971
and 1973, from 7.8 pints per head to 11.2 pints a year.
Beer remains the most popular alcoholic drink in Britain,
consumption per head in 1973 being nearly 197 pints.

Expenditure on food now accounts for a smaller share
of total consumer expenditure than it did ten years ago.
Increases have taken place, however, in expenditure on
motor vehicles, housing, alcoholic drink, recreation and
entertainment. The proportion of expenditure on clothing
and footwear has fallen, but there have been noticeable
developments such as the growing range of leisure clothes,
the more adventurous styling in men's wear, and the large
turnover in mass-produced fashions for young people, with
frequent changes of style. In this branch of fashion, British
designers have gained an international reputation.
From Britain 1975. *An Official Handbook. H.M.S.O.*
(The Institute of Bankers, Part 1.)

15. Give a clear summary *in about 100 words* of the following
letters. Supply also a heading, in which names and addresses
may be given.

ROBSON & SILLS, LTD.
120 Newbury Road,
Reading,
Berkshire.

12th March, 19 .

The New World Advertising Agency,
14 Fenchurch Street,
London, E.C.2.

Dear Sirs,

We have recently perfected in our Laboratory a new
preparation for cleaning all kinds of fabrics which
will, we think, revolutionize the industry. It is in
liquid form and has been subjected to the most

exhaustive tests on all kinds of materials with
complete success.

Ample stocks will be available shortly but before
placing this product on the market we should like you
to carry out an intensive advertising campaign on our
behalf.

We should be glad, therefore, if you would let us
know at your earliest convenience what medium you
suggest.

Yours faithfully,

R. Brown
General Manager

THE NEW WORLD ADVERTISING AGENCY
14 Fenchurch Street,
London, E.C.2.

14th March, 19 .

General Manager,
Robson & Sills Ltd,
120 Newbury Road,
Reading, Berkshire.

Dear Sir,

We thank you for your letter of 12th March and
shall be glad to undertake the campaign you suggest.

We could arrange for television coverage and
advertisements in the national press. We feel, however,
that for a product such as yours - in which you
obviously have the fullest confidence - the greatest
impact upon the public would be made by extensive
door-to-door canvassing and the distribution of free
samples. If you agreed, we could arrange for all
three media to be used simultaneously, with the
canvassing taking place over as wide an area as you
desired.

It would be necessary for you to supply simple,
non-technical details of the make-up of the product
together with an exposition of the main selling points.

We should be pleased to send a representative to
discuss this matter with you at your convenience.

Yours faithfully,

F. SIMPKINS
For THE NEW WORLD ADVERTISING AGENCY.

ROBSON & SILLS, LTD.
120 Newbury Road,
Reading,
Berkshire.

16th March, 19 .

The New World Advertising Agency,
14 Fenchurch Street,
London, E.C.2.

Dear Sirs,

    We thank you for your letter of 14th March and
appreciate the promptitude with which you have replied
to our enquiry.
    The line of action you suggest sounds as though it
would be most effective and we suggest that you send a
representative to discuss details early next week.
Monday afternoon would be most convenient.
    Meanwhile we enclose simplified details of the
formula and examples of its success on various fabrics.

                            Yours faithfully,

                            R. Brown
                            General Manager.

(Note: a convenient pattern for a heading is "Summary of the
correspondence between (name) of (address) and (name) of
(address) on the subject of (subject)". The summary should
contain only *essential* facts.)

Chapter 10

Business letters

Efficient communication is always highly desirable but in business and other formal correspondence it is essential. Inefficient communication may be not merely unfortunate but positively disastrous.

Accordingly, business letters should be complete, concise, logically planned, clearly and politely expressed in grammatically correct modern English, and tidily and attractively presented.

Completeness

The writer of a business letter should make sure that every part of his letter is complete in every way. He should make sure that everything he wishes to state and that everything which the recipient wants to know or might conceivably want to know or needs to know or should be told is included.

Content of the letter proper

The writer should make sure that all the information, questions, requests, apologies, thanks, etc., which he wishes to include are in fact included; and that all the necessary or helpful facts, names, dates, quantities, prices, figures, etc., are stated. It is all too easy to omit something important, through forgetfulness or inattention or through assuming that the person to whom one is writing knows more than he does.

A letter which is one of a series or a follow-up to a previous letter may be regarded as incomplete unless it contains a reminder to the recipient of the topic of the correspondence and of the stage which has been reached in the correspondence, even if the sender considers that these things ought to be obvious. This should be done as a courtesy to the reader and as a precaution — lest the reader is forgetful or less efficient than the sender.

All replies of course are incomplete unless they contain full acknowledgements.

2. *Addresses, date, signature, etc.*

Letters from commercial or official sources have not only the sender's address but also the recipient's name and address — which are essential for filing purposes. Even letters from private individuals often contain both addresses if the correspondence is on a commercial or official matter.

These addresses should of course be complete! This completeness is particularly desirable in international correspondence, where the names of countries should be included. A failure to supply complete addresses always causes delays and inconvenience. Examples of inadequate addresses:

Laburnum Villas	17 High Street	The Old Court House
Little Puddleton	Manchester	Norfolk
		(England or Va.?)

Most commercial and official correspondence will contain a reference, often consisting of the sender's initials and those of his or her typist and some indication of the date of the letter. This is essential for filing purposes. It should be quoted on replies.

The date on which the letter was written should be stated. It is not necessarily the date on which the letter was posted! The date should be written *in full*, e.g. October 24th 1976, not just October 24th and certainly not 24/10/76 — a form which may give an impression of laziness and may be misread. The date usually appears below the sender's address.

Finally we may note here that a letter is incomplete unless it is signed! As so many signatures are legible only to the people who write them, it is customary in business correspondence for the signature to be followed by a typed version of the writer's name. The sender's position in the firm should be made clear, e.g. Regional Sales Manager; Publicity Department.

Conciseness

Letters should be long enough to serve their purpose — and no longer. No-one wants to waste his or her time laboriously reading long-winded and repetitive letters.

Planning

In order to write a complete and concise letter one must plan it first. It is advisable to draft out a plan for any letter in which more than one point is to be made. In examinations, it is almost always essential to write a preliminary version.

The reader should not be expected to find the important points for himself. As a general rule, one should put the main point first or, in a reply, immediately after the acknowledgement. Then should follow material related to this main point (e.g. details, reasons, explanations) or other points in descending order of importance.

Common sense and initiative have of course to be employed: the material should if possible be organized in such a way that each paragraph leads on naturally to the one that follows it, thus avoiding the awkward use of "Regarding" and "With reference to" to introduce new subjects; sometimes it might be desirable to present the material in chronological order (though only after a general introductory opening sentence); at other times it might be advisable to give the good news first!

Tone

It is very difficult to define tone. One definition of the tone of a letter might be that it is the impression given to the recipient of the sender's attitude to him and to the subject of the correspondence. The letter should be polite but not too formal, friendly but not "chatty". The writer should be firm, if necessary, but not rude; if he is making an apology he should not "crawl".

Even if the contents of the letter are arranged very well, failure to adopt an appropriate tone will make the letter inefficient as a means of communication since the reader's attention will stray from what is being said to the unsuitable manner in which it is being said.

Language

The use of formal but unaffected language will go far towards achieving the right tone. The degree of formality of the language will vary with the subject of the correspondence, but in general business letters should be free of slang and other colloquialisms — expressions used only in conversation. The use, for example, of expressions like "up to you" and "give us a ring" would give a casual tone to the letter.

An equally unsuitable tone would be created by the use of "commercialese", the sort of language which used to be called "Business English". The following are examples of this outdated and awkward jargon:

- Yours to hand of 4th instant
- I have to acknowledge receipt of
- We are in receipt of your esteemed communication of the 29th ult. and would respectfully beg to acknowledge same.
- Please find enclosed
- and oblige
- advise (for "inform" or "tell". Still very firmly established)
- under separate cover
- as per the aforementioned letter
- your goodself (in use for internal correspondence in one well-known British firm in 1960!)
- Assuring you of our best attention at all times

Even today this sort of language has its defenders and it is still used and indeed insisted upon in some quarters. It may occasionally create a false impression of extreme courtesy, but the invariable effect of its use is to make letters seem both old-fashioned and insincere and to make them long-winded and difficult to follow. Language should be modern and unaffected.

Words and expressions should be chosen in fact not for their apparent impressiveness but for their suitability for communicating the writer's message to the reader.

One should take care to choose words and expressions likely to be understood by the recipient. One should bear in mind that the recipient may have only a small vocabulary or may be unfamiliar with the latest vogue terms or with certain specialist terms. For example, a person receiving from a college a letter referring to "vocational courses" might wrongly, but quite reasonably, conclude that this meant recreational ones.

One should also try to ensure that the letter is written in properly constructed and grammatically correct sentences, spelt correctly and punctuated sensibly. Slovenly grammar and poor sentence construction, inefficient punctuation and faulty spelling always impair communication.

Particular care should be taken to exclude non-sentences, especially those of the following notorious types:

- With reference to your letter.
- With reference to your letter of April 14th in which you enquired as to the possibility of your finding employment with this company.
- Regarding your application of August 17th.
- Looking forward to hearing from you.
- Hoping to hear from you soon.
- Assuring you of our best attention.
- Thanking you in anticipation.
- Thanking you.

Presentation

Business letters should be legibly hand-written or well-typed. The various parts of the letter should be suitably and attractively spaced. It should be noted that the paragraphing required in most letters helps to improve their appearance. A long letter written in one enormous paragraph is not only likely to have been illogically put together, but also will probably be daunting to the recipient.

Lay-out

No attempt is made here to discuss lay-out or the punctuation,

spacing and style of addresses, salutations (Dear . . .) or subscriptions (Yours . . .), since people and companies have their
own preferences and conventions.

In handwritten examinations the traditional spacing and
punctuation should be used. For example:

34, Graeme Road,
Bargate,
Dorset.

January 27th, 1975

Smith and Co.,
Colonial Drive,
Swindon,
Wilts.

Dear Sirs,

. . . .

Yours faithfully,

Some points to note

1. *Headings* are often used in:
   (a) Letters between companies, especially for a series of
       letters on the same subject.
   (b) Letters between the departments of a company.
   (c) Letters from firms, government departments, associa-
       tions, etc., to private individuals when the use of headings
       is felt to be particularly convenient and appropriate, for
       example, in circular letters and in final demands for
       payment.

The use of headings for correspondence between firms and
within firms is unexceptionable and often desirable, especially
when the correspondence is lengthy; but the use of headings in
letters to individuals too often creates an impression of unfriendliness and coldness. In final demands for payment, however, a certain amount of unfriendliness is no doubt justified!

It is incorrect to use the Latin word "re" (meaning: "about
the matter") before the heading, or indeed anywhere else in the
letter.

2. *Dear Sir, Dear Sirs?*
Dear Sir (or *Dear Madam*) is used when the writer knows that he is writing to one person only (e.g. *Mr Smith; the Chief Education Officer; Her Majesty's Inspector of Taxes; The Secretary, Hazelwood Tennis Club*). *Dear Sirs* is used when the writer is writing to a whole firm or to any other group of people. *Sir* alone may be used in letters to Editors.

Addressing people by name (e.g. *Dear Mr Smith, Dear Miss Jones*) is a way of achieving a friendly and polite tone and is increasingly used nowadays for all but the most formal correspondence, especially when the writer and receiver have already made each other's acquaintance in earlier letters.

The use of first names is rare in business letters and usually confined to correspondence between people of equal status. Certain commercial concerns, trying vainly to create an impression of close friendship, produce a ludicrous effect by writing in Christian names in mass-produced letters (e.g. *Dear John, It seems a helluva time since I last dropped a line . . .*).

3. *Yours sincerely, Yours faithfully?*
Letters beginning with *Dear Sir(s)* or *Dear Madam* should conclude *Yours faithfully*. Letters in which the salutation includes someone's name (e.g. *Dear Mr Lloyd*) should conclude *Yours sincerely*.

4. If you are a lady it will not be enough to write *Pamela* or *Christine* or whatever in your signature. You should write *(Mrs)* or *(Miss)* or even *(Ms)* before or after your name so that the letters sent to you will be appropriately addressed. Despite recent legislation in Britain, signatures or printed names which show no indication of sex (*K. L. Green, Jo Hammond*) will be taken to be those of men!

Expressions useful in business correspondence

1. *Further to my letter of* (date) . . .
This sounds perhaps a little old-fashioned, but it is useful for telling the reader that the writer is following up a previous letter. For example:
Further to my letter of March 18th in which I expressed interest in your scheme, I am writing to ask whether you

would care to visit our London office next Wednesday.

2. *Perhaps you would be kind enough to . . .*
   I should be grateful if you would . . .
   These are pleasant ways of making requests or of asking for information. Direct questions (e.g. *When do you want to travel?*) are best avoided.

3. *We enclose with this letter.*
   Not *in* it! *We enclose* on its own is usually enough.

4. *We note from your letter of* (date) *that . . .*
   A good way of referring to a point made in one's correspondent's letter.

5. *We are wondering whether . . .*
   This is a tactful way of making a suggestion which may displease the reader, e.g. *We are wondering whether you have perhaps concentrated too much on the academic aspects of the matter.*

6. *We were sorry to hear that . . . We were pleased to learn that . . .*

7. *We trust that . . .*
   Trust here expresses a combination of hope and belief, e.g. *We trust that the matter has been explained to your satisfaction.*
      The phrase is also useful for implying a threat! e.g. *We trust that payment will be made before the end of this month.*

8. To *place* an order *with* someone *for* something.

9. To write a cheque *for* £5.
   Cheques should be *made out to* William Hill & Co.

Some typical openings

The following examples, which indicate several of the main types of business letters, illustrate the principle that one should come to the main point of the letter straight away. This done, the remaining material should fall into place naturally.

1. Dear Sirs,

       It is now three weeks since I placed an order with you for two dozen K 23 deck-chairs, but I have, despite your assurances of early delivery, still not received them.
       Unless I receive them within a week . . .

2. Sir,

      I object most strongly to some of the remarks made in the article by A. W. Kenton in today's ''Daily News''. My reasons for objecting are that . . .

3. Dear Sirs,

      Please supply one dozen copies of ''Home Winemaking'' by Iris Toper as quickly as possible. I enclose a cheque for £7.50 to cover cost and postage.

Note: "I should be grateful if you would supply" in this straightforward order would be a waste of words. Although "forward" as a verb is still widely used in commerce, and even in conversation, it must be condemned as commercialese. Its use instead of "send" or "supply" creates an old-fashioned effect. "Please forward me . . ."

4. Dear Miss Welch,

      As Secretary of the Whiteacres Social Club, I am writing to ask you whether you would be willing to give a talk to our members at some time in the New Year.

5. Dear Mr. Smith,

<u>Account No. 53472</u>

      On March 14th and April 10th, 1975, I wrote to remind you that £27.14 was still outstanding on the above account.
      I am afraid that unless the account is settled by next Wednesday, June 20th, we will have no alternative but to place the matter in the hands of our solicitors.

Note: although the writer has cause for annoyance, his letter is polite. The cliché, "no alternative but to place the matter in the hands of our solicitors", is firmly established and in frequent use.

6. Dear Sirs,

      I must protest to you most strongly about the Gremona GT coupe which I purchased from your Camberwick branch on June 4th.
      After 150 miles one of the doors fell off and shortly afterwards the steering wheel came away in my hands. This was rather annoying as I was driving along the M 18 at the time and I had to take prompt action to avoid a collision.

7. Dear Sirs,

Having heard your advertisement on Capital Radio last Thursday, I should like further details of your package tours to the Bulgarian Riviera.

8. Dear Sirs,

One of our customers, Mr. J. F. Stephens of Stambury, Wessex has asked us to supply five ten-gallon drums of tractor lubrication oil (SAE 70-80). As you know, we deal exclusively in non-industrial lubricants, so we have advised Mr. Stephens to get in touch with you.

9. Dear Fellow Resident,

<u>Proposed Stansgate Bypass</u>

As Secretary of the Stanwell Estate Residents' Association, I am writing to invite you and indeed to urge you to attend a Protest Meeting. The meeting will be held on November 11th at the Community Centre and will begin at 8 p.m.

10. Dear Householder,

We should like to bring to your notice a unique TV rental offer . . .

11. Dear Miss Jones,

We were very sorry to learn from your letter of September 15th that the Eastman washing-machine you recently purchased has not been working satisfactorily.

12. Dear Sir,

I should like to apply for the post of Personal Assistant to the Managing Director, as advertised in "The Guardian" of October 25th.

Two versions of a business letter

It will be useful to compare two versions of a letter. The letter is in reply to a complaint.

A poor attempt

PERMAFROST LTD.
Arlington Estate,
Newport.

L. B. Jones, Esq.,
15 Cadogan Terrace,
Glasgow.

Date as postmark

Dear Sir or Madam,

    We are in receipt of your communication and beg to
respectfully acknowledge same. We were of course
extremely distressed to learn that the lid of your
purchase does not fit and are totally at a loss to
understand how this alleged fault could have occurred.
We will be sending one of our reps to discuss it with
the retailer and to inspect it at your convenience at
your house next week. Would you, therefore, forward to
us in the stamped addressed envelope herein enclosed
confirmation that it will be satisfactory for him to
call. It is unfortunate that the product has in fact
become totally inoperative. Our rep will be looking
into this when he calls and he will investigate the
matter of the defective lid which you also mentioned in
your aforesaid letter. Perhaps you haven't got the hang
of the instructions because you have failed to read the
book properly. Anyway, our man will endeavour to
ascertain whether your freezer may be made to function.
If this is not the case, we will be only too glad to
replace the freezer with a new one, although you might
have to wait a few weeks, in which case it would be
about 10% cheaper. As mentioned above, we deeply regret
any inconvenience caused and can assure you that all
our products are stringently tested to ABM standards
before leaving the factory. Assuring you of our best
attention at all times.

Yours sincerely,

(Complaints Department)

Comments:

(a) The letter proper

The material is badly organized. The breakdown of the freezer
is of much greater importance than the fact that the lid does
not fit, and should have been dealt with immediately after the

acknowledgement. Moreover, the word "freezer" is not used until two-thirds of the way into the letter. That the recipient presumably knows what is being talked about is no excuse. The writer has repeated himself, mentioning the complaint about the lid twice; and he has forgotten what he has said in the second sentence — the regrets about inconvenience caused were not "mentioned above". The absence of paragraphing suggests in itself an unwillingness to organize.

The letter is vague. The following essential or desirable details have been omitted: the date of the complainant's letter, the date when the freezer was purchased, the name and number and price of the model, the name of the retailer, the name of the representative, the date on which he will be calling. The reference to "the book" is vague, as is the expression "about 10% cheaper".

The letter is tactless. The salutation is hardly a good start! The use of "alleged" implies that the writer doubts Mr Jones' word, and it is suggested that perhaps he has "failed to read the book properly". "Properly" is a particularly unfortunate choice of word. "We will be only too glad" implies gracious condescension, rather like someone accepting an invitation to open a fete, instead of an apologetic willingness to put things right. The use of "any" before inconvenience suggests that the writer is unimaginative enough to believe that a breakdown of a freezer in August may not cause inconvenience. The "any" is likely to make Mr Jones snort! It should be noted how the injudicious use of one word may have a disastrous effect on tone. As to the remark "You might have to wait a few weeks"...!

Much of the language is unsuitable. The casual tone of the colloquial abbreviation "reps" and of the expressions "haven't got the hang of" and "Anyway" counteracts the bogus solemnity initially created by the archaic commercialese. The expression "deeply distressed" is obviously insincere. Some of the language is reasonably appropriate, but "herein" (i.e. "in this letter" or rather, "in the envelope") is both unnecessary and pseudo-legal. "Has become totally inoperative" is a coy way of saying that it has broken down. "Endeavour to ascertain" is pompous.

The writer of the letter may know what ABM standards are but it is hardly likely that Mr Jones will. "Stringently tested" is enough.

The style of the letter is not improved by the use of the word "case" twice in one sentence.

(b) addresses, salutation, subscription, etc.

The address of Permafrost Ltd is incomplete. There are at least twenty-seven places called Newport. Glasgow is a large city!

Permafrost apparently function without a filing system, for there is no reference.

The date on which the letter was written has not been stated. "Date as postmark" is irritating.

"Dear Sir or Madam"! This does not of course imply any doubts about the recipient's sex. What it does imply is that the writer cannot be bothered to consider the feelings of the recipient.

The signature is illegible, and there is no indication of the position the sender holds in the firm, not even a "p.p." for someone important.

Here we may note that Permafrost must be a very inefficient firm indeed if they have an entire department to deal with complaints!

This letter has of course been concocted for teaching purposes. It would be difficult to imagine any company sending a letter so full of faults as this one, but business and official letters often contain some of the types of faults which it includes. Moreover, examination candidates often submit letters which are a good deal worse. At least the above letter has no spelling or punctuation mistakes!

A better version

```
                                    PERMAFROST LTD.
                                    Dartington Avenue,
                                    Arlington Estate,
                                    Newport,
                                    Loamshire.

    Ref. HA/RW/DL42

    L. B. Jones, Esq.,
    15 Cadogan Terrace,
    Glasgow, N.35.                   August 3rd 1976

    Dear Mr. Jones,

        We were very sorry to learn from your letter of
    July 30th that you are experiencing difficulty with
```

your Permafrost de luxe "Super 70" freezer which you purchased from Riteway Discount Stores of Stourbridge on July 22nd.

We find the failure of the freezer to function both disturbing and surprising since all our products are checked and tested most thoroughly before they leave our factory. Faults in fact are so rare that we wondered whether perhaps the procedures in the instruction booklet supplied with the freezer are being followed correctly.

Providing that the arrangement is convenient for you, one of our representatives, Mr J. L. Smith, will call on you on Wednesday August 8th between 10 and 11 a.m. so that the failure of the freezer to function may be investigated and the matter of the faulty lid looked into. Perhaps you will be good enough to let us know whether this time will suit you. We enclose a stamped addressed envelope.

Should your freezer prove indeed to be defective, we will certainly supply a replacement. Unfortunately, however, there might be a delay of some two to three weeks. In these circumstances we would certainly be willing to allow a discount of 10%.

We look forward to receiving your reply and we must again express our regrets.

Yours sincerely,

H. Appleton
(Service Manager)

Comments

Clear language has been used. Both old-fashioned "business English" and colloquial language have been avoided. The tone is polite. Regret has been sincerely and politely expressed, but no apology has been made as the sender does not yet know whether there is any reason to apologize.

Some particular points

(a) Paragraph 1 contains a full acknowledgement: the date of Mr Jones's letter has been quoted and its subject mentioned. Another version of the paragraph could have begun: "Thank you for your letter of July 30th. We were sorry to learn that . . ."

(b) In paragraph 2 Mr Appleton has tried to suggest tactfully that Mr Jones may not have followed the instructions correctly. How successful in your opinion has he been?

(c) "Perhaps you would be good enough to ..." is a pleasant way of introducing a request. A plain "Please" might have seemed somewhat curt.

(d) Concluding sentence. Perhaps the two points it is making should not be linked. However, the second expression of regret — justified repetition — is appropriate and courteous, and the reminder that a reply has been asked for is sensible.

Some criticisms

It could be objected that "matter" in paragraph 3 is ambiguous. Paragraph 4: there is doubt in the writer's mind whether the freezer *is* faulty and he has been unable to conceal this doubt. However, he has tried to be tactful. The use of the word "allow" is unfortunate as it seems to imply condescension. It is, however, compensated for to some extent by the words "certainly would be willing".

These criticisms may seem over-fastidious, but the fact that they have been made should emphasize how important it is to take every care in letter-writing, both inside and outside the examination room. Despite the fact that minor criticisms may be made of this letter, it may stand as an example of good business correspondence and of the standard of business letter which is expected in many examinations.

Exercises

1. Write or type out the following letter correctly and sensibly:

A. Sheppard
51, Peyton place
Boston

December 5th

Dear Sir

I'm writting to apply for the position of secretary to the Managing director of A & C ltd. That was advertised in daily telegraph of Monday. I have just compleated a two year's buisness studies course at the

college, where I attained a S/H speed of 120 m.p.h. and
can also type accurately a sixty words a minuet. Whilst
it's true I've had no fultime business experience I
have worked on Saturday's in a well-known dept store in
a clerical capasity in a nearby town. Also on weekdays
during the college holydays, I am eighteen years of
age. In the (G.CE) "O" level I past in Maths; accounts
and commerce, but I failed in english, however I intend
to retake this exam again in December. Your
advertisement mentions a salary of between £1,500 to
£2,300. Despite my excallent qualifications as I'm
quiet young I will except sixteen hundred pounds. I'm
available for interview on any day accept Wednesday,
Friday, Sunday Tuesdays and Saturdays. Hoping to hear
from you soon,

> I remain,
> Your obedient servant
>
> Alice Sheppard (miss)

N.B. It is much easier to point out most of the faults in this
letter than to put all of them right.

2. Improve the following letter in any way you consider
necessary:

Dear Madame,

With reference to your letter of March 9th. We
were sorry to learn that the sweater of our manufacture
bought by yourself appears according to you to have
developed a hole in the left elbow.
If you would be kind enough to forward it to us at
your earliest convenience we will do our best to look
into it, alternatively, if it's all right with you, you
might like to drop it in at the shop where you bought
it - they'll send it to us.
We are very surprised to hear that you are
suffering from this complaint, as all our products are
inspected carefully before leaving our factory.

> Yours,

3. Rewrite the following letter, reducing it to its essentials and
re-organizing it suitably:

17 Manor Crescent,
St. Andrews,
Fifeshire.

15th September 1977

International Optics, Ltd.,
(Dept.14)
Crookes Lane,
Market Blandings,
Salop.

Dear Sirs,

About four weeks ago on August 18th after seeing
your advertisement in the "Daily Post", I sent for
your mail-order catalogue. I have always been
interested in optical equipment-ever since I was given
a microscope as a small boy, as a matter of fact-so I
was considering ordering a telescope or a pair of
binoculars. Since the latter are easier to carry about
I chose them and filled in one of the order forms which
you supplied with the catalogue and sent it off to you
on the same day. I must say that I was rather surprised
to have to wait three weeks before I received the
binoculars, for delivery was promised to quote your
catalogue, "within a few days from receipt of the
order." I had been hoping to take them on holiday
with me. When I received them-two days after I had
returned from Pembrokeshire-I found that they had been
very badly packed-in a flimsy cardboard box wrapped in
one sheet of brown paper. This wrapping had started to
come adrift. This seems a very poor advertisement for
your firm (which was recommended to me by a friend).
The catalogue number of the binoculars was B 5.
Actually, what was really annoying was that one of the
serrated controls which adjust the focus had become
jammed, certainly as a result of the inadequate
packaging. I really think I have cause for complaint. I
should be pleased to hear from you in the near future.

Yours faithfully,

G. Williams

P.S. I ordered a B 5 heavy-duty pair of binoculars at
£26.70. You have enclosed a bill for £32.65.

4. Here is a letter sent out by a firm of insurance brokers in
November 1968. The sender is attempting to explain that it

would be slightly cheaper for the recipient to pay the cost of repairing a car he has damaged instead of claiming under his insurance policy. The names have been changed.

Criticize the letter on grounds of:

(a) old-fashioned language
(b) pseudo-legal language
(c) colloquial language
(d) ambiguity caused by the use of "same" in the first para.
(e) faulty punctuation
(f) misspelling
(g) incorrect use of "yourself"
(h) faulty sentence construction in the third paragraph
(i) the use of a non-sentence
(j) the vagueness of the phrase "in view of the amount involved".

Dear Sir,

<u>re: Accident to DMU 273A on 26.10.68</u>

Further to ours of the first instant and your telephone conversation with Mr. Watson, the writer has been in touch with Mr. Watson and has discussed the matter of your No Claims Bonus and the costs involved should same be lost by claiming under your motor policy.

The loss of No Claims Bonus over a two year period i.e. by loosing two years' no claims bonus this year and one years next year would be in the region of £16.10s., £1 more than the Third Party claim as per the estimate sent to you under cover of our afore mentioned letter.

In the circumstances therefore, it would be fractionally more beneficial to yourself to avoid claiming under your own policy and paying the Third Party amount yourself but since the ultimate decision is up to yourself, and in view of the amount involved we wait your advices as to your intentions in this case.

Assuring you of our best attention at all times.

We remain,
Yours faithfully,

SMITH & JONES & CO. LTD.
John Squeers,
<u>Motor Department</u>

5. You are a famous film star. A company has written to you asking if you would be willing to advertise their product in a television commercial. Write a reply in which you decline their invitation. You strongly disapprove of the product.

6. You have received a letter from a mail-order firm threatening legal action if you do not pay for certain goods. You have never received these goods, and did not order them! You have already pointed this out twice in reply to earlier demands. Write your reply.

7. Improve the English and the tone of the following letter:

> 13, Cadogan Mansions,
> Horton Street,
> Moreton,
> Leics.
>
> June 12th
>
> Dear Sirs,
>
>   In reply to your letter of June the tenth. I note you wish to quote from my article on lesser known British lepidoptera found in the Sunday Herald colour magazine on May 30th in your book The World of the Butterfly. Tell me which parts you wish to quote and I may find myself in a position to consider your request.
>
>   Yours truly,
>
>   James Carter, Ph.D., M.A.(Oxon), B.Sc.

8. You have recently purchased, for £15, a transistor radio from a local shop. It has now stopped working and the dealer from which you bought it has advised you to write to the makers of the radio, Court Radios, Court Road, London E 31. Write the letter, giving the name and address of the dealer who sold it to you, details of the radio and what appears to be wrong with it, and ask what you should do with the radio as it is still under guarantee.

Your letter must be set out correctly. Do not address an envelope.

(R.S.A. 1)

9. Imagine you live in a town the centre of which consists of narrow winding streets and old-fashioned buildings, some being of historical interest. The town council has plans for redevelopment. The first, and cheaper, plan is to widen and straighten the main street. The second is to construct a ring road. Write a letter to the editor of the local newspaper, stating your choice with reasons. Make it clear that though it is necessary to reach a decision as soon as is reasonable, yet there must be opportunities for public discussion. The body of your letter should not contain more than 200 words.
(R.S.A. II)

10. Rewrite this letter, retaining the letter form and expressing the facts as concisely as possible.

                                          St. Anne's College,
                                          Camford.

                                          13th July, 19 .

Dear Miss Anderton,

    Thank you for your letter of July 10th asking me to give some talks to the Camford Girls' Club on the evenings of Oct. 5 and Nov. 2 and 16 this autumn.
    I regret that I am not sure that I shall be free on every one of these evenings. I shall be available on Oct. 5 and Nov. 2; but on Oct.19 I shall be engaged and possibly on Nov. 16 also. I can, however, come on Nov. 23 and Dec. 7.
    I understand that the sort of talk you have in mind is something in the nature of a course on some literary or historical subject. I have given a number of such courses to groups of young people like the members of your Club and have found them popular with my audiences. But in this case I am not sure that such an arrangement would be a good one, as the length of time which must elapse between the separate talks might lead to a slackening of interest in the subject matter. In the circumstances it might be better to have four talks, each of which would be complete in itself, but all of them having some connexion.
    For, example, if you preferred to have talks on literary subjects only, I could begin on Oct. 5 with "The Pleasures of Reading". This makes a good introduction to a literary course. I point out, first, what one may expect to gain from reading both the classics and the best of the moderns, in fiction and non-fiction. Then I explain how one may obtain books

from local libraries and from County and Students'
Libraries. This could be followed by three talks on any
particular writer or period about which your members
might like to hear in more detail.

If you thought that a historical series would be
more popular, the first talk could be "The History
of Camford", a subject on which many inhabitants
of our town are surprisingly ignorant. That could
be followed by a visit, on the next evening when
I am to come to the Club, to the Camford Museum. As I
am one of the Trustees of the Museum I should
be able to show you some of the treasures which
are not usually on show to the public, some because
they are too valuable or fragile, others because
they are too large to be staged in the public
rooms. As in the case of the literary talks, I
could on the other two evenings take as my subjects
anything in which your members had a particular
interest.

I should be glad if you would let me know which
of these suggestions appeals more to you.

Yours very truly,

Allen Bowles

Miss H. Anderton,
Hon. Sec., Camford Girls' Club,
5, Trevor Road,
Camford.

11. Your Certificate has arrived from the Association of
Medical Secretaries and you would like it framed. Unfor-
tunately, your small son accidentally spilled tea over it so you
really need another one. Write a suitable letter to the Association.
(Association of Medical Secretaries — Certificate in Medical
Reception.)

12. Write a courteous version of the following letter:

Dear Sir or Madam,

I have to inform you that your application for a
home-improvement loan (August 17th) has been received
and is receiving consideration.

Complete the form enclosed herein <u>legibly</u> and <u>in
ink</u> and return it to the undersigned without delay.

I am, Sir,

Your obedient servant,

13. *Either*

(a) As an official of a charity, political, student or similar organization you are planning a fund-raising event such as a sponsored walk/swim, jumble/bring-and-buy sale, Christmas fair, carol-singing tour or street collection.

Compose TWO letters: (1) for publication in the press to detail the aims of your organization; (2) for distribution to members of your organization outlining the help needed. The body of each letter should be about 10 lines.

Or

(b) You are travelling abroad and read an article in a newspaper/magazine that is very critical of some aspects of your homeland.

Write a letter (in English!) to that publication giving your informed views on the subjects criticized. (You may find yourself dealing with such matters as tourist facilities, public transport, food and drink, dress, police, officials, attitudes to foreigners.)

The body of your letter should contain about 20 lines.

(R.S.A. English Lang. II.)

14. Your local Council has bought a fine Victorian mansion in its own extensive grounds. The councillors are considering whether they should convert the house for use as a youth club and recreational centre or whether they should convert it into flats for old people. Write a letter to your local newspaper expressing your views on what the house should be used for.

(Joint Matriculation Board English Language Ordinary Level Paper A, Part I.)

15. Write a letter to the manager of a travel agency, explaining your reasons for wishing to alter holiday bookings already made. State your new requirements.

16. Here is some information about a house, 26, South Road, Browton, Staffordshire, owned by Mr John Norris.

Built 1910 – semi-detached.
Brick with slate roof.
Cellars (rather damp).
Bathroom (in original state).

Three reception rooms (lounge, dining room and one other).

Small kitchen (unmodernized).

4 bedrooms.

Outside:

Rear garden of approximately ⅓ of an acre — with dilapidated potting-shed and greenhouse — very overgrown and in need of attention.

Front garden almost non-existent — paved area with entrance to coal cellar.

No garage or garage space.

Situated within ½ a mile of town centre, a ¼ of a mile from nearest school.

Once a good area — now two factories close by.

Mr Norris was trying to sell his house, and inserted a very brief advertisement in the *Browton Herald*.

Mr Dennis Johnson, who lived in Hawley, Lancashire, saw the advertisement and wrote to Mr Norris requesting further details. Mr Norris's reply, *though strictly truthful*, made the house appear a very desirable property: he was anxious to sell.

Either

(a) Write this letter, as from 26, South Road, Browton. You may add to the points given above if you wish. Write about 25 lines of average handwriting, not counting the address, etc.

Or

(b) Mr Johnson visited the house described above, and soon decided it was not suited to his needs. As he did not meet Mr Norris, he wrote to him explaining why he did not intend buying the house. Also, feeling that Mr Norris's letter had given a false impression, Mr Johnson politely told him so, describing the house as it had appeared to him.

In about 25 lines of average handwriting, write Mr Johnson's letter, as from his home address in Hawley.

(J.M.B. English Language Ordinary Level, Paper C.)

17. *Either*

(a) You have been employed for five years by your present firm as a private secretary in a post which you have enjoyed and where you have been able to progress, but you now wish to resign.

Write your formal letter of resignation to your employer at the same time requesting a reference you may use for any future job. (In your letter invent your own reasons for your resignation.)

Or

(b) As Secretary of your local literary and arts society, write a letter to a well-known figure (of your own selection) inviting him or her to address your society at the first of the next season's meetings.

In your letter give some brief introductory details of your society as well as the arrangements for the lecture and for the reception of your speaker, who will be travelling some distance and will have to stay overnight. (London Chamber of Commerce Private Secretary's Certificate.)

18. As a private customer you have just received a letter from your bank manager, the text of which is given below. You wish the facility to be extended for an indefinite period. Write a reply, giving convincing reasons for your request. Include all appropriate formalities, and do not let the text of your letter exceed 120 words.

In October last, I agreed to mark up an overdraft limit of £1,000 on your account for a period of six months, which has now expired. I therefore propose cancelling the facility. If this is in order, there is no need to answer this letter. Should you however require our assistance for a further period perhaps you would be good enough to let me know within the next fourteen days.

(Institute of Bankers.)

19. *Either*

(a) The regional branch of your Association of Personal Assistants, of which you are secretary, has arranged a series of meetings for its members over the winter months.

You have just heard, however, that Mr James Grey who was to have given the first talk on 18 September 1972 will now be abroad on behalf of his company at that time. Write a letter to Miss Jane Hurleigh, who would have some distance to travel to the meeting, asking her if she would mind bringing forward her talk from 23 October 1972 to take Mr Grey's place.

Or

(b) Your company, which produces electrical goods, has reorganized its regional offices and service centres. Write a circular letter to your trade customers with this information, and also telling them that a new Sales Manager has been appointed in your particular region. You are his secretary. The Sales Manager intends to call on all customers during the next few weeks to introduce himself and to distribute details of a newly designed domestic cleaner to be available in the Autumn.

(Invent any names and other details you consider necessary to make your letter as realistic as possible.)

(London Chamber of Commerce Private Secretary's Certificate.)

20. You believe that you have left your bag or case on the bus on your return from school or college or work. Write a letter to the bus company explaining the details and requesting their help. Then write the letter you would hope to receive in reply. (A.E.B. English Language Ordinary Level, Syll. I.)

21. *Either*

(a) Write a letter of not more than 100 words offering your services to the local organizer of a campaign to teach illiterates to read.

Or

(b) Draft a circular letter of about 100—120 words appealing to local employers for help in solving the problem of unemployed school-leavers.

(Institute of Bankers.)

22. Your employers, manufacturers of cosmetics, are about to market an entirely new range of products intended to appeal primarily to the budget-minded teenager. They plan to launch a selling campaign through department stores who normally stock their products. The shops will be asked to supply space for a special display stand to be set up in a prominent position in the store, coupled with a window display and the distribution of samples by a beautician representing your firm. The selling campaign will be supported by newspaper, magazine and television advertising, and would be concentrated in the space of

one week; the dates are yet to be determined, but the month of September has been chosen.

Write a letter to be sent to stores outlining your proposals and requesting their co-operation. Special discounts will be available to them on initial orders.

(L.C.C. Junior Secretary's Certificate, June 1975.)

23. Write a letter on your employer's behalf accepting an invitation for him to lecture to a learned society in London on the latest developments in his industry — plastics. Since this will entail an over-night stay request accommodation and any provisions you consider necessary for his lecture which is illustrated and to be given at three in the afternoon.

Or

Your factory, manufacturing furnishing fabrics, has been damaged by fire and production badly affected. Prepare a letter to be circulated to all your customers who are awaiting orders stating that delivery will be delayed by about two weeks and asking for their co-operation.

(L.C.C. Private Secretary's Certificate.)

24. Qualbest Pharmaceuticals Limited is a British company which manufactures drugs and medicines. These have saved many lives in British and European hospitals. Some of the drugs have been invaluable in curing diseases in the developing countries. Of course, it is not possible to cure every sick patient, whatever drug is used. The high cost of research makes the drugs very expensive.

An (imaginary) British newspaper has recently published an article attacking the company for overcharging and for marketing drugs which do not cure people. This attack is unjustified when all the facts are known. For example, the company donated a large consignment of drugs after an earthquake disaster in one of the developing countries.

Either

A Director of the company decides to write a letter to the newspaper, which he hopes the editor will publish, in which he will defend the company against the attack. He asks you as his secretary to draft a suitable letter which he will use as a guide when he writes his final draft. Prepare a letter as requested, basing it on the facts given above. You may invent minor details to lend realism. No expert knowledge of drugs is required,

and you should *not* discuss diseases except in general terms.
Or

An official working for an international relief organization asks you as his secretary to draft a letter from him to Qualbest Pharmaceuticals Limited. He wants to express his gratitude for the firm's generous help during a recent disaster, and to comment on the newspaper attack which he has just read. Prepare the draft as requested, basing it on the facts given above. You may invent minor details to lend realism. No expert knowledge of drugs or relief work is required.

(London Chamber of Commerce Private Secretary's Certificate.)

25. Answer both parts of this question.

(a) As medical secretary working in the casualty department of a large hospital, reply to a letter of complaint by a patient. He claims that there was considerable delay in giving him treatment, during which time he was in considerable pain from a fractured arm.

(b) Imagine you are the medical secretary for a general practitioner whose surgery has been badly damaged by fire. Some valuable equipment has been destroyed. Write to his insurance company explaining the extent of the damage and seeking information about the procedure for submitting a claim.

(Association of Medical Secretaries — Diploma Examination.)

Letters of application for jobs

The most important fact is that you are applying for a certain post. Accordingly, this should come first.

Alternative types of openings:

1. *Dear Sir,*

    I am writing to apply for the post of Personal Assistant to the Public Relations Officer, advertised in "The Times" of July 10th.

2. *Dear Sir,*

    I should like to apply for the post . . .

3. *Dear Sir,*

   In response to your advertisement in yesterday's "Daily Telegraph", I am writing to apply for the post of Assistant to the Works Manager.

4. *Dear Sir,*

   With reference to your advertisement in "The Scotsman" of April 11th, I should like to apply for the post of Assistant Buyer.

5. *With reference to your advertisement in "The Guardian" of July 17th. I should like to apply for the post of Private Secretary to the Managing Director.*

Numbers 1, 2, 3 and 4 are all acceptable but 5 is not as it begins with a non-sentence.

Remarks on these ways of beginning a letter of application:

1. The objection made by some people that it is obvious that you are writing is not important. The inclusion of the comma, one hopes, removes any impression that it is the P.R.O. who has been advertised in "The Times".

2. Surely by writing you are in fact applying? This objection is pedantic.

4. This opening sentence is clumsy but acceptable.

N.B. It is essential that the name of the post for which you are applying should be stated and that you should name the publication in which you saw the post advertised.

After this direct and specific opening sentence you should state, in an order you think appropriate, some or all of the following particulars; according to the instructions in the advertisement or to your judgement.

> details of your education
> details of your commercial or professional experience
> your reasons for applying
> your reasons for considering yourself a suitable candidate
> your reasons for wishing for a change of job
> availability for interview
> the names of referees.

(Referees are people to whom reference may be made by a prospective employer and who will be willing to vouch for you.)

Curricula vitae

Some professional bodies ask, rather grandly, for a curriculum vitae. This is simply a tabulated list which should state your full name and address, your sex and your date of birth, and give details (with dates) of your education and academic and commercial qualifications and a summary of your career since completing your full-time education.

Tone

Generally speaking, the tone of a letter of application should be one of modest optimism (or optimistic modesty!). One has to appear neither "big-headed" nor pessimistic, e.g. "I think I may claim that my qualifications and experience are appropriate to the advertised post."

Examination qualifications

1. The names of all examinations (not "exams"!), certificates and diplomas and of all subjects (French, Art, Bookkeeping, Shorthand, Mathematics, etc.) should begin with capital letters.
2. Inaccuracy of expression should be avoided. For example, "I got three G.C.E.'s — French, Maths and Art". "I passed three 'O' levels in French, Maths and Art. (Three in each subject?) A correct version: "In summer 1976 I passed in French, Mathematics and Art at the Ordinary Level of the G.C.E."
3. It is not necessary to write in full the names of well-known qualifications like the C.S.E. and G.C.E., but lesser known ones should be written in full, for example, *The Civil Service Commission Interpretership Certificate in Russian.*
4. You *pass* an *examination*. You *gain* or *obtain* a *certificate* or *diploma*. You *achieve* a shorthand or typing speed.
5. The dates when qualifications were obtained should be clearly stated.

Exercises

1. Imagine that in today's *Daily Chronicle* you have seen a job advertised. This job interests you and you decide to apply for it. Write a letter of application to R. L. Pryor, Esq., Personnel

Manager, Martin and Co. Ltd, 100–104 Firm Road, Westhampton. Lay out your letter correctly and include in it details of the job for which you are applying, where you saw it advertised, why you are applying for the job, your schooling and previous work experience (if any) and the name and address of somebody who has agreed to provide a reference for you. (R.S.A. I.)

2. You have seen advertised a job which seems exactly what you are looking for. Certain educational qualifications are stated in the advertisement to be essential. Unfortunately, you do not possess these qualifications, but you are sure that your practical experience of the type of work involved would enable you to do the job very well. Write a persuasive letter of application.

3. You have decided to apply for the post of Administrative Assistant to the Manager of a small firm of oriental carpet importers. In drafting your letter of application you have prepared the following notes. Delete unnecessary repetitions, and then (i) arrange the remaining items to form a connected plan for the letter, and (ii) write the letter. Your application should be addressed to The Manager, Eastern Carpets Ltd, Western Road, Brighthelmstone, BN4, NS7.

Notes

1. Age	8. Experience
2. Qualifications	9. Education
3. Reference to advertisement	10. Testimonials and references
4. Outside interests	11. Promise of loyal service
5. Family	12. Hope for interview
6. Examinations passed	13. Length of notice
7. Single	14. Start work if application successful.

(The Associated Examining Board Ordinary Level, English Language — Professional and Business Use, June 1976.)

4. You are seeking a senior secretarial post and have seen the following advertisement in a national newspaper:

"International Chemical Company requires a secretary for Export Manager with good qualifications and experience, personality and ability to work on own initiative. Fluent French necessary and German if possible. Driving licence

useful but not essential. Hard work, but interesting duties and visits abroad. Apply in writing to Box 546 (Ref. E.M. 632), *Morning Clarion*, E.C.4."
Write your letter of application.
(London Chamber of Commerce Private Secretary's Certificate Examination, 1969.)

5. Answer the following advertisement:
    "Join us at Supermart Head Office in Barford and we'll save you all the time and money you waste on commuting and give you an excellent job in superb surroundings.

    Carrying out varied and interesting secretarial work you will have your own special responsibilities and excellent prospects for promotion.

    There are a large number of young people at Supermart so we've a warm friendly environment and exceptional working conditions — air-conditioned carpeted offices with plenty of open space. There's a choice of restaurants and coffee-bar facilities, a special bus into town at lunchtime, a bus service bringing staff in from some areas, an excellent pension scheme and our very own country club — how many London companies can offer all that?

    Stop wasting valuable time and money.

    Apply in writing, stating your educational qualifications and secretarial experience, to the Personnel Manager, Supermart House, P.O. Box 17, Athelstan Road, Barford, Middx. BA9 6 SL."
    (Adapted from a newspaper advertisement.)

6. Answer the following advertisement:
    "We require a young person to train as an Inspector in our Customer Service Department to undertake the inspection of goods returned under complaint.

    Applicants should have a good "A" Level standard of education with particular emphasis on both written and spoken English as considerable contact with customers is involved.

    Applicants should apply in writing to:
    The Personnel Department,
    International Leisure Products Co. Ltd.,
    Ambleside Road,
    Exwell,
    Wessex."

7. Write a letter of application for the following post, advertised in *The Steeply News*:

"Medical secretary urgently required for busy suburban group practice. The successful applicant must be competent both in secretarial and reception duties; she should have had a good general education and hold certificates of competence in shorthand and typing. Apply in writing to: The Group Practice, High Street, Steeply."

(Association of Medical Secretaries — Diploma Examination.)

A telegraphic interlude

The following telegrams were sent by Richard ("Bingo") Little to Bertram Wooster of Berkeley Mansions, London W.1. Write out an economical version of each.

I say Bertie old man I am in love at last. She is the most wonderful girl Bertie old man. This is the real thing at last Bertie. Come here at once and bring Jeeves. Oh I say you know that tobacco shop in Bond Street on the left side as you go up. Will you get me a hundred of their special cigarettes and send them to me here. I have run out. I know when you see her you will think she is the most wonderful girl. Mind you bring Jeeves. Don't forget the cigarettes — Bingo.

Bertie old man I say Bertie could you possibly come down here at once. Everything gone wrong hang it all. Dash it Bertie you simply must come. I am in a state of absolute despair and heartbroken. Would you mind sending another hundred of those cigarettes. Bring Jeeves when you come Bertie. You simply must come Bertie. I rely on you. Don't forget to bring Jeeves. — Bingo.

(From *The Inimitable Jeeves* by P. G. Wodehouse.)

"Make-up letters"

In the Royal Society of Arts Shorthand-Typewriting and Audio-Typing Certificate examinations candidates are shown a letter to which they have to compose a reply, which has then to be typed. The letters of reply are composed from dictated notes. They may conveniently be described as "make-up letters". In certain other examinations there may be a question in which the main points of a first letter are supplied together with points which are to form the basis of a reply.

"Make-up letter" questions provide valuable practice not only for secretarial students but also for other Business Studies students.

The remarks made on page 172 apply, as they do in all business letters. Here is a plan which may be followed for all make-up letters:

1. Acknowledgement of the letter to which you are replying.	This will normally include thanks and the date and topic of the letter to which you are replying.
	It will certainly consist of only one paragraph and probably of one sentence.
2. Information to be supplied or requests to be made.	One or more new paragraphs.
3. Suitable polite conclusion.	One paragraph and probably one sentence.

This plan is ideal, for example, for letters in reply to enquiries. For example:

Thank you for your letter of November 21st in which you ask for details of our day trips to Boulogne.

There are daily sailings from Ramsgate at 8 am and arrival at Boulogne is at 1 pm. The return journey commences at 5 pm and disembarkation at Ramsgate is usually complete by 10.15 pm.

Our modern motor-cruisers are luxuriously appointed and passengers may of course avail themselves of our duty-free shops and bars. There is a reasonably priced restaurant and ample seating accommodation in comfortable lounges. The fare for adults is £10 and that for children under fourteen £6.60.

If there is any further information you require please do not hesitate to contact us again.

It is true to say that the above plan is ideal for any letter of reply. The following points about all make-up letters should be carefully noted.

1. You are composing the letter as if you were the person by whom the letter is to be signed.
2. The material in the notes for the reply may not be in the

best order. You should arrange the material in the best logical order, so that your letter will have continuity.

3. When composing your reply you should keep the contents of the first letter constantly in mind and where necessary refer to those contents in your reply, so that no misunderstanding or vagueness can occur. For example, "Thank you for your cheque for £3.50.", not "Thank you for your cheque." It is certainly advisable to mention all the facts and figures, dates and times which appear in the original letter, e.g. when confirming your acceptance of an appointment.

4. The notes for the reply are *notes*. They will probably not consist of complete sentences. In particular, "the" and "a" may be omitted. You should make sure that you use in your letter complete grammatical sentences.

5. You must not invent material which does not appear in the notes for the reply, although such expressions as "unfortunately", "accordingly", and "we are pleased to inform you", and suitable conclusions like "We trust that this arrangement is satisfactory" are permissible and indeed in most cases essential. Expressions, then, should be added which express feelings which it would be reasonable to ascribe to the sender, which give continuity to the letter, and which help to provide a neat and reasonable conclusion.

6. None of the facts in the notes should be omitted!

Style

(a) By far the best beginning is "Thank you for your letter of (date) . . . In suitable cases one may start: "We were sorry (glad) to learn from your letter of (date) . . . or, in less formal letters, "Many thanks for your letter of (date) . . .

(b) Do not normally use both "We" and "I" in the same letter. This may, however, be done if the writer is both writing on behalf of his or her firm, college, etc. ("We") and elsewhere in the letter making a personal statement ("I").

(c) It is advisable to avoid direct questions. For example, instead of "When do you wish to travel?", say "I should be grateful if you would inform me . . .". Care should be taken that requests do not sound like orders.

(d) Use friendly but formal language (i.e. without slang or other language used only in conversation). Avoid old-fashioned "business English" like "We are in receipt of your esteemed communication of 4th instant and would respectively beg to acknowledge same."

(e) Avoid the use of non-sentences, e.g. "With reference to your letter of June 12th.", "Trusting this answers your queries.", and "Thanking you in anticipation."

(f) I *should* be grateful if you would . . .

(g) Letters in which the salutation includes a name (e.g. *Dear Mr Peters, Dear Miss Morgan*) should end with "Yours sincerely". "Dear Sir" or "Dear Madam" are followed by "Yours faithfully".

Tone

The use of formal but friendly language should go far to achieve the right tone, but one should keep in mind the desirability of courtesy and politeness. Direct criticism of one's correspondent and sarcasm should be avoided.

Even if the correspondent has made an unjust criticism or been abusive, one's reply should be courteous. Accordingly, it would be quite wrong to say, for example, "If you had taken the trouble to read the instructions you might not have made such a mess of it." Instead one would say something like this: "Perhaps we may point out that in the instruction booklet it is clearly stated that . . ."

Two versions of a make-up letter

Here is a question set in the R.S.A. Shorthand-Typist's Certificate Examination, Stage II:

                                        18, Dale Road,
                                        Weymouth,
                                        Dorset.

Whitney Buildings Ltd.,
Holbrook Lane,
Wellington,
Shropshire.   24th June 1970

Dear Sirs,

    I recently purchased from you a greenhouse, Model SB/126, measuring 10ft x 8ft, and wish to heat it during the cold weather for raising seeds.

I have a small coal-stove complete with chimney, and would like to know whether I could use it inside this greenhouse. Would there be any damage to the plants from fumes, or would the heat be too dry?

Any information you can let me have will be greatly appreciated.

Yours faithfully,

J. Lawson

Notes for the reply
Acknowledge inquiry. Greenhouse cannot be heated satisfactorily as suggested. Although stove has chimney, fumes would escape into greenhouse when stoking and seriously damage plants. Special types of oil heaters available, capable of heating different sizes of greenhouse. Several designs shown on enclosed illustrated leaflet. Suggest dividing off part of greenhouse for raising seeds, thus possible to maintain higher temperature at reasonable running cost. Five per cent discount on all orders received before the 1st August.

A bad answer
(Despite the absence of spelling mistakes.)

Whitney Buildings Ltd.,
Holbrook Lane,
Wellington,
Shropshire.

18 Dale Road,
Weymouth,
Dorset.   26/6/70

Dear Sir/Madam,

Thank you for your inquiry. The greenhouse cannot be heated satisfactorily as suggested. Although the stove has a chimney, fumes would escape into the greenhouse when stoking and seriously damage plants. Special types of heaters are available capable of heating different sizes of greenhouse. Several designs are shown on the enclosed illustrated leaflet. We suggest dividing off part of the greenhouse, thus it would be possible to maintain higher temperatures at a reasonable running cost. There is a five per cent discount on all orders received before 1st August. Hoping to hear from you soon.

Yours sincerely,

W. R. Smith
For Whitney Buildings Ltd.

What criticisms may be made of this letter?

A better answer
Here is a much better answer. It would certainly satisfy the examiners, although perhaps one or two slight criticisms could be made.

Whitney Buildings Ltd.,
Holbrook Lane,
Wellington,
Shropshire.

J. Lawson, Esq.,
18 Dale Road,
Weymouth,
Dorset.   June 26th, 1970.

Dear Mr Lawson,

Thank you for your letter of June 24th in which you enquire about the possibility of heating your SB/126 greenhouse.

Unfortunately it would not be possible for you to satisfactorily heat the greenhouse with your coal-stove despite the chimney, since while the stove was being stoked, fumes would escape into the greenhouse and seriously damage the plants.

Special types of oil heaters, capable of heating different sizes of greenhouse, are in fact available and several designs of such heaters are shown in the illustrated leaflet which we enclose.

If such a heater were used, it would be possible to divide off part of the greenhouse specially for raising seeds, so that a higher temperature could be maintained and yet running costs kept at a reasonable level.

If you are interested in the possibility of purchasing an oil-heater you may perhaps like to know that we are offering a 5% discount on all orders received before 1st August.

Yours sincerely,

W. R. Smith
for Whitney Buildings Ltd.

Exercises

1. Compose and type a reply of appropriate length to the following letter. Your reply should be set out in the correct form ready for signature by the Sales Manager as for dispatch today.

25 Rochester Drive,
OTTLEY,
Lincs.
HA3 1AH

12th May, 1971

The Sales Manager,
The Deep Freeze Refrigeration Co. Ltd.,
Station Road,
OTTLEY,
Lincs.

Dear Sir,

I have seen your advertisement in today's Ottley Gazette, and I should be much obliged if you would send me details of your selection of home freezers.

I have a family of four, and we live a long way from the shops, so perhaps you could make suggestions as to size and type. Although I should like to put the freezer into the garage, this will not be possible until a new extension is built, and until that time it will have to be placed in the kitchen where the space is rather limited.

Perhaps you would be kind enough to let me know where it would be possible to see your freezers on display.

Yours faithfully,

(signed) Mary Dyer (Mrs)

Notes for the reply

Acknowledge letter. Send list of freezers available from us. Possible to buy slightly marked cabinets at lower prices; these not listed; will have to telephone for details. Advise not to think small when considering freezers, choose fairly large one. One cubic foot will store about twenty-five pounds of frozen food. No purchase tax over twelve cubic feet, so these better value. Top-opening type more economical to run, but upright ones take less space. Suggest visit to warehouse; please telephone for appointment with Mr Allen.

(R.S.A. Shorthand-Typist's Certificate, Stage II, May 1971.)

Note: The wording of the instructions for this and the other R.S.A. questions in this section has been slightly altered, since the notes for the replies are, in the examination, dictated at shorthand speed.

Some points to remember when answering this question:

(a) "Of appropriate length". This means long enough to incorporate clearly all the material in the notes in courteously worded and grammatically complete sentences. Too short or too long a letter would in differing ways be an inefficient means of communication.

(b) "Think small". This phrase should not be used in a formal business letter. Why?

(c) Students have been known to refer to a one cubic foot freezer!

(d) It is necessary to decide exactly what the notes mean, particularly "No purchase tax over twelve cubic feet". It is just the sort of thing someone might well say in giving notes for a reply or in conversation, but it could not be used in a written reply, as it would not make sense.

2. Compose and type a reply of about 150 words to the follow-

ing letter. Your letter should be set out in the correct form
ready for signature.

> Allgood Manufacturing Co. Ltd.,
> Haverstock Works,
> Blackpool.
>
> 7th July, 1960.

Dr. H. Martin, M.D.,
The Firs,
Mount Road,
Blackpool.

Dear Dr. Martin,

As arranged with you during our telephone
conversation this morning, I have instructed Mr George
Hawkins to attend at your Surgery at 10 a.m. on Tuesday
morning next for a medical examination.

Up to a few months ago he was a most reliable
employee, but since then he has shown a marked falling
off in efficiency and seems to be unable to concentrate
on even routine jobs. We are unable to account for
this, since as far as we can tell, he has no domestic
worries and insists that there is nothing wrong with
his health.

He is only fifty-three years old and so is not
approaching the age of retirement; yet his present
standard of work is so low that we do not feel that we
can continue to employ him. In view of the type of
machinery we use I am justified in saying that it would
be dangerous to do so. We are most reluctant to dismiss
a man who has hitherto given us such good service and
sincerely hope that you will be able to help him – and us.

> Yours sincerely,
>
>
> CHARLES SHOESMITH,
> Personnel Officer

Notes for the reply

Type a letter as from Dr Martin saying that Mr Hawkins has
been thoroughly examined. He injured shoulder on football
field some years ago necessitating operation. Recently fell from
bus, aggravating former injury and causing shooting pains near

heart. Feared heart trouble, loss of employment, and retirement on inadequate pension. X-ray reveals no damage. Condition due solely to anxiety. Recommend fortnight's rest and reassurance regarding employment.

(R.S.A. Shorthand-Typist's Certificate, Stage II, 1960.)

3. Compose a reply to the following letter:

> 14 Worcester Road,
> Birmingham 8.
>
> 21st November 1974
>
> The Area Manager,
> Clan Hotel Group,
> High Street,
> Worcester,
> WO6 4BS
>
> Dear Sir,
>
> ### White Lion Hotel, Worcester
>
> Last week I spent the week-end at the above-named hotel. I arrived at 9.00 p.m. on the Friday evening having previously telephoned the Manager to ask if a meal or sandwiches could be kept for me. I was told that this would be arranged.
>
> When I arrived, I was told that no food was available. I then went to my room (booked by telephone), and found that the bed had not been made up. When I complained, I was told that owing to a shortage of staff this had been overlooked but would be put right immediately.
>
> The following morning I was served with the worst breakfast I have ever had in one of your hotels. The toast was hard and burnt, the coffee almost cold, and the egg so undercooked that I had to ask for another but I did not get one. Dinner that night was of an equally poor standard.
>
> As a result of such poor service I left the hotel early on Sunday morning.
>
> I trust that you will look into the matter to ensure that such an incident does not arise in the future.
>
> Yours faithfully,
>
> (Signed) J. H. Coleman

Notes for the reply

Acknowledge. Matter investigated. Very disturbed to find situation did exist. Acute staff problems at that time. Manager White Lion most apologetic. Send cheque £5 in compensation. Thanks for drawing attention to situation. Hope he will continue to use hotels. Assure high standards will be maintained in future. Trust no further cause for complaint.
(R.S.A. Shorthand-Typewriting, Stage II, Nov. 1974.)

4. Compose a reply of appropriate length to the following letter. Your letter should be set out ready for signature by the Chief Estimator.

> 21, Hill View Avenue,
> South Common,
> Worcs.
>
> 12th May, 1970.

Messrs. P. Atkins & Sons, Ltd.,
514 Lower Road,
South Common,
Worcs.

Dear Sirs,

    I wish to have four rooms of my house at the above address redecorated, namely the lounge, dining-room, bathroom and separate toilet.

    Perhaps you would be kind enough to send me a rough estimate for re-painting and re-papering these rooms. If the cost of this work is not excessive, I may consider having the study emulsion painted.

    If possible I should like to have the work carried out within a few weeks.

    It may interest you to know that your name has been given to me by Mrs. Rogers, who was very satisfied with the work which you carried out for her about a month ago.

> Yours faithfully,
>
> (Signed) Brenda Phillips (Mrs.)

Notes for the reply

Acknowledge Mrs Phillips' letter. Would be possible to start work in a month's time. Approximate estimate for rooms mentioned in first paragraph — £210. This includes choice of wallpapers at a set price; more expensive wallpapers would be added to cost. Emulsioning of study would cost about £25. Would be pleased to send estimator to make a thorough examination and give detailed estimate. Mrs Phillips to notify a convenient date and time. Work would take about a fortnight.

(R.S.A. Shorthand-Typist's Certificate, Stage II, May 1970.)

5. Compose a reply to the following letter:

Royal Hospital,
Inn Road,
London, W.C.4.

26th June, 1972

PRIVATE AND CONFIDENTIAL
Head of Business Studies Department,
College of Further Education,
London, W.C.1.

Dear Sir,

<u>Miss Elizabeth Brown</u>

The above-named has applied for the post of Personal Secretary (Medical) at this hospital and has given your name for reference.

We should be most grateful if you would let us have your opinion of her character, ability and general suitability for this position.

We apologise for troubling you, and enclose a stamped addressed envelope for your reply. We should like to take this opportunity of thanking you for your assistance.

Yours faithfully,

(Signed) R. West (Mrs)
Personnel Officer

Notes for the reply

Acknowledge letter. Miss Brown has been attending a full-time Medical Secretary's Course. Her examination successes to date include six "O" levels and "A" level English, R.S.A. Shorthand at 100 wpm and Typewriting II. Examinations taken in June for which results are pending: Diploma of the Association of Medical Secretaries, Medical Shorthand-Typewriting Stage II, Medical Audio-Typewriting Stage II, Medical Stenography 100 wpm, Shorthand 120 wpm and Advanced Typewriting. During her course Miss Brown has made very good progress; she is intelligent, efficient, industrious and has a pleasing personality. (R.S.A. Medical Audio-Typewriting, Stage II, July 1972.)

6. Compose a reply to the following letter:

> World Interlines Ltd.,
> 27 Seaford Street,
> London, W.C.1.
>
> 26th June, 1973

Dr L. Taylor,
56 Oak Grove,
Hillside,
S.W.5.

Dear Dr. Taylor,

Following my telephone conversation with your secretary, I have looked into the question of the flight itinerary for your lecture tour in the United States of America but before giving you definite dates and times I would like the following information:

approximate date of your departure;
the names of the States which you intend
to visit and the length of time in each State;
how many will be in your party;
whether you will be taking any equipment
with you?

As soon as I have this information I will draw up the flight itinerary and let you have it together with our account.

Yours sincerely,

(Signed) T. L. Andrews
Overseas Travel Manager

Notes for the reply

Acknowledge letter. Date of departure middle of September. Intend to visit Tennessee ten days, Georgia two weeks, Alabama two weeks and New York three weeks. Return to England beginning of December. Number in party five adults. Will be taking slides and special projector, 250 mm x 450 mm. Ask whether these can be treated as hand baggage or whether they should be specially packed and treated as heavy luggage. Insurance cover will be required. Ask for quotation. Shall be pleased to receive flight itinerary and their account as soon as possible.

(R.S.A. Medical Audio-Typewriting, Stage II, July 1973.)

7. Compose a reply to the following letter:

> St. Mark Ambulance Brigade,
> Haltford Section,
> 18 Wells Farm Road,
> Haltford,
> Somerset.
>
> 13th November 1973

The Hospital Secretary,
General Hospital,
Bowater,
Somerset.

Dear Sir,

    A number of our cadets have never seen the inside of a hospital.

    As your hospital is a large General Hospital with a variety of departments, including a Casualty Department, I wonder if it is possible for you to arrange such a visit. This would help the cadets to gain some knowledge of hospital life.

> Yours faithfully,
>
> (Signed) L. Atkins
> Superintendent

Notes for the reply

Acknowledge letter. Ask how many cadets would be involved in this visit and whether this must be a week-end visit or could they attend any day, perhaps during school holidays. The visit to last two hours per party, including a break for refreshments. The following itinerary suggested: 1000 hours meet at Reception Office and proceed to Lecture Hall for talk by Hospital Secretary. 1020 hours visit to Casualty Department. 1050 hours Coffee. 1110 hours Physiotherapy Department. 1135 hours Out-patient Department. Six cadets accompanied by one adult the maximum size of group possible.

(R.S.A. Medical Audio-Typewriting, Stage II, November 1973.)

8. Compose a reply of appropriate length to the following letter:

106 Downs Crescent,
Lewes,
Sussex.

24th June, 1971

S.L.M. Products Ltd.,
26 George Street,
Ipswich,
Suffolk.

Dear Sirs,

Shortly after I treated the water in my fish pool with your special chemical ''Puron'', to clear it of excess weeds, my 30 fish, worth about £20, died.

I followed carefully the instructions on the packet, using the exact quantity of "Puron" stated, and throwing it over a quarter of the pool at a time.

I shall be glad if you will explain how this chemical could have proved poisonous. I feel that the fault lies entirely with your product.

Yours faithfully,

(Signed) G. S. WILLIAMS

Notes for the reply

Reply to Mr Williams that this chemical definitely not poisonous. Extensively tested before marketing. This is first complaint received. If used in too great a concentration all oxygen eliminated from water. Lack of oxygen killed fish. Possibly instructions not followed that pool should have been treated a quarter at a time over a period of ten days. Our representative will telephone to make arrangements to call. (R.S.A. Shorthand-Typist's Certificate, Stage II, June 1971.)

9. Compose a reply of appropriate length to the following letter. Your letter should be set out in the correct form ready for signature.

Apex Works,
Rockingham Way,
Exbridge,
Middlesex.

5th June, 1975.

Messrs. Lineham and Company,
23 The Hill,
BENFLEET,
Surrey.

Dear Sirs,

I am enclosing a drawing showing the proposed fitting of doors to shelving in the Efficiency Office at this factory. This matter was discussed with your representative, Mr. James Marten, on his last visit here. I shall now be pleased if you will let me have a quotation covering the manufacture and fitting of these doors according to the enclosed specification. Arrangements for viewing the shelving can be made by telephoning the Efficiency Engineer, Mr. Robert Stott (Extension 5).

I have to draw your attention to an error in your quotation (Requisition No. 20976) for one Four-drawer Unit Card Index Cabinet. The enquiry was for a cabinet to take cards eight inches wide and five inches deep. Your quotation gives the size as five inches wide and eight inches deep. I assume that the sizes have been transposed accidentally but should like your assurance that the price quoted is for a cabinet of the correct size.

Yours faithfully,

John Smith
Works Manager

Notes for the reply

Type a letter from Sales Manager thanking writer for inquiry. Representative will phone for appointment to check measurements and show samples. Apologize for error in quotation. Price given is correct for size required. Transposition of numbers a typist's error. Enclose catalogue of new cupboards to be shown at national exhibition. Ask how many free tickets to this are required.

(R.S.A. Shorthand-Typist's Certificate, Stage III, 1969.)

10. Write a courteous reply to the following letter:

> 14 Carnarvon Drive,
> Barford,
> Essex.
>
> September, 1st 1976.
>
> Mrs. Christine Jones,
> 60 Church Road,
> Cold Christmas,
> Nr. Amberleigh,
> Wessex.
>
> Dear Madam,
>
> I enclose an estimate from a local garage for repairs to my car. You will see that the cost (including V.A.T.) of having a new bumper fitted is £23.15.
>
> As I explained to you on the day of the mishap, I am in the process of trading my car in for a new one and in the circumstances I think that you, the person responsible for the accident, should pay all expenses.
>
> In view, however, of the fact that you were good enough to inform me of what had occurred and did not simply drive away as so many people would have done, I will be prepared to consider the matter settled if you will send me a cheque for £20.
>
> Yours faithfully,
>
> H. A. Thornton-Smythe

Notes for the reply

Don't think new bumper necessary. Dent on your bumper

hardly noticeable, not surprising as only moving about 2 m.p.h. when collision occurred. Even if bumper not replaced selling price of your car will hardly be affected. Certainly not to the extent of twenty pounds. Very upset about affair but feel that £5 more than covers any depreciation suffered by your vehicle. Enclose cheque.

11. Write a reply to the following letter:

St. James' Hospital,
Chelsea Crescent,
London, S.W.1.

22nd October 1976

Dr. J. A. Morgan,
Carlton House,
Long Lane,
ONGAR,
Essex.

Dear Dr. Morgan,

I am writing to invite you to address a group of our students, although I realise that you have retired from practice.

Your research into cardiac disease has earned you a national, indeed an international, reputation and I am sure that both teaching staff and students would be delighted if you would be kind enough to give them a talk on any subject of your choice.

I would like to suggest 3 p.m. on July 1st, 2nd or 3rd and if you should choose to accept our invitation, perhaps you would care to lunch with members of the Hospital Management Board at 1 o'clock in the Board Room.

We would of course defray all your expenses and arrange for you to stay in a nearby and comfortable hotel.

Yours sincerely,

L. P. Smithers
(Hospital Secretary)

Notes for reply

Delighted to attend. Plenty of spare time at the moment. Lecture will last an hour. Shall arrive at 12.30, July 2nd.

Subject of lecture: "Some Modern Developments in the Treatment of Cardio-Vascular Conditions." Don't bother about hotel
as will stay with son's family in Kensington for a few days. Will
be bringing 35 mm slides and film strips. Please make available
slide projector, film-strip projector and screen. Hope it'll be
possible to darken lecture room. What stage in studies have
students reached? How many attending? Accept offer of lunch.

12. Your employers, manufacturers of kitchen utensils, have
received complaints that the handles of some of their saucepans
are not heat-resistant as claimed. In some instances the material
used has cracked.

An investigation has shown that this defect is confined to one
particular batch. At the time of production, supply difficulties
necessitated the substitution of a material slightly different
from the usual one.

Write a suitably apologetic letter to the aggrieved customers.
In your letter you should:
  (i)   Assure them that the defect is not dangerous.
  (ii) Offer immediate free replacement of goods, all charges
        paid.
  (iii) Thank them for writing about the complaint.
  (iv) Explain the cause of the problem.
        (L.C.C. Junior Secretary's Certificate, 1973.)

13. Compose a reply of appropriate length to the following
letter:

Flat 14,
23 Russell Street,
London, W.C.1.

16th May, 1966

The Banqueting Manager,
Royal Hotel,
Dover Street,
London.

Dear Sir,

    I should be glad if you would inform me if you can
accommodate a Wedding Party on 2nd July.
    My daughter will be getting married at Holy
Trinity Church, Clarence Road, at 11 a.m. and
approximately eighty guests will be present. I should
like to have details of your menu for both a buffet and

a full luncheon. Perhaps it would be a good idea for me
to come in to discuss with you the question of wines,
etc.
      I will let you have a table plan as soon as I know
the actual number of people expected. I assume that
table decorations and wedding cake stand will be
provided.
      I look forward to hearing that you will have a
room available for the reception. My husband and I were
very pleased with the arrangements you made for our
Silver Wedding party – the service and food and wines
were excellent.

                              Yours faithfully,

Notes for the reply

As Secretary to the Banqueting Manager, write saying that you
are pleased that the previous function was a success. Suggest
that Mrs Hill should make an appointment with Mr Belloni to
inspect the rooms available. Enclose sample menus which range
in price from 22/6 to 42/- per head, plus 10% service charge.
Suggest that a sherry bar be provided for arriving guests.
The question of wines with the meal can be discussed. Wine list
is enclosed. Enquire how long the reception will last. Floral
decorations and a cake stand and knife will be provided.
(R.S.A. Shorthand-Typist's Certificate, Stage III.)
Note: "plus 10% service charge" should not be included in the
letter in this form. Something like "There is an additional
service charge of 10%" is suggested.

14. Compose a reply to the following letter:

                              Jameson Engineering (U.K.) Ltd.,
                              Overhill Works,
                              Cannock,
                              Staffs,
                              WS11 2TQ

                              13th March, 1973.

K.Z. Tubes Ltd.,
Oldbury,
Worcester.

Dear Sirs,

      We placed our order No. SS10789 on 2nd January,

1973 for 100 lengths of stainless steel tubes, 26" by
2" outside diameter with 1⅞" bore.
    Delivery was specified within six weeks. This
period has now been greatly exceeded and I should be
glad if you would let me know when you intend to
deliver.
    The tubes are wanted in connection with an
important export order.

                          Yours faithfully,
                          JAMESON ENGINEERING (U.K) LTD.

                          (Signed) J. Hadlow
                          Sales Manager

Notes for the reply

Apologise for delay in delivery. All customers notified in
September nineteen seventy-two of intention to move early in
nineteen seventy-three to a new address — old premises having
proved inadequate. Notification obviously not received by you.
New factory near railway depot and main road. Modernized
equipment will result in trebled output. New factory has been
operational for six weeks. Backlog of work nearly cleared.
Order should be dispatched within ten days. New arrangements
will mean better service. Look forward to continued business.
(R.S.A. Shorthand-Typist's Certificate, Stage III, March 1973.)

15. Compose a reply to the following letter:

                          65 High Street,
                          Isfield,
                          Sussex.

                          14th November, 1973

The Editor,
The Handyman's World,
71 Lauderdale Road,
London W1B 7RB

Dear Sir,

    My neighbour, a grocer, also sells paraffin which
he stores in a building on the boundary between our
respective properties. The building is of cement blocks

and two of the walls are boundary walls. The 250-gallon
tank of paraffin is situated on top of this 8ft high
building with a supply pipe leading down inside the
building.

I do not know whether this pipe is leaking, but I
have noticed recently that paraffin is seeping through
the bottom of the wall on to my property where I have
various flowering bushes growing. It is also spreading
upwards on the wall.

I intend to write to my neighbour about this and
should be glad if you would advise me as to whether I
should report the matter to my local authority.

                    Yours faithfully,

                    (Signed) S. L. WELLARD

Notes for the reply

Reply saying we assume neighbour aware of leakage. If not, first
step is to speak to him about it. If no action, should then write
to neighbour and call at local council offices. Speak to a health
inspector or building inspector. Could be danger if large amount
of paraffin leaking. Obviously neighbour's responsibility to
prevent this. May find that he needs local authority help to get
neighbour to act. Is entitled to expect this.
(R.S.A. Shorthand-Typewriting III, November 1973.)

16. Compose a reply to the following letter:

                    Maryland General Hospital,
                    Maryland,
                    Oxted.

                    16th June, 1975

Dr. I. Johnson,
Community Health Physician,
Town Hall,
Oxted.

Dear Dr. Johnson,

        Last year you consented to present the prizes to
the nurses at the end of their training but
unfortunately had to cancel and you arranged for your

Deputy to attend the prize giving in your place. At this time you stated that you would be willing to attend next year if the date was convenient.

The date for this year's prize giving is 18th July, 1975 at 1400 hours. I should be grateful if you could let me know whether you would be able to present the prizes this year.

Yours sincerely,

(Signed) C. R. Davies (Miss)
Chief Nursing Officer

Notes for the reply

Acknowledge. Will attend. Ask how many nurses; what kind of prizes; who else will be speaking and on what topics.
(R.S.A. Medical Audio-Typewriting II, June 1975.)

Chapter 11

Report-writing

The word "report" has several meanings, most of them associated with the idea of "carrying back" (RE-back, PORT-carry) information. In business a report may be defined as the delivery of information in response to an instruction.

A very short report may be oral. A long one is likely to be written.

Written reports may be divided into routine reports and special reports.

Special reports, i.e. reports on special matters, are often asked for in business and secretarial examinations. Examinees are asked to make the sort of reports which are often called for in reality.

They may, for example, be asked to report on the mislaying of a file, on the failure of a shop to increase its profits, on the suitability of a hall for a discotheque, on an item of equipment being considered for purchase by a club, on students' opinions of college food, on the advisability of replacing manual typewriters with electric ones, on a visit to an exhibition, on a course recently attended — on almost anything in fact which is not a routine matter.

A useful and frequently-used plan for a special report

The types of plan used for reports will vary according to the nature of the material being dealt with. However, here is a plan very commonly used:

Heading
Terms of Reference
Procedure
Findings
Conclusions
Recommendations
Date and signature.

Heading

The heading should leave the reader in no doubt as to the subject of the report. A lengthy and specific heading is a great deal better than a short and vague one; cf. "Report on Student Discontent with the Refectory at South Wessex College" with "Report on Food". It does not matter if the words of the heading are repeated in the Terms of Reference. There is of course no need to write the word "heading".

Terms of Reference

This section states *exactly* what was to be reported on and who asked for the report to be made and on what date and possibly by what means (e.g. letter) it was asked for. A useful pattern for the Terms of Reference is:

To report on (subject) as requested by (person) in his letter of (date).

Procedure

This section lists the steps taken to collect the information. In an examination a candidate will be expected to think of the various methods and various sources by and from which information might be gathered in a real situation. Information might be obtained from written sources such as sales records or articles in trade journals; it might be obtained from question-naires or censuses; it might be obtained from interviews and discussions; it might be obtained by observation. Every detail which could possibly be relevant should be stated. For example, "A number of students were interviewed." is no good. How many were interviewed, and when were they interviewed?

Findings

This part of the report presents the information collected. It is the central and almost always the longest part of the report, and the information should be clearly presented in sections arranged in a suitable order, e.g. in order of importance or in order of time.

Note that there is no need to say "It was found that . . .". This is not part of the findings but a sort of repetition of the heading "Findings".

Conclusions

This part of the report consists either of a summary of the Findings or of conclusions which may reasonably be drawn from the Findings. Normally it should contain nothing for which there is no evidence in the Findings.

Often the Conclusions are grouped under headings which "match" those in the Findings, but this need not always be done.

Recommendations

These are recommendations for action — or possibly for no action! They are made by the reporter on the basis of the Findings and Conclusions. Care should be taken not to mix up the Conclusions and Recommendations.

Date and signature

The report should be dated and signed. The date serves two purposes: to show that the person making the report has not "hung about" before making it (cf. date in the Terms of Reference) and of course to show to a future reader what period the report refers to.

As well as writing his signature and perhaps supplying a more legible version of his name, the reporter should state his status, for example, Social Secretary, Regional Sales Manager, Officers of the Student Union.

Example:

Report on the Fall in Profits at
Cisco Ltd., High Street, Barchester.

TERMS OF REFERENCE

To report on the reasons for the fall in profits at the Cisco Supermarket, 19-23 High Street, Barchester, in the period January 1st 1976 to June 30th 1976, as requested by the Managing Director of Cisco Ltd., in his letter of July 4th 1976 (Ref.EK/JBS 4/7/76) and to make recommendations.

PROCEDURE

1. The sales records for the period from January 1st to June 30th 1976 were inspected and compared with those for the second half of 1975.

2. Fifty customers were interviewed by the Regional Sales Manager over three days (August 3rd, 4th and 5th).

3. The premises, both inside and outside were carefully inspected.

4. The Manager, the two general assistants, and the three cashiers were interviewed.

5. Recent developments in the High Street and the surrounding area were noted.

FINDINGS

1. Extent of the fall in profits

    Profits fell from an average of £1,200 a month in the second half of 1975 to an average of £850 a month in the first six months of 1976.

2. <u>Causes of the fall in profits</u>

    A. Internal

        i Since December 1975 the Manager, Mr L. B. Clark, has had a number of domestic problems which have made him less efficient than in the past, particularly in the supervision of other members of the staff. However, the allegations of a few customers that conditions were no longer hygienic were not justified.

       ii One of the cashiers, Miss S. Rogers, has been discourteous to customers. A majority of the customers interviewed complained of her discourtesy and she certainly made an unfavourable impression when interviewed. Miss Rogers stated that since March this year she had been suffering from emotional problems.

     iii The two general assistants appointed in March to replace those who left for other employment are inexperienced and inefficient. The R.S.M. found that shelves had not been kept properly stocked and that old stock has been kept on display after the last permissible date for sale.

    B. External

        i The opening in January 1976 of a new branch of Continental Groceries in Station Road half a mile from the Cisco branch has probably attracted custom away from us, chiefly by means of special offers and intensive advertising in the local press.

       ii The improvements to the A 514 completed in February 1976 have diverted some trade from Barchester as a whole, as the new shopping centre at Ambridge is now easily accessible.

     iii New parking restrictions in Barchester High Street, in effect since April 1976, have probably further reduced custom, especially from those who like to buy their groceries in bulk. Unfortunately the new multi-storey car park will not be completed until early in 1977.

CONCLUSION

The decline in profits is partly the result of external
developments but the decreased competence of the
Manager together with the inexperience or discourtesy
of some of the staff is certainly a very important
cause.

RECOMMENDATIONS

It is recommended that:

1.　an advertising campaign be mounted in the
local press.

2.　the two general assistants and Miss Rogers be
warned that they must raise the standard
of their work.

3.　the situation, including the competence of
the Manager, be reviewed in six weeks' time.

August 8th, 1976　　　　　　　　Alan B. Edwards
　　　　　　　　　　　　　　　　Regional Sales Manager

Notes and comments on the foregoing report

Language and tone

As in almost all reports, the language is formal — the sort of
language which should be used in business correspondence.
There is no slang or other colloquialisms (e.g. *weren't too
pleased*, *quite a few*) and no shortened forms like *hadn't*, etc.

Complete sentences are used, or (as in the Recommendations) parts of sentences which fit onto a common introduction
(Here, *It is recommended that*:). Notes — which are usually
ungrammatical — should never appear in any report.

The report is objective and not coloured by any prejudices
which the reporter might have. The personality of the reporter
does not obtrude; it does not glare out at the reader. A main
reason for this is the use of the passive (e.g. *The premises were
carefully inspected*) and of the Third Person (e.g. *The R.S.M.
found that . . .*) instead of the First Person (*I*).

The tone of the report is restrained. Perhaps Miss Rogers had
been disgracefully rude, but the reporter has chosen to use the
softer word "discourteous".

Organization

The material has been presented in a logical order. The reporter considered it advisable to indicate to what extent profits had fallen. This was an essential preliminary to the presentation of the causes.

The causes have been classified, logically, into *Internal* and *External* and the numbered points under these headings have been arranged in what seems to be the order of importance.

The reporter could of course have used alternative headings, for example: *Inefficiency of Staff* and *Unfavourable External Factors*. If there had been other causes besides those listed, perhaps a fourfold classification might have been used; e.g.:

Increase in Costs
Decrease in Efficiency of Staff
Increase in Competition
Miscellaneous Factors

Classification of material in any section of the report should always be as logical as possible, even though it is sometimes very difficult to do this with very complicated material. Whatever classification is used, the most important points should, in general, be made first.

Spacing and notation

The spacing of the various parts of the report is consistent throughout. All the main headings (Terms of Reference, Procedure, etc.) are at the same distance from the edge of the paper. The subheadings (Extent, Causes) are indented equally. The numbers 1, 2, 3, 4, 5 in the Procedure and 1 and 2 in the Findings and 1, 2 and 3 in the Recommendations are vertically in line with one another, as are A and B, and i, ii, iii, etc.

The notation (i.e. lettering and numbering) is consistent throughout. N.B. It does not matter what system of notation is used as long as it is consistently observed.

Consistency is also essential in headings. Headings of equal importance and indentation should be in the same type of lettering; if the first such heading is in capitals and underlined, for example, the others should be.

Grammatical parallelism

The principle of grammatical parallelism has been observed, as it should be in all reports.

Just as spacing, notation and typography should be consistent, all sentences in a series should consistently follow the same grammatical pattern (e.g. *Fifty customers were interviewed, The premises were inspected, Recent developments were noted*); parts of sentences which share the same introduction (as in the Recommendations above) should follow the same grammatical pattern; and headings of similar importance should be grammatically parallel (e.g. *Extent* of the fall in profits, *Causes* of the fall in profits — two *nouns; Internal, External* — two *adjectives*).

Observance of the principle of grammatical parallelism makes for clarity and gives a good impression of the author of the report to the reader.

Content

Only six causes are listed, but to introduce them, deal with each reasonably adequately and to add conclusions and recommendations has taken more than 500 words — more than the number required in most examinations.

All facts and figures and all names and dates which might reasonably be required by the person asking for the report have been included.

As retailing students might realize, the person who made this report had no special knowledge of retailing practice or terminology. In most English and Communication examination papers, expert knowledge of the subject being reported on is not often required, for the Report question is regarded mainly as a test of the candidate's ability to organize material efficiently and to express his meaning clearly in good English.

However, candidates are often expected to invent a certain amount of material, even when material which is to form the basis of the report is provided in the instructions which accompany the question.

Probably all the material in the above report could have been invented by a student who keeps his eyes and ears open and his imagination lively.

Imaginativeness, however, must be tempered with verisimilitude: it would not, for example, have been realistic to state that the Cisco shop was haunted, or that the entire staff had been "taken over" by invaders from Outer Space!

Other types of plan for reports

The plan which has been described on pages 227—9 and used in the report on the shop's losses is very often used, particularly for reports on serious and important matters, but it will not always be suitable.

The person making the report could decide to combine the terms of reference and the procedure in an unheaded introductory paragraph; he could decide to omit the Procedure, if no special steps had to be taken to gather the information; he could present the Findings in one undivided section; he could decide that the conclusions were too obvious to be mentioned; he might not have been asked to make recommendations.

He might decide that certain sections, or perhaps all the sections, in a particular report might be better dealt with in continuous prose than in numbered points.

In other words, one may use *any* plan as long as it is clear and logical. The best plan for any report is the plan best suited to the matter being reported on. For example, a report on an unfortunate occurrence like the loss of a file and the delay in retracing it might well consist of an introductory paragraph followed by an itemized narrative in order of time and a list of recommended precautions which could be taken to prevent a recurrence. A report on a club's social programme could take the form of an introductory paragraph followed by a list of functions against the dates on which they are to take place, the name of each function being followed perhaps by a short explanatory paragraph.

Another example of a report

The following example of a report was produced by an examination candidate. It will be noted that the student decided, quite justifiably, to write in the First Person (*I*) and to use a friendly but correct style. The essentials of good report-writing are all present. It is to be noted that in the subheadings the principle of grammatical parallelism has been observed.

The report contains over 500 words, and yet he has not mentioned some points (e.g. ventilation, emergency exits, acoustics) which could have been dealt with. Clearly most students should be able to think up sufficient material for reports in examinations.

The report is perhaps slightly open to criticism — there is, for example, a mistake in the English in the section on parking — but it would certainly get a good mark in most examinations.

<u>Report on St. Peter's Church Hall, Trentwood:</u>
<u>Suitability for Student Union Dance</u>

As Social Secretary of the Student Union, I was asked by the president at the General Committee Meeting of January 4th 1976 to assess the suitability of St. Peter's Church Hall, Trentwood, as a venue for the Spring Disco to be held on April 10th. Accordingly, I visited and thoroughly inspected the Hall, on January 10th, and learnt of the conditions of hire from the Church authorities. My findings are as follows:

<u>Location</u>

The full address of the Hall is:

St. Peter's Hall,
Valley Road,
Trentwood,
Middlesex.

The Hall is situated just over half a mile from Trentwood Town Centre and could be easily reached by most members of the Union. It is well served by bus routes until 11 p.m.

<u>Size</u>

The area which could be used for dancing measures 30 feet by 50 feet. This is perhaps rather small, for over 300 people are expected to attend. However, I suggest that a crowded hall is better than an underpopulated one.

<u>Suitability for a Dance</u>

The floor of the hall is rather worn, and not ideal for dancing. However, it is not dangerous.
The stage, just large enough to accommodate disco equipment, is fitted with three sets of 13 amp. electric points.
From the front door, the hall proper is approached via an entrance hall which is ideal as a place for checking tickets. Cloakrooms are situated on either side of this entrance hall.

Refreshment Facilities

To one side of the main hall there is a kitchen which may be used for the provision of tea, coffee and soft drinks. These may be served direct to people in the hall who queue up by a serving hatch.

St. Peter's Hall is not licensed, but the "Red Lion" is five minutes' walk along Valley Road.

Cloakrooms and Toilets

If 300 people did in fact attend the cloakrooms might prove inadequate, since there is provision for only 200 coats.

Toilet facilities are just adequate without being luxurious.

Parking

There is a car park, which will hold no more than twenty cars. About five cars could be parked in the road outside the Hall but if parked anywhere else in the road they would cause inconvenience to residents. It might be thought that in view of the accessibility of the Hall by public transport and the nearness of the "Red Lion" that the shortage of parking space should not greatly worry us.

Conditions of Hire

The cost of hiring St. Peter's Hall for one evening, from 7.30 until midnight is £50, this to be paid three weeks in advance. Hirers are required to sign an undertaking to make good any damage they cause to the premises or to equipment stored there.

Conclusion

Despite its one fairly important disadvantage, the uneven surface of the floor, St. Peter's Hall seems more suitable than the other two suggested venues – the College hall, which would be free of charge but which is too far from the homes of most students; and the Town Hall, which is too large and too expensive (£300) to hire.

January 21st 1976   Barbara Jones
                                     Social Secretary

Report-making summarized

The process of making a report can be conveniently summarized in the following instructions:

1. Make absolutely clear to yourself what has to be reported on and note whether conclusions or recommendations are asked for.
2. Decide on suitable ways of obtaining the required information.
3. Having obtained (or, in an examination, invented) the information, classify it under appropriate headings so that it may be presented in a logical way in the report. Think up your conclusions and recommendations if necessary.
4. Decide on a suitable plan for your report, remembering that all reports must be headed, must state what instructions were given to the reporter, and must be signed and dated.
5. Write the report, making sure that nothing essential is omitted, using suitable and grammatically correct language, ensuring that spacing and notation are consistent, and observing the principle of grammatical parallelism.

Exercises

1. The following report is unsatisfactory in several ways. Rewrite it, making any corrections and adjustments you consider necessary.

Fall in Sales of Viscol

Terms of Reference I was asked to report on the fall in sales of Viscol between 1/1/76 and 30/9/76 in Kent, which is covered by the territories of W. Simpson and G. Foster, as requested by the regional Sales manager in his letter of October 10th.

Procedure

(i) talked to both reps.

(2) I visited twenty garages in Kent. (October 12th)

Findings:

Sales have fallen by approx. 30% (On average over the whole area)

Causes (as far as one can tell)

A. Simpson has some family trouble and finds he can't concentrate on selling.

b Foster, as you know, new to area—has adopted rather aggressive approach and put people's backs up.

C.Two large petrol companies, Mogul and Olio, have embarked on a campaign to drive us off the face of the earth in this area. They're offering low-interest loans to garage proprietors to improve facilities on condition that they "push" their products. So in many garages Viscol signs removed from forecourt. Another effect—customers only get Viscol if they ask for it special.

RECCOMMENDATIONS

A.See if we can help Simpson in any way.

(2) R.S.M. to have a word with Foster to put him right.

c. We ought to point out to garage owners the advantages of continuing to stock more than one make of lubricant.

D. Some battered Viscol signs to be replaced by new ones.

E Garage proprietors' cut could be upped.

R. Cranston   October 15th 1980
(Representative-East Sussex)

2. As Safety Officer of J. Nosnibor & Sons, Steel Stockholders of London S.W.35, you have to submit to the Personnel Manager a report on an accident in which an employee, Mr John Edward Smith, aged 27, was injured.

You may present your report as a routine form appropriately completed or in any other format you consider suitable.

The only eye-witness of the accident was another employee, Mr Alan Walters. Base your report, which must contain all *essential* details, on Mr Walters' account, which is reproduced below:

"Well, I suppose it was about eleven, or just before. No, wait a minute — it was eleven on the dot 'cos I heard the clock striking just when it 'appened. We was carrying one of them four-metre lengths of galvanized sheet steel — and they weigh a ton, well, it feels like it anyway — from the Works entrance — the Camborne Road entrance — to the van. Me looking forward, Smithy facing me so he was walking backward. All of a sudden Smithy suddenly gives a hell of a shout and keels over. It was part of the Dartford order. I couldn't keep 'old of the steel and it crashes down on his knee — not the knee down the manhole, but the other one, his left knee. Some comedian had left this manhole cover off. The manhole's in the road a yard or so from where the van was parked. He's yelling like hell and no wonder 'cos he's got a fractured knee cap, hasn't he? Lucky it wasn't a damned sight worse. We got him up, me and the driver, Steve Manton, gave him a fag and rang for an ambulance. They took him to the War Memorial and, like I said, they said the knee cap was broken. Rotten thing to happen, especially as he's off to Torremolinos Saturday — well, he would've been. Pity we can't find out what clown left the thing uncovered — the cover was a foot or so from the hole. Anyway, it's been reported to the Union. I reported it after I'd got back from the hospital. They say he'll be off work for about three weeks."

3. The Principal of the Barset College of Arts and Technology has received a complaint from the Manager of the College Bookshop that many of the books ordered by staff for purchase by students remain unsold. As the lecturer responsible for submitting to the Manager a consolidated list of orders, you have been asked by the Principal to report on the reasons for this.

You have jotted down the following points:

"Sometimes students can get cheaper editions from outside shops. Exact size of classes never really known until 3 months after the orders have to be placed. Orders placed in June. Size of classes not known till September. Some deliberate over-ordering to be on the safe side — staff don't want students to be without books. Some students get second-hand books from past students. College bookshop has hardback editions only — of some books. Paperbacks (cheaper) available elsewhere. Some students decide to drop a subject or change courses in the first week or two in September, before they've bought any books. Occasionally the bookshop doesn't get the latest edition. Sometimes books arrive too late for the start of courses — this unavoidable. Occasionally orders have been duplicated because individual members of staff renew their orders separately — not as an addition to the list sent in by me."

Make a report for submission to the Principal. You may include examples to illustrate any of the above points and may make recommendations which seem appropriate.

4. The Business Studies Department of the college you attend is housed in premises built at the end of the last century. Work on a Business Studies wing at the main college, which is two miles away, is due to begin at the end of this year but may be postponed for financial reasons.

Several members of staff have a sentimental regard for the old building, and claim that facilities for staff at the main college are already inadequate; and both the staff and students who use the old building like being near the town shopping centre.

They admit, however, that there are defects: the buildings are rather gloomy, the refectory accommodation and refectory facilities limited, the classroom acoustics bad, the neighbouring engineering works noisy. There would be certain advantages for staff, students and college as a whole in having all departments together.

As Chairman of a committee of staff and students, write a report in which you advance reasons for urging the County Council not to postpone the building of the new wing. You may introduce points other than those listed above.

5. To save money, the number of newspapers and magazines taken by your college library is to be reduced. Submit a report to the Chief Librarian urging the retention of some publications and suggesting those which could be dispensed with. Base your report on the views of library users and state the reasons for your recommendations.

6. You are Secretary to your local Youth Club. Write your report for presentation at the Annual General Meeting on this year's events, which included a tennis tournament, a summer

camp and a drama presentation, as well as the usual social activities.
(London Chamber of Commerce Private Secretary's Certificate, alternative to memorandum.)

7. Your employers, a large international chemical company, provide social facilities for the employees. It has now been suggested that there should be a separate youth club for all young people under 21 and the company will provide premises for their use. The company has invited views from a committee of young employees, of which you have been elected secretary. Prepare, in report form, the ideas, conclusions, and recommendations your committee wishes to submit to the company for the setting up of the youth club.
(London Chamber of Commerce Private Secretary's Certificate, alternative to memorandum.)

8. Three teenagers have been found guilty of stealing a car, deliberately driving it into a canal, and causing damage to the car estimated at £300, and of stealing a radio and clothing from the car valued at £60. The magistrates have asked for a report on the culprits recommending the action you consider most suited for each one. You have information on the three which is given below. The possible punishments are in order of leniency, (a) a conditional discharge (i.e. punishment will be given only if in trouble again. It will be added to that given to the next offence); (b) Fine up to £150; (c) Probation up to two years; (d) Detention Centre for up to three years.

As a social worker write a report to the Magistrates stating the action you recommend for each person and making very clear your reasons.

Brian Manning Age 17. Middle of three children. Mother a permanent invalid, frequently in hospital. Father illiterate, out of work. Elder brother in prison for robbery with violence. Has two previous convictions for stealing cars and is on probation. Has had several jobs since leaving school; at the moment is in the dispatch department of a cigarette factory.

Janet Thomson Age 15. Schoolgirl. Only child of an overseas sales director who is frequently away from home. Is intelligent but unruly and totally opposed to school and school discipline. Intends to leave before taking any examinations. Hopes to work in a beauty salon. Is sexually promiscuous. Parents express concern but have made no positive effort to control her. No previous police record.

David Wilcox Age 16. Schoolboy. Has a 13-year-old sister. Father killed in a car accident three years ago. Mother works as a part-time canteen supervisor and occasionally in the evenings at receptions as a waitress-barmaid. Is intelligent and expected to do very well at "O" level. Wishes to take "A" levels and go to University, probably to study medicine. Has an excellent school record but although having no previous police record is known to them as being closely associated with "undesirables".

(R.S.A. II.)

9. As Captain or Manager of a club team, write a report on the past season for publication in the club magazine or for distribution at the A.G.M. Your report should include a general introduction describing the past season, a tabulated summary of the team's record, commendation of outstanding players, thanks for the voluntary work done by some non-playing members and a recommendation that subscriptions for playing and non-playing members should be increased by 25%.

10. Your Social Club, of which you are Honorary Secretary, wishes to raise funds for improvements and redecoration. You have received some helpful suggestions such as raffles, dances, and a fashion show. Present these proposals with your recommendations, and a possible programme of events, in the form of a report for the next meeting of your committee.

Or

The typewriters in your office which have been in use for some years are to be replaced. Submit a report to your manager in which you urge that the replacements should be electric rather than ordinary typewriters. Establish your case by putting all the points you can in their favour.

(L.C.C. Private Secretary's Certificate.)

11. You work for a long-established department store with a tradition of "high-quality goods for discerning customers" — as its advertisements in the press constantly emphasize.

Owing to recent town re-development the store can no longer

be regarded as being in the main shopping area; but this regrettable fact does not fully explain the disturbing and accelerating decline in trade during recent months. Other factors have been suggested — for example, a failure to attract younger shoppers. Produce a report in which you recommend measures by which the downward trend in trade may be reversed.

12. Your firm has sent you to an exhibition to report on any items of interest. Write your report.

13. Support for social functions organized by the Student Union has been declining recently. Several members of the Student Union Committee maintain that functions have not been adequately advertised, but others state that many students are not happy with the programme of social events.

You are requested by the Committee to report on the views of students, and discover that many are complaining of a lack of organization at the two dances which have been held, while others think that there should be more varied activities and suggest in particular debates, visits to theatres and coach outings. Make your report.

14. You have been asked to assess the suitability of the Warwick Hotel, Thamesford, for your company's Sales Conference, which is to run from the evening of Friday, September 3rd until midday on Sunday 5th.

Your investigations reveal that in most respects this hotel is suitable. There is a large room suitable for conferences and equipped for the use of audio/visual aids, and a smaller room which may be used as a Company office. There is sufficient comfortable accommodation for those attending and standards of catering and service seem high. The hotel is licensed and situated in pleasant countryside.

Prices are rather high, but you consider that the hotel's advantages make it preferable to the two other suggested venues. Make your report, which should briefly indicate why the Warwick is preferable.

15. You are Secretary to a group dental practice. A patient's file has been mislaid and this has resulted in inconvenience and delay. Write a report on what has been done to trace the missing file and recommend improvements to filing procedures.

16. On the instructions of the committee of the club to which you belong, report on an item of equipment which the club is considering purchasing. You should take into account the quality and cost of the equipment and its usefulness, and you may make comparisons with the products of other firms or with completely different items which may also be under consideration.

17. You are the secretary of the Residents' Association on a new and developing housing estate. Investigate the existing educational and social facilities, which are said to be inadequate, and prepare a report embodying your findings and recommendations for submission to the local council.

18. Write a report on a course or conference you have recently attended. The following details should be included: when and where it was held; what the object was; whether it was successful; whether it was well organized; any point worth special mention; any conclusion to be emphasized.

19. You have been asked to prepare a report on magazines suitable for the waiting-room of the medical centre where you are employed. Write the report, bearing in mind the types of patient who attend and the need to keep expenditure within reasonable limits. Justify your choice of magazines.
(Association of Medical Secretaries — Diploma Examination.)

Memoranda

The word "memoranda" is the plural of "memorandum", which is the Latin for "something to be remembered". Unfortunately and ironically, the contents of all memoranda are more easily remembered by the senders than by the receivers!

"Memoranda" is a term used in fact to denote two very different types of communication.

Unsolicited memoranda

These may be described as documents in which suggestions are made, sometimes to those who are equal in status to the sender but more often to a superior. Such memoranda will often be prompted by ambition — by a desire to "catch the boss's eye", or by a zeal for efficiency or perhaps by a sense of grievance. They may contain tactfully and clearly expressed suggestions for improving or expanding in some way some activity of a firm or other organization, for example, office procedures, marketing, advertising.

Such memoranda may be regarded as unsolicited (i.e. not asked for) reports. At the start of a memorandum the names of the sender and of the recipient should appear against the words FROM and TO. Against the word SUBJECT there should be a clear and explicit heading. This should be followed by a very well-thought-out introductory paragraph in which the sender explains his reasons for submitting the memorandum.

The body of the memorandum should consist of clearly and appropriately headed sections containing grammatically correct continuous prose or numbered points. The principles of good report-writing apply, and tact, good organization, clarity and conciseness are essentials. If any one of these qualities is missing your memorandum, instead of being remembered, may be consigned to oblivion — in the waste-paper basket or in some dusty file.

Internal correspondence

More commonly, "memoranda" denotes the internal correspondence of a company or some other organization. Most of this correspondence will be intra-departmental (between people in the same department) or inter-departmental.

These internal letters may convey or request information, may introduce or announce, remind or confirm, give instructions or offer advice or, in the nicest possible way, reprimand.

Broadly speaking, these communications range from very brief messages, often written by people equal or nearly equal in status to the recipient, to important documents of several hundred words such as those sent out by the head of a department to his subordinates. The briefer the message, the more likely it is that it will be called a "memo"; the more important and longer it is, the more likely it is that it will be dignified by the full name of "memorandum" and that a file copy will be kept.

Whether or not office memoranda are written on printed forms, the following items should appear at the top: the name of the sender and of the recipient or recipients against the headings FROM and TO, the date on which the memorandum is sent, and the subject of the memorandum. It is not usual for a memorandum to be signed.

Usually one subject only should be dealt with in one memorandum, though there may be several aspects of one subject to be dealt with. In such cases, the use of subheadings and/or numbered points may be advisable. In this respect an internal memorandum differs from most external letters. However, the same standards of courtesy, clarity, conciseness and correctness should be maintained. The only place for a rough note is a rough scrap of paper.

Exercises

A.

1. The company for which you work advertises in your local newspaper. You consider that the design and wording of the advertisements do not have sufficient appeal. Submit to your employers a memorandum in which you set out your criticisms and in which you suggest improvements.

2. The walls separating the classrooms in your college building are not soundproof. Submit to the Principal a memorandum in which you point out the inconvenience of this and enquire whether some form of soundproofing could be installed.

3. As an active member of your firm's social club you have been invited to serve on a panel to consider how its facilities, which already include a bar, dance floor, and games room, might be improved to prove more attractive to the considerable number of young people — some 300 — between the ages of 16 and 21 your firm employs.

   Each member of the panel has been asked to prepare a report or memorandum which should be submitted to its Chairman, the Company Secretary, in two weeks' time, giving ideas and suggestions on matters which should be given priority for discussion at the panel's first meeting.

Put forward your opinions, using your imagination to invent any details you think necessary.
(The London Chamber of Commerce Private Secretary's Certificate Examination, 1969.)

4. You are critical of the way in which ingoing and outgoing mail is handled by your firm. Submit a memorandum in which you suggest ways in which mail could be handled more efficiently and speedily.

B.

1. Your firm has decided to remove its commercial offices to a country market town. Premises are available but before a final decision is made the Personnel Director, your employer, with one or two other executives, is visiting the area to investigate availability of labour, housing, transport facilities, etc. His visit will cover three days.

   As his secretary prepare a memorandum detailing the arrangements with which you have been concerned for hotel bookings, appointments with Town Clerk, Youth Employment Officers, transport officials, etc. (Add as much detail as you can to your memorandum to make it as informative as possible to your employer for his visit.)
   (London Chamber of Commerce Private Secretary's Certificate.)

2. You are responsible for organizing a weekend conference on career possibilities in your company. Draft a memorandum to departmental managers asking for the names of employees who have applied to attend. You require details of applicants' educational qualifications and of their business experience before joining the company, as well as a brief description of their present duties. This information is required within one week of the date of the memo.

3. As secretary to the hospital administrator, who is concerned with the national need to conserve energy:
   (a) Draft a memorandum for circulation to departmental heads urging economy in the use of electricity.
   (b) Draft also a suitable notice for general display throughout the hospital.
   (Association of Medical Secretaries — Diploma Examination.)

4. Imagine that you are the head of a department. Write a memorandum to all staff, informing them of the time and place of the departmental Christmas luncheon. Tell them what will be on the menu and state the cost. Ask staff to let your secretary know whether they will be attending. This must be done by December 15th.

5. You are the manager (or manageress) of a large department store. Recently some shop assistants have been arriving late, advancing the spurious excuse that bus services in the early morning have become unreliable. Moreover, some employees have taken to wearing clothes which you do not consider suitable. Write an admonitory memorandum for distribution to all junior staff. Copies are to be sent to supervisors.

6. As the Chairman of an interviewing board, write a memorandum to the other members of the board confirming the time and place of the next meeting and detailing the names of the three interviewees.

Chapter 12

Comprehension exercises

All English exercises are in a sense comprehension exercises. It is, for example, not very likely that anyone could make a good summary of a passage without comprehending (i.e. fully understanding) it. Even essay questions may be regarded as comprehension tests — tests which are failed by those students who misinterpret essay titles!

The traditional Comprehension Question which appears in many English Language examinations consists of a passage followed by questions based on it. If the Comprehension Question has been well-chosen by the examiners (and occasionally such questions, it seems, are not!) it is a test not only of a candidate's understanding of one particular passage and of his ability to demonstrate that understanding, but also a good test of the candidate's general command of English.

Consequently it is wrong to say that the examination comprehension question cannot be prepared for: one prepares for it every time one reads or writes. And one can and should prepare for it by doing comprehension exercises and comprehension questions from past examinations. Such practice obviously must improve one's command of English to some extent; but also it provides training in the techniques of answering comprehension questions, i.e. in the methods which should be employed. Without such training a highly literate person could fail an examination even though he might have the ability to pass it with distinction.

Yet comprehension practice is valuable for another reason: it accustoms us to the close and careful study of pieces of writing — something most of us have to do very often in our everyday lives.

Finally it should be said that, although many students regard comprehension exercises as something given to them to keep them quiet, something with no relevance to anything outside school or college, something to be got through as quickly as possible by means of guesswork and a pocket dictionary, it is possible to enjoy the challenge of comprehension questions: to derive satisfaction from getting a passage to yield up its meaning, and from correctly, clearly and completely answering the questions based on it — even though the subject matter might seem uninteresting or uncongenial. The interest can come from the challenge of the task.

How to answer comprehension questions in examinations

It is essential to adopt the right attitude: be careful and cautious but also optimistic. Do not be demoralized by the sight of unfamiliar words. It may not be necessary to understand the meaning of these words; it may, on the other hand, be possible to work out their meaning.

Having resolved to be optimistic:

1. Read the passage very carefully indeed at least twice so that you understand as well as possible what the author is saying, and try to keep the main theme or themes in mind.

2. Read the questions very carefully and, equally carefully, read the instructions for answering them and make sure that you understand both the questions and the instructions.

3. Write your answers correctly and in full, taking care to look back frequently to the part or parts of the passage on which they are based, and remembering that some questions may require a careful re-reading of a large part of the passage or even of the entire passage.

Two rules must be obeyed: (i) answers must be based only on material which is found in the passage — except on those very rare occasions when the instructions state otherwise; and (ii) answers must be complete in every way. If an examinee thinks that part of the answer is obvious he must nevertheless include it in what he writes. Everything must be explained to the examiner.

The following advice should also be borne in mind:

1. Answers must be grammatically correct and suitably punctuated. Particular care should be taken to use quotation marks when parts of the passage for study are being quoted.

2. Answers should be correctly spelt. Many students misspell words which appear in the passage on which the questions are based!

3. Unless the instructions explicitly state otherwise, all answers should be expressed in complete sentences, not in parts of sentences. For example:

   (a) *Why did John think that Mrs Brown was ill?*
   John thought that Mrs Brown was ill because he saw the doctor's car outside her house.
   NOT *Because he saw the doctor's car outside her house.*

   (b) *What were the contrasting qualities combined in Shakespeare to a remarkable extent?*
   The contrasting qualities combined in Shakespeare to a remarkable extent were poetic imaginativeness and commercial shrewdness.
   NOT *Poetic imaginativeness and commercial shrewdness.*

4. Answers should follow the pattern suggested by the form of the questions. Consequently, the following answer to the second of the questions in (3) would not be ideal:

   Shakespeare had a poet's imaginativeness and was very shrewd in commercial matters — these were the qualities which were combined in him to a remarkable extent.

Great care should in fact be taken to ensure not only that one's answer is factually correct and that there is no chance that it will be misunderstood but also that it is expressed in the most suitable way.

We may note here that when answering multiple-choice questions one should take care to select the best answer rather than an answer which from a careless reading looks approximately correct.

Types of question

Most comprehension questions are devised to test a candidate's understanding of what the author of the passage has to say; most others may be loosely but conveniently described as questions on the manner in which he has said it.

Questions on what the author has to say may in effect ask the candidate to reproduce in different words the statements of the writer. Hence, examinees may be faced with questions like:

Describe in your own words . . .
State the writer's views on . . .
What, according to the writer, are the chief reasons . . .
How does the author explain . . .
Summarize the author's views on . . .

Such questions may seem straightforward but they require very great care, as do those questions found in very elementary tests which ask for simple facts. For example:

In what country were the goods being made?
How many men were employed in the task?

Other questions may ask *Why*? For example:

Why does the author say . . .
Why does the writer conclude . . .

Here it is important to make sure that one supplies all the reasons which may be found in the passage and none which are not!

Some questions may demand not only great care and thoroughness but also some hard thinking. For example:

What may be deduced from the statement . . .
What does this tell us about the author's attitude towards . . .
What does the author imply in his remark . . .
Indicate the contrast in thought between the first and last sentences of the passage.

Questions asking for the meaning of words and phrases

In some examinations candidates are asked to supply words or phrases which could be used to replace words or phrases in the passage without altering the meaning. Examinees should take great care to think up expressions which could fit *exactly* into the passage. Consider the following sentence:

He was *popularly supposed* to be an expert in all branches of mathematics but in fact *was ignorant of* the principles of geometry.

Suitable replacements for the italicised expressions would be:

"believed by many people" or "thought by most people"
"had no knowledge of", "knew nothing of" or "did not know"

The following answers, however, would not fit:

"Many people believed", "It was thought by many"
"had no knowledge", "unfamiliar with"

Unfortunately, many students are content to supply an answer which does not fit exactly into the sentence.

Sometimes examinees are not expressly asked to suggest replacements but to supply synonyms (words of the same or very similar meaning) for, or write expressions of the same meaning as, words which are used by the author of the passage.

Even with this type of question it is a good practice, whenever possible, to supply expressions which could act as replacements. Then, one is more likely to keep firmly in mind the sense in which the specified words are used in the passage; and more likely to write answers in the appropriate grammatical form.

The synonyms or equivalent expressions must "match" the words as closely as possible: e.g. verbs in the past tense must be matched by verbs in the past tense, nouns by nouns or by phrases in which the chief word is a noun, plurals by plurals, adjectives by adjectives or adjectival phrases, adverbs by adverbs — and so on. The words in the right-hand column below might well be accepted by some students as good synonyms of those on the left, but although the central meanings have been conveyed the grammatical forms are wrong:

assess	—	to estimate
intentionally	—	deliberate
convictions	—	firmly held belief
dreaded	—	fear greatly
shrewdness	—	clever
scornful	—	contempt
monopoly	—	exclusively controlled
essentials	—	you cannot do without them

This is not a technical point: if the grammatical form is wrong the meaning is not accurately conveyed.

Another common task of examinees is that of stating in their own words the meaning of long phrases, clauses or even whole sentences which are in the passage for study. Usually all that is required is a faithful "translation" into different words. Great care should be taken to ensure that *all* the meaning of the original is conveyed and also that no other meaning creeps in. For example:

State the meaning of the following:

"appeared to be in a state of alcoholic intoxication"

A correct answer would be "seemed to be drunk". All of the following answers would be incorrect, or at least only partly right:

He seemed to be drunk.

He was drunk.

Was drunk.

Drunk.

The author said that he seemed to be drunk.

("The author said that he" does not appear in the original statement.)

But judgement has to be exercised here. It may be that a word-for-word "translation" will not do: certain additions and adjustments may have to be made to convey an implied or un-usually expressed meaning. So, if asked to express the meaning of this sentence (from *Oliver Twist*), "He was alternately cudgelling his brains and his donkey", one might write: "He was in turn racking his brains and beating his donkey with a cudgel".

We cannot list here all the problems of "stating the mean-ing". The guiding principles are: keep the context in mind, and exercise judgement and common sense.

We may note here that one thing which is in effect tested by comprehension questions is the ability to understand and follow instructions. Carelessness in reading one part of one question may turn a borderline pass into a failure. Misreading, misunder-standing or plain disregard of the instructions seems particularly common with the "supply synonyms" type of question. When-ever, for example, examinees are asked to state the meanings of four words or expressions out of six, there are always some people who persist in stating the meaning of all six. In such cases only the first four would be marked and consequently it would be possible to get four answers correct but to score only half marks.

Other types of question

As has been suggested already, most comprehension questions test examinees' understanding of *what* the author of the set passage has said but others test examinees' appreciation of *how* he has said it or their ability to decide *how well* he has said it. The following types of question sometimes appear:

1. Questions asking for comments on the author's reasoning

These are designed to test candidates' ability to think clearly. Such questions might possibly begin:

- How far has the author justified his opening remarks . . .
- Do you find any contradiction between . . .
- Pick out a sentence which seems to disprove the author's main contention . . . and explain . . .
- Comment on the conclusion . . .
- Using only material found in the passage, state whether you think that the author . . .

It should be noted that when a question of this sort is set it is likely that there is some ground for criticizing the author's reasoning. Accordingly, examinees should be bold enough to state what they find at fault. They must relentlessly examine the author's reasoning and confidently and clearly and fully and correctly write their answer.

2. Questions on the author's choice of words

Such questions might well ask examinees to comment on the author's use of certain words. A word may perhaps be used in an unusual way — to achieve a special effect like irony or humour; or it may even have been used incorrectly — even some of the greatest writers use words incorrectly, or at least in ways which are not generally accepted. The ability of students to answer questions of this type depends greatly on their general command of English.

Examples of answers:

Q. *Hopefully*, the new project will be completed by next spring.

A. There is no grammatical justification for the use of the adverb "hopefully" here. There is no verb to which it can apply. However, "hopefully" used in this manner is now an idiom which means "it is hoped" or "I hope", "we hope", etc.

Q. When the land route to the Indies was blocked, the Europeans looked for an *alternate* route.

A. Here, the author has used a word that means "every other" instead of using the correct word, "alternative".

Q. When I offered him the rubber bone, the dog barked *sarcastically*.

A. The author is using "sarcastically" to achieve a humorous effect. He is pretending to ascribe to a dog the human capacity for sarcasm.

Again it should be noted that all quoted words should be enclosed by quotation marks.

3. Questions on grammar and sentence construction

Examinees are occasionally asked to comment on the grammar of a group of words or on the way in which a sentence or part of a sentence has been put together. This usually means that there is something wrong — for example, the use of a singular verb with a plural subject, the omission of a word, the wrong preposition after an adjective, or words placed in the wrong order. The fault should be tracked down and then described in complete sentences. For example:

Q. Shaw was not only the author of "Pygmalion" but also of "Saint Joan" as well.

A. The words "not only the author" might lead us to expect that Shaw was also perhaps the publisher. "Not only" should immediately precede the noun to which it refers — "Pygmalion". However, the writer's intended meaning is quite clear. A more serious criticism of the sentence is that "as well" is not wanted, as the word "also" has already been used.

4. Questions on punctuation

Occasionally one is asked outright to criticize the punctuation used by the author, but more often one is asked *why* the author has used certain punctuation. Sometimes, for example, one is asked why the writer has placed an expression in quotation marks, or asked to justify the placing of an apostrophe. It is usually essential to try to point out how the punctuation used has affected the meaning of what the author has sought to say. Such questions should not be regarded as punctuation exercises which have somehow strayed into the wrong part of the paper but in truth as tests of comprehension.

5. *Questions on figures of speech*

Personification and hyperbole and rarer creatures like onomatopoeia and zeugma are occasionally asked about, but questions on metaphors and similes are the most common.

Examinees may be asked to show the appropriateness of a metaphor or simile as it is used in the passage, to explain the force of a metaphor (i.e. what effect it has), to state in non-figurative (literal) language the meaning of figurative language, or perhaps point out how a metaphor or simile is sustained or developed throughout a passage. On the other hand, one might be requested to state why a metaphor or simile chosen by the author is *not* suitable.

Every care should be taken to ensure that such questions are answered thoroughly and exhaustively. In one set of comprehension questions Ordinary Level candidates were asked to describe how the author of the passage had compared the atmosphere of a forest to that of a cathedral. Probably, some candidates contented themselves with the statement that the author had compared the quiet of the interior of a forest to the quiet of a cathedral, without noticing other comparisons made later in the passage — trees and spaces like columns and aisles and over-arching branches like parts of a cathedral's ceiling.

Here are two examples of answers to questions on figurative language:

Q. State why the simile in the following sentence is suitable: Like a cue across a billiard table, the railway line stretched out across the green plain towards the horizon.

A. The simile, "like a cue across a billiard table" suggests the straightness of the railway line and compares the green plain to the green and perfectly flat surface of a billiard table. Moreover, a billiard cue is tapered and this makes us think of the railway line appearing, as an effect of perspective, to become narrower as it stretches away into the distance. For these reasons the simile is very suitable — and effective.

Q. People were programmed by this training to act in an utterly predictable way.

Explain the metaphor "programmed".

A. The verb "to program" is used in computer technology. The metaphor suggests that people can be caused to act in a certain way which has been arranged by someone else and that their capacity for independent thought or judgement has either never existed or may be destroyed. Like computers, they can be made to respond exactly and predictably.

6. Questions on the author's style

Style, rather a vague term, may be defined as the manner of writing — suitable, unsuitable, simple, complicated, fluent, awkward, clear, obscure, formal, colloquial, figurative, literal, plain, ornamental, pompous, unaffected, concise, circumlocutory, pleasant, irritating — or whatever.

Questions on style are not asked very often nowadays. They demand a high degree of literacy if they are to be answered competently, but examinees should not be afraid to speak their minds: if, for example, a writer has obscured what he has to say by using unnecessarily complicated language, this should be boldly pointed out. Examinees should ask themselves the following sorts of questions:

Is the author's style appropriate to the subject? (e.g. was he justified in using a racy colloquial style in a discussion of capital punishment?)

Has the style, though apparently unsuitable, been chosen for a special effect?

Are the words well chosen?

Is the language clear or involved?

Do the sentences flow smoothly or lurch jerkily?

Are the sentences of a suitable length? (e.g. Has the author succeeded in creating a dramatic effect by his use of a number of short staccato sentences, or has he merely fragmented his story?)

Is the language pedantic, pompous, affected, voguish, slangy, lively, etc.?

What use is made of metaphors, similes, repetition, personification?

What use does the author make of irony and humour?

Be on the look-out for other types of question

It is not practicable to list every variation of comprehension question one is likely to encounter, but we have probably noted the main ones.

Examination candidates should not be thrown into a panic when they are faced with types of question with which they are not familiar or with traditional types of question expressed in an unusual way, for it is extremely rare for an unfair question to be set. Nor should they be too annoyed by questions which ask them to draw upon their own knowledge and experience to develop or further illustrate some point made by the author of the passage. It may reasonably be objected that such questions are not, strictly speaking, comprehension questions, or rather that they test other things besides the ability to comprehend the set passage; but such questions usually require not encyclopaedic knowledge but initiative and common sense.

It is perhaps less reasonable of examiners to ask candidates to state an opinion on what the author of the passage has said — unless it is an opinion which is to be based on an acceptance of the facts as stated by the author, i.e. to decide whether the author has been logical in his argument.

Questions which ask for opinions may create the suspicion that what is being tested is not the candidate's command of English but his attitudes. After answering a number of true comprehension questions a candidate, on finding a question asking him to state his opinion (e.g. What, in your opinion, should be the role of trade unions in society?) may first wonder whether he is to refer to the passage or draw solely on his own experience, and then wonder whether he is expected to agree or disagree with the author, and finally suspect that his answer will be marked on the views expressed instead of on the English used to express them. All that can be recommended is an honest and well-argued answer clearly and grammatically stated.

Even that advice might not have been much help on one occasion, when candidates were asked to *refute* (probably used incorrectly since "refute" means "prove wrong") the author's views — unfair for an examinee who happened to agree with the author!

Ambiguity of questions

Occasionally, particularly when candidates are asked to *describe* or *explain*, the instructions may be open to more than one interpretation. On such occasions it is advisable to offer an answer which meets all the possible requirements. For example:

- In one examination, in which the comprehension passage described a market scene and the activities of the vendors, this request was made:
- Explain "They squabble eloquently with one another to collect a crowd in their mutual interest."

Perhaps all that the examiners expected was a sort of translation, for example:

> They argue fluently and skilfully with one another to attract the attention of people so that they, the vendors, will all benefit.

Probably, however, it would have been advisable to add explanatory material, for example:

> This means that the vendors, with great command of language, pretended to argue with one another in order to attract people's attention, so that, having stopped to listen and watch, the people might notice the goods which were for sale and decide to make purchases. Consequently all the vendors might benefit.

It is in fact advisable to include in one's answers everything which could *reasonably* be considered relevant to the question.

Some advice to remember

1. A comprehension question is a test of your command of English and of your ability to demonstrate that command.
2. Be optimistic, even if the subject of the passage seems uninteresting or unfamiliar and the vocabulary seems too advanced.
3. Read the passage, the instructions and the questions very carefully indeed.
4. Note that many questions are framed in such a way that

they can be answered adequately only if the candidate uses his own words. Except in quoting evidence, the wording of the author should not be used. Usually candidates are explicitly instructed to use their own words: they must use sentences which they have composed themselves and words and expressions which come naturally to them. Note, however, that this does not mean that you may not use *any* of the words which occur in the passage!

5. Answer the required number of questions, neither more nor fewer.

6. Base answers only on material to be found in the set passage — unless requested otherwise.

7. Note that the ideal number of words for any comprehension answer is the number of words which is required to answer the question! If you are sure that you have answered a question in full, do not worry if your answer consists of only a few words. A short, clear sentence or phrase may get full marks; a long, rambling, irrelevant paragraph, none.

8. Do not leave any questions unanswered. Write down something for every question.

9. Quickly but carefully read through your answers after you have written them so that you may correct avoidable errors of spelling and punctuation.

Comprehension practice

As has been suggested earlier, doing comprehension questions, whether or not they are from past examinations, is certainly a very useful activity and can be an enjoyable activity, providing that it is regarded as a challenge and not as a chore.

No doubt for exercises not done under examination conditions most students will consult dictionaries — certainly a useful activity in itself — but they are strongly advised not to rush to the dictionary at the sight of an unfamiliar word (or when asked to state the meaning of a familiar word, as so many do!) but to turn to the dictionary as a last resort, or perhaps as a means of confirming what they have worked out for themselves. After all, there will be no chance of using a dictionary in the examination room. When a dictionary *is* used, the general theme of the passage for study and the context in which the difficult word or expression is being used should be kept firmly in mind.

Exercises in comprehension

1. Read the following passage carefully and then the questions which follow it. Each question is followed by an answer. The answers are factually correct but in various ways unsatisfactorily expressed.

Having carefully re-read the passage and the questions, write out a properly expressed set of answers.

In the earliest stages of Man as a commercial animal, his trading consisted entirely of barter. The hunter exchanged his hides and pelts and meat for the corn and straw of the tiller of the soil. And both, in a slightly later stage, traded their products for the wares of the village craftsman. Now barter as a method of trade has several grave defects. One of these is the difficulty of settling on terms. The relative values of two or three of the more important articles of trade may be well known. It may for example be a convention of long standing that ten bushels of corn exchange for one cow. But how are the values of less actively traded commodities to be established? How many bushels of corn should exchange for one tiger-skin? And how many bananas for a goat? And how many pigs for a new wife? These are the commercial problems of private barter, and they are obviously not easy to solve. The first function of money is to help with the solution of these problems. Suppose that everything is valued in terms of one commodity. Let us suppose that this one commodity is the goat (as it is today among some East African tribes). Everything is valued in terms of the goat, and the terms of exchange between any pair of commodities can thus easily be established. A hunting-knife is worth ten goats, fifty bananas are worth one goat, five bushels of corn are worth two goats, a wife, if she is young and comely, is worth six goats — and so on for every commodity. To us this invention seems very simple. It is merely the application to the sphere of value of the same idea that has produced the foot or the metre to measure length, the pound or gram to measure weight, the degree to measure temperature, and so forth. But at the same time it was doubtless radical — the invention, perhaps, of some lazy genius who found himself oppressed by the task of calculating how many bushels of corn should exchange for one tiger-skin, if three bushels of corn were equal to five bananas, twenty bananas to one goat and twenty goats to one tiger-skin. And it undoubtedly was an invention; it needed the conscious reasoning power of Man to make the step from simple barter to money-accounting.

This is the first of the three primary functions of money. It serves as a unit of account. It acts as a yardstick, or standard measure, of value to which all other things can be compared. Trading is still a simple exchange of goods for goods: bananas are still exchanged for corn, ox-hides for straw. But the terms of exchange are now fixed by reference to one standard commodity. The community is on the goat-standard. Money has arrived.

(From *An Outline of Money* by Geoffrey Crowther.)

(a) Write in one sentence a definition of barter.
It's changing things for things, for example you might want to change a bicycle for a lawn-mower, you don't use money.

(b) The author points out a great disadvantage of barter as a method of trade. Without using examples, say in your own words what this disadvantage is.
Well, it might be a bit difficult to find out the exact value of things in relation to each other. Especially if they weren't all that often traded. There was nothing to go by.

(c) State in your own words the function of money indicated here.
Something to go by, if you had an ass its value could be worked out in money-goats (in this case). The author says that money measures things, or rather there value.

(d) The Latin for "money" is "pecunia", which is derived from the word the Romans used for "cattle". Suggest a reason for this derivation.
Probably because they used cows etc for money. Or maybe if you owned a load of cattle you were considered rich. Probably the word originated like this. Just as an East African with many goats is rich.

(e) Comment on the words "if three bushels of corn were equal to five bananas".

Corn can't really be equal to bananas, like 2 + 2 is equal to four, for example, the author should have said equal in value. But we know he means that. Strictly speaking the wording should be if three bushels of corn were equal in value to five bananas.

(f) State in your own words the meaning of the following:
   a convention of long standing
   It means that it was a very long established understanding that they could exchange ten bushels of corn for one cow. A sort of customary agreement, this had been going on for ages.
   The community is on the goat-standard.
   Everything measured in goats. Goats were a sort of money.

(g) Supply words or phrases, which, without a change in meaning, could be used to replace FOUR of the following words in the passage:
   wares; relative; established; comely; radical; genius; oppressed; yardstick
   Wares means products, goods for sale
   relative means comparative
   established — settle
   comely — probably good-looking
   radical — tending to change at the root, revolutionary
   genius — extremely intelligent
   oppressed means he was burdened
   yardstick is to measure things with

2. Read the following passage carefully and then answer the questions that follow. Answer as far as possible in your own words and in complete sentences, with the exception of (h), (i) and (j).

Organizing a major expedition, whether it be to the Himalayas, the polar regions or darkest Africa, is a formidable business. I have experience only of the first of these undertakings, but I can now sympathize deeply with those who have the cares of planning and preparing missions in other realms of adventure or research. Imagine that you are charged with the task of fulfilling, in company with others, a long and exceptionally arduous task, in some remote and uninhabited corner of the earth's surface, where climatic conditions are extreme. The success of your mission depends primarily on the human factor on the joint efforts of every man in your team, and failure — moral or physical — by even one or two of these would add immensely to its difficulties. You have the responsibility of seeking and selecting these men, in whom you are looking for a happy combination of qualities which are difficult to reconcile. You will not be able, in most cases at any rate, to test these qualities, at least in conditions comparable with those which will <u>confront</u> you — it is unlikely that you will even be <u>acquainted</u> with most of them beforehand. You have to ensure that the party is suitably clothed and equipped to carry out its job in the especially <u>rigorous</u> conditions, and that it takes with it all the tools it is likely to require for the job, bearing in mind that communications will be so extended, slow and difficult that you must be entirely self-contained for the duration of your mission. Some of this equipment is <u>highly specialized</u>, and difficult questions of design and <u>quantities have to be</u> decided. Provisions have to be calculated for the whole period of your absence from civilization and they must be carefully chosen; a diet must be established suitable to the climate and the nature of the work. All these numerous items of equipment and food must be ordered, many of them only after thorough testing in conditions as nearly as possible approximating to those likely to be met. Arrangements must be made for packing, <u>cataloguing</u> and moving them, as well as the party, to the starting-point in a distant land, and from that point onwards by more <u>primitive</u> <u>transport</u> to the area of operations. Last but by no means least of these <u>manifold headaches</u>, and governing the whole enterprise, is the problem of financing it; it is your job to calculate the costs. To complete this picture, suppose that you are given a bare minimum of time to launch the expedition and that you take it on with the ever-present possibility of its being cancelled when the preparations are well under way. You also realize that it will be necessary for you to make provision for a second expedition to carry on in the event of failure. In such a <u>predicament</u> you would, I fancy, be inclined to think that you were faced with as tough an assignment as any you had ever undertaken or were ever likely to in the future.

(a) On what does the success of a major expedition mainly depend?

(b) What kind of expedition has the writer organized?

(c) Why does the writer sympathize with people who are responsible for "planning and preparing missions in other realms of adventure or research"?

(d) Why does an expedition to a distant and uninhabited place have to be "entirely self-contained"?

(e) For what reason does the organizer of an expedition have to make preparations for a second expedition?

(f) Suggest two qualities which you think would be desirable in members of an expedition.

(g) Why should equipment and food be tested in conditions very similar to those that will probably be met on the expedition?

(h) Explain the meaning of the following phrases as they are used in the passage:

exceptionally arduous   highly specialized
primitive transport   manifold headaches.

(i) Quote the words from the passage which indicate that finding the money to pay for an expedition is of the greatest importance.

(j) For *each* of the following words, taken from the passage, give a single word with a meaning similar to that of the word as it is used in the passage:

confront   rigorous   cataloguing   predicament.

(Royal Society of Arts, English Language I.)

3. Read the following passage carefully and then answer the questions that follow. Answer as far as possible in your own words.

I was now being asked to photograph weddings and children. I set up a studio at home. This was good training for later years, especially the child photography. I believe that anyone who wants to be really successful at bird photography should start with child portraiture. It is ten times more difficult to get a really good photograph of a child than of a bird; one is self-conscious, the other not.

The greatest problem in child photography is to overcome shyness. I allowed an hour for each child, telling the mother (fathers seldom came) I would leave them alone in the studio at first. Various toys were scattered about and by the time I came in most children were happily playing. The mother stayed in the room all the time. With particularly shy children I ignored them completely and talked to the mother. Few children like this and soon even the shyest child tried to attract attention.

Next I asked the child to sit on a pouffe in the right position for the portrait. As the dark unwinking camera lens can be upsetting to a child (some Eastern peoples regard it as the evil eye) I had bookcases built all round the camera to hide it as much as possible. When all was ready I brought out the special toy which would usually bring the desired expression to a child's face. This is when a smile is developing; taken too soon the photograph is dull, too late and the result is an unphotogenic grin. The toy was a monkey climbing a ladder which, when it reached the top, always balanced <u>precariously</u> before falling down — the high spot of the performance. The toy was manually operated and I controlled it with my left hand, the shutter release with my right.

After the monkey had performed several times the child knew what to expect, and there was a moment — no more than a second or so — when the smile of anticipatory delight was forming, a sparkle coming into the eyes, which was the exact instant to press the shutter.

The photographing of weddings proved to be as <u>hazardous</u> in one respect as photographing birds — both are subject to the vagaries of the weather. Just as sometimes happened when I had waited for weeks for a clutch of eggs to hatch — the climax ruined by rain — so it became near-calamity when, instead of being blessed by sunshine, bride and groom were met by torrents of rain. Sometimes the situation could be saved by using flash, but the general dreariness and greyness took the excitement and glitter from the occasion. Wedding photographs, of course, cannot be repeated, so it is vital to be successful first time. Yet it is necessary to work quickly, especially in winter.

(Reproduced from *An Eye for a Bird* by kind permission of Eric Hosking and Frank Lane and the Hutchinson Publishing Group Ltd.)

(a) How does the author think that a person who wishes to be very successful at bird photography should start? (2 marks)

(b) Where was the writer's studio? (2 marks)

(c) Why is it more difficult to get a good photograph of a child than of a bird? (2 marks)

(d) Why did the author leave a mother and her child alone in his studio before photographing the child? (2 marks)

(e) Why was the camera hidden as much as possible when a child was being photographed? (2 marks)

(f) When is the best time to photograph a child? (2 marks)

(g) How was the toy monkey operated? (2 marks)

(h) What can sometimes almost ruin photographs of weddings and photographs of birds? (2 marks)

(i) Why did the author undertake to photograph children and weddings? (2 marks)

(j) What do you think is the author's present job? (2 marks)

(k) In the book from which this passage is taken, Eric Hosking is telling the story of his own life. What do we call this kind of book? (2 marks)

(l) What is the meaning of "various"? (2 marks)

(m) What is the meaning of "precariously"? (2 marks)

(n) What is the meaning of "hazardous"? (2 marks)

(o) What is the meaning of "vital"? (2 marks)

(30 marks)

(Royal Society of Arts, English Language I.)

4. Read the following passage carefully and then answer the questions that follow. *Answer as far as possible in your own words.*

When I was a schoolboy of eleven or twelve, an incident happened which has remained in my mind ever since.

There was in one of the main streets of the town where I went to school a very large and prosperous pawnbroker's shop. It was got up like a silversmith's in front, and only a side entrance showed that it was a pawnbroker's. One of the advertisements in this side window said that the pawnbroker was anxious to buy foreign stamps. I collected foreign stamps, and it struck me that this would be a good way to make money with some of my swaps. So, one afternoon, when school was over, I plucked up my courage and went in to the pawnbroker with a selection which I offered him.

He gave my stamps one <u>scornful</u> glance, and said, "I am afraid those would be of <u>no use</u> to us. But perhaps you would like to see some of our Approval Sheets."

And in a few seconds I, who had come to sell, found myself invited to buy, and stood gazing dumbfounded at the sheets of stamps which he laid on the glass counter before me.

"Perhaps you would like to look over those and make up your mind," the pawnbroker suggested: and he went off to attend to the one other customer in the shop.

This was an elderly lady, who was standing nervously down at the far end. The pawnbroker went to her, and asked what he could do for her. She began to speak in a low, agitated voice that at once caught my attention: and while I stood pretending to stare at the sheets of stamps I both listened to and saw what followed.

The lady was neatly dressed, but I could see at once that she was not well off. She opened her bag, took from it something wrapped up in tissue paper, and unwrapped it. It was a long gold chain with a locket on the end, and I heard her ask the pawnbroker, little above a whisper, what he could give her for it.

I could guess at once that she had never done anything of the kind before, and what resolution it had taken to bring her to the pitch of trying to sell her treasure.

The pawnbroker picked up the chain and ran it through his fingers.

"Gold — ah, yes," he said peering at it through a glass. "May I test it, madam?"

The lady looked startled, then recovered herself and said, "Of course."

The pawnbroker took a little bottle and poured something on to one of the links of the chain, and rubbed it with a file. Then he looked up.

"I am sorry, madam," he said, "but this chain is not gold."

The lady stepped back as if he had hit her, and uttered a sharp cry.

"Not gold! Are you . . . are you sure?"

"Positive, madam."

She stood for a moment, then snatched up the locket, crammed it into her bag, and ran out of the shop.

(From *English for Pleasure* by A. E. G. Strong.)

(a) Where did the incident described by the author take place? (3 marks)

(b) What attracted the author to the pawnbroker's shop? (2 marks)

(c) Why did the author visit the shop? (2 marks)

(d) How many people were in the shop? (2 marks)

(e) Why was the author "dumbfounded"? (2 marks)

(f) Do you think that the shop did much business? Why? (2 marks)

(g) What did the lady want in the shop? (2 marks)

(h) Was the lady in the shop rich? How do you know? (2 marks)

(i) What drew the author's attention to the lady? (2 marks)

(j) What was the author doing while the shopkeeper attended to the lady? (2 marks)

(k) Why did the lady run out of the shop? (2 marks)

(l) What is the meaning of "scornful" as used in the passage? (2 marks)

(m) What is the meaning of "agitated" as used in the passage? (2 marks)

(n) What is the meaning of "resolution" as used in the passage? (2 marks)

(o) What is the meaning of "startled" as used in the passage? (2 marks)

(p) What is the meaning of "crammed" as used in the passage? (2 marks)

(33 marks)

(Royal Society of Arts, English Language I.)

5. Read the following passage carefully, and then answer the questions on it in your own words.

Death of a Village

By any standard the village was beautiful. Its narrow street contained well-preserved Tudor houses and one or two from the Middle Ages. London lay nearly forty miles away, and a journey into the city took almost two hours.

5 A handful of people did commute, but the rest worked at or near their homes, and many were farmfolk.

During the 1950's, however, the village began to show disturbing symptoms. Commercial travellers took to using the street as a short cut, which meant that the street

10 became a main road. More commuters arrived, bristling the picturesque station, famed for its dahlias, with briefcases.

Meadows disappeared because the strangers demanded dormitories. Yet still the village retained some beauty, set among hills, watered by a stream. Unfortunately, they des-
15 troyed the stream in order to provide water for the new-comers. Then the stream ran dry and left only a green hollow.

Unfortunately, too, the commercial travellers so multi-plied that a by-pass had to be built because the village
20 could no longer cope with the cars. This by-pass might have been a blessing but it proved otherwise, for it had to be linked to the village by a shorter by-pass, which lay like a scar on the heart. From 8.30 a.m. to 7 p.m. the High Street was a permanent car park. Elderly pedestrians
25 dithered on the kerb, seeking a lull among the roar which drowned their conversation.

Villagers hoped for some respite during the 1960's when the place was declared part of an area of outstanding natural beauty, protected by an Act of Parliament which
30 encouraged the preservation of hale old houses. The effect of the Act was interesting: somebody promptly pulled down one such house and built a block of flats on the site — country life with a window box, but no garden. In due course another handsome old house was destroyed, this
35 time causing an outcry in the Press. For two years the site was a mass of weeds, gravel, bricks, plaster. There even-tually arose a block of flats, to clash with the hills above them. Today, estate agents advertise "Executive Homes", with all the vulgar snobbery which that phrase implies.
40 Also during the 1960's the slow steam trains were replaced by fast diesels, so the tide of Londoners became a flood. Next the motor trade drove up. Six petrol stations were the result. Soon after that, somebody demolished a seventeenth-century house — the finest of its kind in the
45 High Street — and converted the space into a bank. The village now has three banks.

A twisting, narrow lane leads from the village. I used to walk there, and was amazed if I met four vehicles an hour. Now it is so dangerous that many people refuse to walk
50 along it; some decline even to drive. In order to keep up with the times, the council inserted a stretch of wide road, where speeds of seventy are common among maniacs racing for first place at the narrow bend.

Many of the country folk have fled, some of them at a
55 time of life when it is painful and perhaps impossible to
take root in strange soil. Those remaining occupy a nether-
world, not quite in nor ever wholly out of London. In
short, the village has become a suburb. Now suburbs are
sometimes inevitable and occasionally pleasant. But to a
60 village they bring death; and anyone who pretends otherwise is equating "life" with shops, season tickets, and
estate agents. Of course, the village is only one of thousands that now lie within reach of an industrial octopus.
None of them needs to ask for whom the bell tolls. The
65 issue is not whether, but in what manner, the old order
shall change and give way to a new.

Note. In your answers to (a), (b) and (c) below you must not
quote whole phrases from the passage. The length of answers
suggested for (a), (b) and (c) is meant as a guide to candidates.
There will be no penalty for not answering within the suggested
limits.

(a) Using the evidence of the whole passage, show what
aspects in the appearance and life of the village, before
its destruction, appealed to the writer.
(Answer in about 60 of your own words.) (8 marks)

(b) Explain how the process of destruction began during the
1950's.
(Answer in about 60 of your own words.) (8 marks)

(c) During the 1960's the village became a suburb of
London. Show how this happened and what changes
have taken place as a result.
(Answer in about 100 of your own words.) (12 marks)

(d) The writer is sceptical about the effect of laws and
public protest in preserving villages such as this. How
does he illustrate his point? (4 marks)

(e) What is the comparison which the writer is making in
each of three of the following phrases, and in what ways
is it appropriate?
(i) lay like a scar on the heart (lines 22—3);
(ii) the tide of Londoners became a flood (lines 41—2);
(iii) to take root in strange soil (lines 55—6);
(iv) an industrial octopus (line 63). (9 marks)

(f) Explain carefully what is meant by:
"Executive Homes", with all the vulgar snobbery which
that phrase implies (lines 38—9) (3 marks)

(g) What warning seems to be conveyed in the last two
sentences of the passage? (3 marks)
(Compulsory question, G.C.E. Ordinary Level, Paper B,
Joint Matriculation Board.)

6. In the following passage, the underlined words and phrases
are all expressions which have recently come into use. Choose
THREE of these, write each one down, and beside it write its
meaning as it is used in the passage. Do not use more than two
complete sentences for each meaning.

In an attempt to curb the wages spiral and escalating
prices, the Chancellor has inflicted upon us yet another
credit squeeze. This may well prevent the Smiths from
struggling with hire purchase to show off their most recent
status symbol to the Joneses; but what is the point of the
Government's trying to put the brake on spending when
hoardings, newspapers and TV commercials so insistently
tell us how wonderful it is to own this, that and the other?
Surely the most logical way to boost the economy and
close the trade gap is to increase production by banning
wild-cat and all other strikes. Let the back-room boys
work on this for a while! Forget the break-through and
avoid a break-down!
(R.S.A. I.)

7. Read the following passage carefully and answer the
questions that follow:

The townsman envies the villager his certainties, and, *in
Britain, has always regarded urban life as just a temporary
necessity*. One day he will find a cottage on the green and
"real values". To accommodate the almost religious inten-
5 sity of the regard for rural life in this country, and to
placate the sense of guilt which so many people feel about
not living on a village pattern, the post-war new towns
have attempted to incorporate both city and village —
with, on the whole, disheartening results. A number of
10 such towns are spreading into East Anglia, arriving
suddenly on the loamy flats where there never was habita-
tion before, and claiming that they can offer the best of
both worlds. Trees are landscaped into the concrete. There
are precincts, ways, conurbations, complexes . . . enlight-

15 ened civic nouns. There are open spaces, air, and every
amenity. Yet the inhabitants, many of whom are the descendants of the great village exodus of the nineteenth
century, often look bewildered. They have, in three or
four generations, over-filled London and are now spilling
20 back home. Except that the estate-towns aren't home, so
more than ever *the old, settled, recognizable village rep-*
resents the ideal community. More and more are making it.
With general car-ownership, perhaps the greatest single
factor in village change since the war, a vital new class of
25 countryman has come into existence. Only a generation or
so ago a villager who had to "go away to work" was
obliged to give up the close-knit and meaningful village
background of which he was an important part for
lodgings in an Ipswich or Norwich back street. Or, con-
30 versely, *village life became so suffocating and inhibiting*
because he had no way of occasionally getting away from
it, that a young man would join the army or simply the
age-old drift away from his home village which was also his
prison. The new villagers commute to the country and
35 market towns. In Akenfield they include school-teachers,
technicians from the Ipswich factories, office workers and
an architect. These "young marrieds" go less and less for
the converted cottage and more for picture-windowed
bungalows set in *gardens so spectacularly neat that they*
40 *look as though they had been bought by the yard from a*
nurseryman — which many of them have. They travel to
work daily in Ford Anglias and on mopeds. The towns are
numerous and near. There are as many as twelve to choose
from and none much more than twenty miles off. Three,
45 Framlingham, Woodbridge and Wickham Market, are
almost within walking distance, or would have been
thought so when walking was a normal human activity.

But the villager who works in the nearby town does not
think of himself as belonging to an urban district any more
50 than his ancestor was very conscious of belonging to a
Hundred*. The first thing a newcomer does when arriving
in a village is to begin to claim it. He doesn't state or stake
his claim, he simply starts to feel his way towards the
village's identity, recognize it for what it is and shape him-
55 self to fit it. He will often envy the old indigenous stock —
there are eighteen families in Akenfield descended from

people living in the village in *c.* 1750 — but in effect his life will be far freer than theirs. The sometimes crushing, limiting power which the village exerts on families which
60 have never escaped will be unknown to him.

The new villager's attitudes are deeply coloured by the national village cult. In Akenfield, evidence of the good life, a tall old church on the hillside, a pub selling the local brew, a pretty stream, a football pitch, a handsome square
65 vicarage with a cedar of Lebanon shading it, a school with jars of tadpoles in the window, three shops with doorbells, a Tudor mansion, half a dozen farms and a lot of quaint cottages, is there for all to recognize. Akenfield, on the face of it, is the kind of place in which an Englishman has
70 always felt it his right and duty to live. It is patently the real country, untouched and genuine.

*Note: A Hundred is a sub-division of a county.

(Taken from *Akenfield Portrait of an English Village* by Ronald Blythe.)

(a) Select three of the following statements and bring out their meaning *in your own words*:

  (i)   "The townsman in Britain has always regarded urban life as just a temporary necessity." (Lines 1—3)

  (ii) ". . . the old, settled, recognizable village represents the ideal community." (Lines 21—2)

  (iii) ". . . village life became so suffocating and inhibiting because he had no way of occasionally getting away from it." (Lines 30—2)

  (iv) ". . . gardens so spectacularly neat that they look as though they had been bought by the yard from a nurseryman." (Lines 39—41) (9 marks)

(b) What is the writer's view of "New Towns"? Supply as much evidence as you can from the passage to support your answer. (6 marks)

(c) Summarize, using your own words as much as possible, the second and third paragraphs, i.e., from "But the villager . . ." to ". . . untouched and genuine." (Use about 80 words; the original contains about 250) (20 marks)

(d) In about 12—15 lines write in support of town life. (10 marks)

(R.S.A. English Language II.)

275

8. Read this passage and answer the questions which follow it.
    "In the Arab states the huge increases in oil prices since 1973 have caused social upheaval as well as bringing material progress. Saudi Arabia, for long a closed kingdom trying to preserve the old ways, has been forced to open up to Western industry and technology. With hundreds of businessmen crowding the hotels of Jeddah or Riyadh, the Saudis, and the deprived portion of the Saudi Arabian population, the million labourers imported from Yemen, have been brought into contact with new ideas and different life styles.
    In Oman, on the southern rim of Arabia, the Sultan has built apartment blocks, hotels and offices which have all but destroyed the charm of his capital Muscat, once one of the world's most attractive cities. In Iraq and Iran, at the head of the Gulf, the millions pouring in have enabled the two governments to diversify their whole economies, to set up industries unconnected with oil, and to take water and electricity to some of the most remote areas. The result has often been deserted villages, as people who scratched a living in tiny rural communities have been moved to new centralized villages, to which the water and electricity can be taken, and where schools and clinics can be set up.
    Only in Kuwait and some of the United Arab emirates has the new-found wealth really filtered down, and even in those places, there are first-class and second-class citizens — those able to claim nationality, and those on temporary work or residence permits, or with no papers at all."
    (From the *Daily Telegraph* Magazine.)
  (a) Which groups of people referred to in the passage are likely to benefit greatly from prosperity and progress?
  (b) What evidence is there to show that progress is not always achieved without loss?
  (c) Which of the benefits brought by immensely increased wealth is likely to have the greatest long term impact on Arab society? Give reasons for your choice.
  (d) What do you understand by each of the following expressions as it is used in the passage:
      (i)   social upheaval
      (ii) material progress
      (iii) a closed kingdom
      (iv) diversify their whole economies

(v) second-class citizens
(London Chamber of Commerce Junior Secretary's
Certificate.)

9. Read the following passage and then answer the questions
below.

The skies have suddenly clouded over for the world's
60,000 airline pilots. While the industry has fallen victim
to the oil crisis and world recession, increasing use of
wide-bodied jets, each carrying 300 or more passengers,
5 means that fewer aircraft, and therefore fewer crews, are
needed. Pilot-miles flown dropped last year by 5 per cent.
There is also a move to use more two-man crews in
long-haul jets. Before inertial navigation (a computer-based
system that accurately locates an aircraft's position any-
10 where in the world) there used to be four men in the
cockpit of long-haul airliners. Today the usual figure is
three; and Boeing, for one, argues that with reliable computers even that is more than is needed. Not surprisingly,
the pilots' unions are resisting the two-man trend.
15   The economic climate could also bring more collapses
and not necessarily just among the smaller outfits. Pan
American is in sufficient trouble for its pilots to have for-
gone an 11 per cent pay increase. In return, the company
has agreed to drop out of the American airlines' pact to
20 help each other withstand a strike, but that is a poor *quid
pro quo* for accepting well below the going American rate.
However, if Pan Am had gone broke last November,
instead of fixing up a borrowing facility of $125m, 2,500
more pilots would have joined the 1,000 already
25 redundant in the industry.
Newly-fledged pilots just out of training schools,
including those from the government-sponsored British
college at Hamble, are having to wait for a job. British Airways, which has 100 pilots on permanent leave (i.e. laid
30 off with pay), cannot take a large number of last summer's
graduates. And when 400 senior British Airways captains
retire during the next three years, many of their jobs will
go with them. They will collect their pensions, grateful
that throughout their 30-year career they enjoyed regular
35 expansion of a sort unlikely to be repeated for the next
generation of pilots.

The gloom should not be overdone. Growth in commercial aviation will be resumed. The questions are when, and how much slower than in the past. One forecast, from 40 Boeing, last October, was that the demand for flight crew in 1985 would be 80 per cent. higher than it was in 1970, even assuming a more widespread use of two-man crews than, in fact, seems likely. If so, the training schools should not be cutting back their intake as much as they 45 are. But the forecast may well be too hopeful, and does not seem to have allowed fully for the slowdown that began even before the oil crisis.

America and Britain dominate the supply of pilots. Their training facilities are partly responsible. So, too, is 50 their language: English is the official international aviation language, even, except for domestic flights, in eastern Europe. Operating procedures, examination standards and safety regulations also usually follow American or British patterns, though there are some minor variations, par- 55 ticularly in Europe. Over half of all civil pilots are either British or American, especially the latter, thanks to the increased numbers trained for the Korean and Vietnamese wars.

Arab countries, spending new-found oil wealth on air- 60 lines, are the latest to want American and British pilots. They offer pay at least up to American scales, but the posts are never permanent. As locals gain experience, they naturally want to take over the well-paid and glamorous top jobs. Iran has shown the way to the Arabs. It has its 65 own highly trained pool of expert military pilots, and its airline, Iran Air, has a close working association with Pan American but an increasing number of its own Iranian pilots.

This process has in the past been hurried, sometimes for 70 political reasons, often with disastrous results for safety. Japan promoted inexperienced nationals to captain big jets and there was a series of accidents; the Japanese have since stiffened up job qualifications to western standards but, in the meantime, they re-employed expatriates, to improve 75 safety.

Even if they remain healthy, most pilots have to retire at 55 on half-pay with little training to help them get a reasonably good desk job. The surprise is that their side-

lines are so ordinary. Many have small shops selling baby
80 wear or hobby equipment, launderettes, a pub or an
insurance agency. Some even take up concessions for one
of the patent drain-clearing systems. It is the rare spirit
who decides to run a disco or a night club. A pilot's life
ends unglamorously.

(From *The Economist*, February 1975.)

(*You will lose marks if your answers are unnecessarily
long. Except for* (b), (d), (g), (h), (j), (m), *questions can be
answered in ten words or less. Use your own words, except
when you are asked to quote from the passage.*)

(a) How do the pilots feel if the "skies have clouded over"
(Line 1)?

(b) List on separate lines three reasons for a decrease in the
number of air-crew required. (Lines 1—14).

(c) Why are some of the words in brackets in paragraph
two?

(d) List on separate lines the steps which American and
British airlines respectively have taken to overcome their
difficulties. Do not copy directly from the passage.

(e) What are "newly-fledged" pilots? (Line 26).

(f) What is meant by "many of their jobs will go with
them"? (Lines 32—3).

(g) According to the passage, what mistake are the training
schools making? Explain why it is a mistake.

(h) On separate lines, list four reasons given in the passage
for there being more American and British pilots than
pilots of other nationalities. (Lines 48—62).

(i) What phrase indicates that non-English pilots speak
English when piloting aircraft? (Lines 48—58).

(j) Which countries will employ fewer people of a different
nationality?
Why will they do this? (Lines 59—75).

(k) What disadvantage does the passage say there is in dis-
placing foreign pilots hurriedly? (Lines 69—75).

(l) What makes the author say a pilot's life ends unglamorously? (Lines 83—4).

(m) Explain very briefly, in fewer than six words wherever
possible:
long-haul jets (line 8).
a borrowing facility (line 23).
redundant (line 25).

desk job (line 78).
sidelines (lines 78—9).
rare spirit (line 82).
(n) What word in the same paragraph could be used instead
of "unglamorous"? (Lines 76—84.)
(The Institute of Bankers, Part I.)

10. Read the following passage carefully and then answer the
questions on it.

It is popular (and totally mistaken) to see tomorrow's
woman as a stockbroker or an engine driver. This illogical
conclusion comes from the shaky belief that to be more
free, a woman must somehow be more like a man. Men are
5 in no way liberated. They are, if anything, more mercilessly enslaved by their cog-like role in the nation's
economy than women have ever been.

Today's woman is angry because she believes she is despised and exploited by men in her traditional role of wife
10 and mother. In a society that measures status by the
pound sterling her non-earning function renders her contemptible, but what women do not always seem to understand is that the traditional role was once entirely dignified
and honourable. It is only the development of a modern,
15 industrial society that has reduced it to emptiness.

Just as today's train drivers are bitterly and stubbornly
angry because technical development has made their skills
redundant (and thus shaken their self-respect), so today's
women are angry because they have been made redundant
20 as human beings.

Their anger, however, is best understood as the anger,
not of aggression, but of bewilderment, and some of this
bewilderment no doubt stems from the fact that they are
told they have been freed by the science and machinery of
25 their time. Certainly the washing machine, the vacuum
cleaner, frozen foods and cans have removed drudgery,
contraception has removed continual fear of pregnancies,
and cheap synthetic fibres have removed the persistent
need to make and mend, but the science that has altered
30 their lives is a most ambiguous wonder. It has also destroyed the very real skills that were best performed by
women, and demanded far more of them than purely
manual dexterity.

You can still see in the country woman some of the
35 fundamental knowledge that dignified a woman's role. She
must know her seasons, her growing times to preserve the
fruits and vegetables that will last a family the entire
winter, and when she digs her garden she is not pursuing a
hobby to fill the sagging hours, but making a very real con-
40 tribution to the well-being of those for whom she is
responsible.

Women have not been increasingly freed by machinery:
they have simply had more free time, and they have filled
it in ways that have intensified the neurotic uncertainties
45 they have felt about themselves. They tend to their make-
up, their clothes, the colour of their hair, to meet whatever
current ruling is deemed most feminine; or they devote
more of their time to following (i.e. worrying about)
educational or child care theories and feeling guilty if they
50 fail to achieve the standard they think proper; or,
increasingly, they go out to work, and there find what
they believe to be discrimination.

All these things magnify firstly their lack of self-
confidence, and secondly their anger about the role into
55 which they feel forced, but to suppose that tomorrow's
woman will be a more unfettered version of today's
woman is to suppose that today's economic structure will
continue pretty well unchanged. There are several reasons
for supposing it will do nothing of the kind. and the effect
60 on women could be formidable.

High unemployment is bad for both sexes and at the
moment it is not quite so bad for women. That is because
they can be found lower paid jobs. When the pay is the
same for both sexes, the problem will be the same for both
65 sexes, and there is little reason to expect unemployment
levels to plunge tomorrow. Nor will the rises in the prices
of food. There are more mouths in the world to be fed and
more of these mouths are demanding better food than
they have had in the past. Already we are trying to cut
70 down our meat consumption, which still leaves us with the
problem of fresh foods whose relative price rise is greater
than that of meat. The best way to ensure cheaper fruit
and vegetables is to cultivate your own or preserve crops in
seasons. Apart from a shortage of meat-producing animals
75 we face a shortage of animals whose hides and pelts have

281

made fashionable shoes and clothes for women. More importantly, we face a shortage of those materials which have so far produced and fuelled women's liberating domestic machinery.

80 If, as I believe it will, affluence deserts us, women may well find themselves far more highly valued in the traditional role that they have been brought to think of as destructive of self.

(a) "Today's woman is angry because she believes she is *despised and exploited* by men in her *traditional role* of wife and mother. In a society that *measures status by the pound sterling* her *non-earning function renders her contemptible*" (lines 8—12).

Express in your own words the meaning of these sentences, taking particular care to explain the expressions in italics. (10 marks)

(b) Explain briefly in your own words what, according to the writer, train drivers and today's women have in common. (4 marks)

(c) "but the science that has altered their lives is a most ambiguous wonder" (lines 29—30).

State how, according to the writer,

(i) science has improved the lives of women (7 marks), and

(ii) science has made their lives less happy. (9 marks)

You should not need to use more than 100 words altogether.

(d) "but to suppose that tomorrow's woman will be a more unfettered version of today's woman is to suppose that today's economic structure will continue pretty well unchanged. There are several reasons for supposing it will do nothing of the kind, and the effect on women could be formidable" (lines 55—60).

Confining your answer to lines 55—83 ("but to suppose ... destructive of self"), list the reasons advanced by the writer for supposing that changes will take place, and state the effects she believes they will have on women.

You should not need to use more than 80 words. (12 marks)

(e) What does the writer say about "the country woman" (line 34) that supports her statement:

"the traditional role was once entirely dignified and honourable" (lines 13—14)? (6 marks)

(f) The writer says that men are "mercilessly enslaved by their cog-like role in the nation's economy" (lines 5—7).

Give TWO reasons why you think a man's role in modern industrial society could justifiably be called "cog-like". (4 marks)

(Joint Matriculation Board English Language Ordinary Level Paper C.)

11. Read the following passage carefully and then attempt the questions given below:

"We are witnessing two simultaneous revolutions: the scientific revolution and the revolution of rising expectations. And the second is the product of the first.

The world has been reduced in time and distance to a small planet round which a man-made satellite can travel sixteen times a day. The astronauts, on their way to and from the moon, reminded us by comment and television pictures that Earth is a minor planet in the solar system. No place in the world is more than a few hours away by jet propulsion, a few minutes away by inter-continental ballistic missiles, and split-seconds away by radio. Within its limits, 3,500 million people have to contrive to live together. It has become a neighbourhood.

Communication, the all-pervading radio, has made people everywhere aware of change. We have seen the *epidemic of freedom*. In 1945 there were fifty-two countries in the United Nations. Today there are 125. Most of the new nations were the subject peoples of the great empires of twenty-five years ago. What Harold Macmillan called the "winds of change" were in fact etheric — radio-winds. The demands for independence spread throughout the world. With each successful claim others followed suit. Events outside a country reverberated in the Council Chambers of the United Nations, and the debates in the U.N. reverberated within the countries themselves.

But independence was not the only change which people assumed was coming their way. To the aspirations, the intangibles of freedom, were added the expectations, the material substance of freedom. As the advanced countries boasted their great achievements people everywhere began to expect that the wit of man could do something about their conditions of life, about their sickness, their hunger, their poverty. And the unfulfilment of these expectations has produced resentments and frustrations. Today the confrontation is not between East and West as it was a few years ago, but between North and South, between the scientific and technologically advanced countries and the scientific and technologically underprivileged countries.

There is little doubt that we could fulfil the expectations. But the scientific and technological revolution is spinning faster and faster and the revolution of rising expectations is turning fitfully like the millstone in a windmill. It is ironical that human ingenuity can send people round the moon and bring them back bang on target but that we cannot solve the problems of this planet and the needs of our common humanity. In the last twenty years I have travelled over two million miles and have been to most places in the world to see how science and technology could be applied to the wellbeing of mankind. One thing I know. It is not a question of lack of knowledge but of lack of intention. If we shared our knowledge and skills we could reduce the disparity between the prosperity of the developed countries and the poverty of the underdeveloped.

We say that ignorance of the law is no excuse. Ignorance of science is no excuse. The first does not mean that everyone has to be articled to a solicitor and the second does not mean that everyone should be a B.Sc. It is not necessary to practise science in order to understand it any more than one has to be able to write poetry or compose music in order to appreciate them. What blocks the understanding of science for ordinary people is the language of science — the *jabberwocky* — and two other things: that if it takes all those clever chaps all those years to learn it, how can the common man grasp it? And, the fear of science. People forget penicillin and remember the bomb. They feel their jobs are threatened and forget that science has simplified their jobs for them.

(From "Science and the Public". Lecture by The Lord

Ritchie-Calder, recorded in *Royal Society of Arts Journal*, March 1969.)

(a) Give the passage a title and summarize the first five paragraphs (i.e. from the beginning to ... "poverty of the underdeveloped") in about 130 of your own words. (20 marks)

(b) The author uses the word "expectations" repeatedly in this passage; he also speaks of "aspirations".

   (i) What do you understand to be the difference in meaning between these two words in their context?

   (ii) Why do you think he uses the expression "epidemic of freedom"?

   (iii) Even if you have not met the word "jabberwocky" before, say, from the context, what you think it means. (10 marks)

   (30 marks)

   (London Chamber of Commerce Private Secretary's Certificate.)

12. Study the following passage, then answer the questions below.

Shampooing rabbits

This year is the centenary of the Cruelty to Animals Act which regulates animal experimentation in Britain. With an R.S.P.C.A. report on vivisection expected soon, activity in both Houses of Parliament, and a pro-vivisection campaign by scientists getting under way, the centenary is certain to be a controversial one.

When the 1876 Act became law *virtually all* animal experiments were connected with medical research. But in recent years this has changed. An increasing proportion are connected to the safety testing of agricultural and industrial chemicals, food additives, and, most controversial of all, lipsticks, shampoos, face creams and other cosmetics.

It is one of the recommendations of the R.S.P.C.A. report, now in draft form, that such *non-medical experiments* should be banned. It is a proposal that is bound to gain public support on the ground that *saving lives is one thing, marketing new brands of deodorants another*.

Earlier this year, Mr Phillip Whitehead, Labour M.P. for Derby North, introduced a Private Members Bill along similar lines. It did not get beyond a first reading but a

Lords Bill, introduced by Baroness Phillips, to ban the use of animals in testing cosmetics has now had its second reading.

A Parliamentary ban on "non-medical" animal experiments would, however, lead to a Gilbertian situation. For most of the recent increase in such experiments has been the result of legislation that makes animal testing obligatory.

Drugs, medicines, food additives, pesticides and weed-killers must now all be tested for toxicity by law. Cosmetic testing is not compulsory, but a manufacturer that marketed, say, a face powder that caused dermatitis would be in serious trouble.

And so it is that shampoos are put into rabbits' eyes and on to the skin of animals partially encased in plaster of paris to prevent them scratching it off. Others are fed chemicals to establish how much is required to kill off half of the test batch.

Even the defenders of animal experimentation have their doubts about some of these bureaucratically rigid trials. *"I wouldn't approve when the dose required is enormously different from that likely to be incurred in practice"* said Professor William Paton of Oxford, Chairman of the Research Defence Society whose aims are "to make known the value and necessity of experiments on animals."

The Society itself is not prepared to be critical of non-medical experiments as such — citing the 10,000 clearly medical poisoning cases a year involving non-medical substances and the continued demand for safe cosmetics. But with the opposing forces getting stronger, its stand may be a bad tactical move in the defence of animal experiments. (From a *Sunday Times* article by Bryan Silcock.)

(i) What does the author mean by "virtually all"?

(ii) Define the term "non-medical experiments" as used in the passage.

(iii) Explain the meaning of "saving lives is one thing, marketing new brands of deodorant another".

(iv) State the dilemma posed by the impending Gilbertian situation.

(v) What does the Professor Paton mean when he says "I wouldn't approve when the dose required is enormously different from that likely to be incurred in practice"? (20 marks)

(Association of Medical Secretaries Diploma Examination.)

13. In the following extract five phrases in common use are underlined. Explain what you understand by these phrases.

"<u>Technological innovation</u> during the last 50 years has led to a decline in <u>the quality of life</u> in the <u>major conurbations</u>. The most <u>obvious example</u> of this is <u>the amount of environmental pollution</u> caused by <u>exhaust emissions</u> from motor vehicles."

(Association of Medical Secretaries Diploma Examination.)

14. Answer both part (a) and (b).

(a) Read the following extract from the instructions supplied with a small electronic pocket calculator and answer the questions below it. No special knowledge is required. Keep your answers brief.

Your calculator uses a standard nine-volt battery type PP3—P available at most camera shops. Do not use any other type. To operate calculator, turn power switch to "ON" position. Switching off clears the machine.

To use mains adaptor, remove battery from calculator. Plug adaptor into electric mains and connect to calculator using the lead provided.

When battery weakens the display figures on calculator will go out. Always remove a worn battery to prevent damage.

The calculator will work out your VAT, trade discounts, tax rebates, etc. To do this, use the percentage key. There is a memory key to enable you to store sub-totals.

If an error is made when entering a figure the C/CE key should be pressed once. This will cancel the entry but leave the rest of the calculation intact. Pressing the C/CE key *twice* will clear the machine ready for a fresh calculation.

The calculator is guaranteed for one year. For service, pack securely and return, carriage paid, to makers. No liability can be entertained for misuse or tampering.

(i) Members of staff in your office are permitted to use the calculator. Prepare a short list of instructions telling them what to do (e.g. what checks to carry out) if they cannot get the machine to work.

(ii) What do you think is the point of using a mains adaptor?

(iii) Your employer decides not to buy a mains adaptor, saying "It will limit the calculator's flexibility." What do you think he has in mind?

(iv) Explain briefly what you understand by TWO of the following:

VAT   trade discount   tax rebate   carriage paid

(v) Rewrite the last sentence of the passage in your own words, paying special attention to the meaning of "entertained" and "tampering".

(vi) The battery has run down. The calculator will not work because the battery has now leaked and damaged the machine. Your employer proposes to send the calculator back to the makers (it is only two months old). Comment on his intended action. (20 marks)

(b) The following passage is taken from *The Shell Guide to England*, a detailed guidebook about English towns.

In every English town much conforms with the norm of modernity. All traffic signs are the same everywhere. The fascias and window-dressing of the chain stores are the same. Advertisements are the same. The brands in the shops are the same. The citizens are also very much the same. All this is very convenient; all urban life flows together, and the approach to an unfamiliar town offers no problems. It might be added that all modern buildings are very nearly the same, or, if they are not, they very soon will be.

In fact, no English town would be better worth visiting than any other, were it not for the enormous legacy of the past. There is so much of it that even the most affluent and rapidly developing town cannot entirely wipe out its old self. This is what gives each town its special "character".

(i) Explain what you understand by TWO of the following:

norm   chain stores   urban   affluent

(ii) The opening of the extract sounds very boring. Suggest how the writer will probably continue his chapter (do *not* write a continuation of the extract, but merely *indicate* what you expect he will say).

Do you think it is ever wise business practice to begin an article in such a negative and dissatisfied way? Give your reasons in a line or two.

(iii) The writer may, later on, comment on the effect of petrol stations and garages on the English town and country scene. Do you expect he will think their effect is good or bad? State clearly what evidence you base your answer on.

(iv) Express the opening sentence in your own words.

(v) How far do you think the argument in the second paragraph is valid? For example, how would it apply to towns built in a developing country or a newly discovered part of the world?

(20 marks)

(London Chamber of Commerce Private Secretary's Certificate.)

15. The damage threatened by Concorde is well enough known. Suffice it to say that the sonic boom — which would almost certainly be sanctioned over Scotland, Wales and other "less populated" areas of Britain if it were seen as a means of selling more Concordes — is now only one problem. Among the more immediate or serious threats which have emerged since the 1960s are its shattering ground noise, its consumption of precious energy (four times that of subsonic jets) and its erosion of the ozone layer which protects us from ultra-violet radiation — a source of skin cancer.

Surely, critics will argue, the Americans can make up their own minds on these matters. Undoubtedly they can; and I think there is a strong chance that Concorde will be banned or cripplingly restricted. But the hearing of British voices opposed to Concorde is important in Washington for two reasons.

The first is that only a British witness (in this case the Bishop of Kingston, appearing on behalf of the Heathrow anti-noise group, HACAN) can give evidence of the devastating impact of Concorde take-offs from London Airport last summer. The second is the need to counter the impression, which has been fostered by the Foreign Office in connection with tomorrow's hearings, that the rejection of Concorde by the American authorities would be seen throughout Britain as an act of discrimination.

This chauvinistic picture is clearly contradicted by the only statistical evidence on the subject — an opinion poll conducted by Business Decisions Ltd, on behalf of *The Observer* in 1974. The finding showed a majority of respondents (57%) in favour of stopping the whole project. Significantly, a similar result was obtained in France a few weeks later by the Paris newspaper *France Soir*.

But the Government's stance is dishonest for quite a separate reason which becomes evident when one examines the public figures on Concorde's production economics.

In asking America for British Airways landing rights, the Government has maintained that the services proposed — one flight a day to Washington and two to New York — would be too infrequent to have serious environmental effects. This, too, is untrue, as noise measurements testify. But the greater dishonesty consists in the fact, admitted by Concorde's makers, the British Aircraft Corporation, that the main purpose of getting these services approved by the US Government is to establish a "bridgehead" from which to expand both services and sales of aircraft.

Just how many planes would need to be sold to recover the cost of building them may be gauged from figures given by Mr Benn, then Secretary for Industry, in March 1974. On the present 16 Concordes being built, he told Parliament, we should lose £200—£225 million; on 35, £260—£300 million; and on 100, £120—£250 million. The "break-even" production figure (which would still bring no return on the £1,200 million spent with France on *development*) has never been published. It is believed to be about 130 — a total which, if ever built, would make environmental damage very serious indeed.

From an article in *The Observer* (January 4th 1976) by David Wilson of the Conservation Society.

(a) Write a summary of the passage in continuous prose. Do not use more than 180 words. State at the end of the summary the number of words you have used. Supply a suitable title.

(b) (i) Explain fully what the writer means by the words "would be seen throughout Britain as an act of discrimination".

(ii) What evidence is there in this passage that opinion

in Britain carries weight in the United States?
(iii) Why has the word "development" been italicized?
(iv) "This chauvinistic picture is clearly contradicted".
To what extent is this contention borne out by
other statements in the fourth paragraph?
(v) *Concisely* answer *either* 1 or 2.
1. What, in your opinion, is to be said in favour of
the Concorde project?
2. How, in your opinion, could the money spent on
Concorde have been more usefully spent?
(Ordinary National Certificate in Business
Studies. Summary and Comprehension questions
set by *one* examination centre, June 1976. The
summary should take about 40 minutes, the
comprehension no more than 20 minutes.)

16. Read the following passage carefully, and then answer the
questions on it. (20 marks)

When supper was finished Mother Sprigg, Madge and Stella
quickly removed the dishes, while Father Sprigg, sepulch-
rally clearing his throat, walked with heavy, deliberate
tread to the dresser, took the Book from the tureen,
5 carried it and laid it down carefully before his chair. Then
he seated himself, took off his spectacles, polished them
meticulously on his handkerchief, readjusted them on his
beak of a nose, wetted his finger and slowly turned the
pages until he found the pressed carnation that marked the
10 place. Mother Sprigg and Stella reseated themselves about
the table with hands reverently folded, whilst Sol, in his
chimney corner, cupped his right ear in his hands.

The only books at the farm were the Family Prayer
Book and the Bible and Father Sprigg, with ineradicable
15 determination, read one chapter of the Bible aloud every
evening. He worked solidly through from Genesis to
Revelation, attacking the difficult words with the same un-
daunted courage with which he took a five-barred gate in
the hunting field, charging as fast and furious as his own
20 bull through the more indelicate passages of the Old
Testament, happy in the New Testament with the parables
of sowing and reaping and with the shepherds in the fields,
but plodding through the last incomprehensible chapters
of the Book with stumbling tongue.

25   He was humiliated by his own inability to read such a story in a manner as befitted it, but nevertheless shirked nothing whatever from the first page until the last.

     What his listeners made of it all, what he made of it himself, would have been difficult to say; perhaps to them it
30 was a soporific before bedtime, to him one of those duties which from generation to generation fall to the master of the house.

     But to little Stella this nightly reading was glory and enchantment. Sitting there demurely, her eyes cast down,
35 she gave no outward sign of her excitement, but the blood drummed in her ears at the tales of old adventures. Even in the dreadful parts of the Book, the language would suddenly affect her like an enchantment. The peculiarities of Father Sprigg's delivery worried her not at all.

40   Old Sol was leaning sideways to bring his cupped hand close to Father Sprigg's voice and he lifted his head a little as a man does who looks at a distant view. Mother Sprigg was dozing and Madge's face wore the vacant look that it always had when she was not engaged in active work.

45   "Amen!" said Father Sprigg in a voice like a thunderclap, and let out a gusty sigh of relief and profound satisfaction. Once more he had performed an uncongenial duty creditably and the mingled feeling of martyrdom and virtue were pleasantly inflating to his ego.

Elizabeth Goudge

(a) State briefly Father Sprigg's preparations for the reading, as indicated in the passage. (3 marks)
(b) Say *in your own words* how Father Sprigg varied his reading of the chapters mentioned in paragraph 2 of this passage. (3 marks)
(c) In what different ways did the four other people present receive the reading? (4 marks)
(d) How does the author indicate in this passage that Father Sprigg was pleased when the daily reading was over? (2 marks)
(e) Explain what you understand by TWO of the following:
    (i)   with ineradicable determination (lines 14—15);
    (ii) humiliated by his inability to read such a story in a manner as befitted it (lines 25—6);
    (iii) he had performed an uncongenial duty creditably (lines 47—8). (4 marks)

(f) Choose FOUR of the following words and for each give a word or a phrase of the same meaning as the word has in the passage.

reverently (line 11)   delivery (line 39)
shirked (line 26)   dozing (line 43)
soporific (line 30)   inflating (line 49) (4 marks)
(20 marks)

(A.E.B. Ordinary Level English Language Syll. 1 Paper 2.)

17. Read the following passage carefully, and then answer the questions on it in your own words.

The First Glimpse of Tutankhamun's Tomb

I suppose most excavators would confess to a feeling of awe — embarrassment almost — when they break into a chamber closed and sealed by pious hands so many centuries ago. For the moment, time as a factor in human
5 life has lost its meaning. Three thousand years have passed since human feet last trod the floor on which you stand, and yet, as you note the signs of recent life around you — the half-filled bowl of mortar for the door, the blackened lamp, the finger-mark upon the freshly painted surface, the
10 farewell garland dropped upon the threshold — you feel it might have been but yesterday. The very air you breathe, unchanged throughout the centuries, you share with those who laid the mummy to its rest. Time is annihilated by little intimate details such as these, and you feel an
15 intruder.

That is perhaps the first and dominant sensation, but others follow thick and fast — the exhilaration of discovery, the fever of suspense, the almost overmastering impulse, born of curiosity, to break down seals and lift the
20 lids of boxes, the thought — pure joy to the investigator — that you are about to add a page to history, or solve some problem of research, the strained expectancy — why not confess it? — of the treasure seeker.

Surely never before in the whole history of excavation
25 had such an amazing sight been seen as the light of our torch revealed to us, the first light that had pierced the darkness of the chamber for three thousand years. Here was a roomful — a whole museum it seemed — of objects, some familiar, but some the like of which we had never

293

30 seen, piled one upon another in seemingly endless profusion.

Gradually the scene grew clearer and we could pick out individual objects. First, right opposite to us, were three great gilt couches, their sides carved in the shape of
35 monstrous animals, curiously attenuated in body, as they had to be to serve their purpose, but with heads of startling realism throwing grotesque distorted shadows on the wall behind them. Next, on the right, two statues caught and held our attention, two life-sized figures of
40 kings in black, facing each other like sentinels, gold kilted, gold sandalled, armed with mace and staff, the protective sacred cobra upon their foreheads.

These were the dominant objects that caught the eye at first. Between them, around them, piled on top of them,
45 were countless others — exquisitely painted and inlaid caskets; alabaster vases; strange black shrines, from the open door of one a great snake peeping out; beds and chairs beautifully carved; a golden inlaid throne; beneath our eyes, on the very threshold of the chamber, a beautiful
50 cup of translucent alabaster; on the left a confused pile of overturned chariots, glistening with gold and inlay; and peeping from behind them another figure of a king.

Whether we noted all these objects at the time I cannot say for certain, as our minds were in much too excited and
55 confused a state to register accurately. Presently it dawned upon our bewildered brains that in all this medley of objects before us there was no coffin or trace of a mummy, and the much debated question of tomb or cache began to intrigue us afresh. With this question in view we
60 re-examined the scene before us, and noticed for the first time that between the two black sentinel statues on the right there was another sealed doorway. The explanation gradually dawned upon us. We were only on the threshold of our discovery. What we saw was merely an ante-
65 chamber. Behind the guarded door there would be other chambers, possibly a succession of them, and in one of them, beyond any shadow of doubt, in all his magnificent panoply of death, we should find the Pharaoh lying.

Note: In your answers to (a), (b), (c) and (d) below, you must not quote whole phrases from the passage. The length of answers suggested for (a), (b), (c) and (d) is meant as a guide to candidates. There will be no penalty for not answering within the suggested limits.

  (a) Basing your answer on the first paragraph of the passage, explain the feelings and thoughts of the writer as he first gazed into the chamber. (Answer in about 70 of your own words.) (7 marks)

  (b) What feelings immediately followed these? (Answer in about 60 of your own words.) (6 marks)

  (c) What did the writer find "amazing" in the arrangement, quantity and quality of the objects which he saw in the light of his torch?

     (You may draw attention to particular objects to support your answer, but do not merely compile a list. Answer in about 100 words.) (11 marks)

  (d) What conclusions did he draw from the fact that the coffin was not among the objects he could see? (Answer in about 50 words.) (5 marks)

  (e) Explain FOUR of the following phrases as used in the passage:
    (i)   little intimate details (line 14);
    (ii) dominant sensation (line 16);
    (iii) overmastering impulse (lines 18—19);
    (iv) seemingly endless profusion (lines 30—1);
    (v) curiously attenuated in body (line 35);
    (vi) magnificent panoply (lines 67—8). (12 marks)

  (f) Give the meaning of TWO of the following, as used in the passage:
    (i)   annihilated (line 13);
    (ii) exhilaration (line 17);
    (iii) distorted (line 37);
    (iv) medley (line 56). (4 marks)

  (g) Examine the second paragraph. Show how the writer has broken down a long sentence in such a way as to convey the thrill and excitement of the occasion. (2 marks)

    Style marks for questions (a)—(d) (5 marks).

    (Joint Matriculation Board English Language Ordinary Level, Paper B. Candidates were recommended to spend not more than 50 minutes on this question.)

18. Read the following passage, which consists of items from a

dictionary of money terms, and then answer the questions below:

John Maynard Keynes (1883—1946) was the most influential economist of his generation and possibly of this century. Educated at Eton and King's College, Cambridge, he was a brilliant student in mathematics, politics and
5 philosophy. He eventually turned to economics in order to prepare for a civil service examination, and in 1906 entered the India Office. Two years later Keynes accepted a lectureship in economics at Cambridge, and during the First World War he did important work at the Treasury.
10 The result was a highly successful book. *The Economic Consequences of the Peace*. His biggest impact, however, came with the publication of his *General Theory of Employment, Interest and Money* in 1936. The timing could not have been better: after the great depression,
15 economic theorists were in disarray and desperately needed a saviour. Keynes adopted basic premises a little closer to reality than those of his predecessors. He argued against *laissez-faire*, and made a strong case for government intervention, to compensate for the uncontrollable vagaries
20 of private capitalism, even if it meant government deficits. He advocated a permanent policy of keeping interest rates low, and put heavy emphasis on the need to maintain full employment. His theories were by no means universally accepted, but his policy suggestions were practical enough
25 to be widely adopted by economists in desperate search of solutions. Keynes gave economics a new lease of life, and his views still command a very wide following today — although, inevitably, some of his arguments are increasingly challenged. Keynes was a skilful writer, but his
30 *General Theory* is hard going for any layman. No matter; what counts is that his ideas had, and still have, practical value. Keynes was not only a brilliant thinker; he also proved himself a highly successful stock market speculator. You can't ask for much more, can you?

35 Karl Marx (1818—1883) was a German socialist, economist, and sociologist who devoted his life to destroying the capitalist system — on paper. His prose was turgid and many of his ideas were impractical, but he must certainly be counted as one of the most influential economists of all
40 time. Marx developed his theories against a background

of high unemployment, low wages, long hours, and deplorable working conditions, and it isn't difficult to see why he detested a system which produced such blatant injustice. Marx himself lived in dire poverty for most of his
45 life and when he died not more than eight people attended his funeral.

The basic point of his long and involved argument was that the capitalist system could not by its very nature survive; that it carried the seeds of its destruction. This
50 reasoning was based chiefly on the view that life is one long class struggle, that workers lack the power to demand a greater share in the new wealth created by capitalism, and that the proletariat in industrialized societies (Marx was thinking primarily of countries like Britain and
55 Germany) would eventually rise and seize power from the ruling class.

Despite superficial appearances to the contrary, most of his predictions have turned out to be wrong. The proletariat has not carried out a socialist revolution in any
60 highly industrialized state; what now goes by the name of communism has won its victories chiefly in backward agricultural regions. The proletariat has not maintained a united front and the system has not destroyed itself, mainly because it has shown a far greater capacity to adapt
65 than Marx thought possible. He did not foresee the growing power of labour unions, the impact of democracy, and the possibility of progress through evolution. The working class has not suffered increasing misery, but has enjoyed, in most industrial nations, a rising standard of living. If
70 Marx could spend a week in some of the American and European suburbs, he would be astonished. Most of the benefits promised labour as a result of "dictatorship of the proletariat", such as the eight-hour day and social insurance, have become fact. Indeed we have gone further
75 than the *Communist Manifesto* envisaged, and this progress has been achieved with the active support of the middle class.

It won't do, though, to dismiss Marx merely because his forecasts contain historical errors. He did have a major
80 impact on social development in large parts of the world, and one is certainly entitled to ask how far his teachings — and the events they inspired — helped to produce the

297

infinitely better conditions we take for granted in the Western world today.

(From *Money Talks* by William Davis.)

(You will lose marks if your answers are unnecessarily long. Most questions can be answered in ten words or less. *Use your own words, except when you are asked to quote from the passage.*)

(a) For each of the words below, give another word or a group of words to express its meaning as it occurs in the context:

predecessors (line 17); deficits (line 20); layman (line 30); proletariat (line 53); adapt (line 64); *Manifesto* (line 75)

(b) In not more than 20 words, explain why the publication of Keynes's most influential book was so timely.

(c) Quote a single word, occurring later in the passage, which has much the same meaning as "made a strong case for" (line 18).

(d) Quote a brief expression that suggests the opposite of a policy of *"laissez-faire"* (line 18).

(e) Re-write the following to show that you understand the italicized words: *"compensate for the uncontrollable vagaries of private capitalism"* (lines 19—20).

(f) The writer says that Keynes's *General Theory* is "hard going" (line 30). From lines 35—44, quote the single word that best suggests that the same might be said of Marx's theories.

(g) What weakness of Marx does the writer seek to emphasize in lines 35—7?

(h) In not more than 20 words, sum up the contrast between Keynes and Marx in the management of their private financial affairs.

(j) What is meant by the statement that the capitalist system "carried the seeds of its destruction" (line 49)?

(k) From the last paragraph of the passage, quote a word that has much the same meaning as "predictions" (line 58).

(l) Why, according to the writer, is it no longer true to say that "workers lack the power to demand a greater share in the new wealth created by capitalism" (lines 51—2)?

(m) Give the reason for the use of italics (i) in line 18; and (ii) in line 30.

(The Institute of Bankers, Part 1.)

19. Read the following passage and answer the questions you will find below it:

Experience is divided into subjects, in every known academic curriculum. When these subjects are called, as so often, disciplines, it seems easy to believe that an understanding of the definitions and boundaries of the subjects
5 is a condition of seriousness. And since academic institutions, almost necessarily, are self-reproducing and self-perpetuating, any questioning of subject divisions — the internal organization of academic studies — can be made to seem an attack on serious study of any kind and even,
10 paradoxically, on academic freedom.

Yet it must always be clear, not only that the division of experience into subjects is arbitrary, but that any particular division is an expression of a particular way of seeing the world: usually a selective combination of past
15 and present. Classification is arbitrary in itself, and the habit of classification, because it lends itself to a particularly straightforward kind of teaching and learning, is deeply rooted in academic method. But the particular classification into subjects has its significance far beyond
20 the walls of academies. It is a prepared, defining framework for the understanding of all experience. To be educated at all is to submit, at least temporarily, to the prepared system. Like everyone else who is writing or reading this book, I have made this submission, to be in a
25 position to work at all. It is then necessary to explain why I now reject the system, in a crisis of experience, and as a condition for continuing and developing my own work.

My centre of interest, from the beginning, had been imaginative literature. I had understood this, since I was a
30 boy at school, as writing novels and plays. And I thought for some time that an academic course in English would be mainly a way of reading other people's novels and plays and poems, and learning what was necessary to understand them. I had two surprises in the course of my education.
35 First, I discovered the shadow line between writing and the study of literature. It amazed me to discover how many teachers of literature regarded writing as something that had already happened, at a safe distance in time, rather than as something that is still happening and that we our-
40 selves can give our main energy to. I found that a critical

299

essay on another writer is taken more seriously, as a contribution to the study of literature, than a piece of what is called — with a slight sideways smile — original or creative writing. Now, in a university, when I tell my scientist
45 colleagues that I am writing a novel they understand me at once; it is what they expect me to do — a practical, experimental, ongoing activity. From most of my colleagues in the arts I more usually get that same sideways smile; it is perhaps no harm that I spend my time in that playful way,
50 but they would like me to know that meanwhile they are getting on with the serious business of editing or collation or criticism. This profound bias against practice, in academic minds that have been trained in what are still called the humanities, is a matter of great significance in
55 the present unrest in education. I do not want to see our arts departments teaching creative practice; in a hierarchical system there is something inescapably absurd about that. But I do want to see the centre of any arts course as practice; free and where necessary co-operative
60 practice; as the only way of defining, at the heart of our studies, the seriousness and the difficulty of the central discipline.

Our present system is against that. And this is not surprising. For its delicate internal balances depend on the
65 exclusion of certain kinds of practice and experience. This, many years ago (I have become hardened now) was my second surprise. To understand works of literature meant necessarily, I thought, understanding the times and societies they had been written in: not as "background",
70 an inert two-dimensional staged society; but as active experience, of the kind I know in my own life in a particular society at a particular time. This is where the division of subjects fell as a second shadow-line. For I was given to understand that only certain kinds of what were
75 called extra-literary facts were relevant to the study of literature. And at a certain point these extra-literary facts became something else: were called politics, sociology or economic history; and there were quite other departments of the academy which dealt with them. Might one then go
80 to those other departments? Well no, you must make your choice. And of course, if you're more interested in those other things than in literature . . .

(From Raymond Williams: *An Introduction to Reading* in *Culture and Society*.)

Note: In answering these questions you should use *your own words* as far as possible.

(a) Explain the sentence: "academic institutions, almost necessarily, are self-reproducing and self-perpetuating" (lines 5—7). (5 marks)

(b) What, according to the writer, are the defects of classifying experience into subjects or disciplines? (5 marks)

(c) Williams refers to "the profound bias against practice" (line 52) and, later, he says: "I do want to see the centre of any arts course as practice" (lines 58—9). What do you think he means? (5 marks)

(d) What, in your own words, constitutes "a second shadow line" (line 73)? (5 marks)

(e) What is the implication of the final sentence ("And of course . . .")? (2 marks)

(f) Explain the following terms in their context:
    curriculum   (line 2)
    paradoxically   (line 10)
    arbitrary   (line 15)
    collation.   (line 51) (8 marks)

(g) Write a brief comment either supporting or challenging any one idea in the extract that strikes you as being especially significant. (Your answer should occupy 10 to 12 lines). (10 marks)

(A.E.B. Advanced Level English, Paper 2, Question 1.)

20. Read the following passage carefully, and then answer the questions printed after it.

The passage is taken from "Revolt into Style — the Pop Arts in Britain" by George Melly (Penguin, 1972).

The word "pop" is clearly an abbreviation of the word "popular". One of the meanings of the word "popular" given by my dictionary is: "adapted to the understanding, taste, or means of the people". This seems to me an
5 adequate if partial definition of what I understand by the phrase "popular culture", but useless as a definition of "pop culture".

Etymology and semantics are often at odds, but if pop culture is in fact more than a recent phrase of popular

10 culture, the first thing to establish is what separates the meaning of the two terms and what, if anything, they share in common. The most obvious way to begin would be to offer a definition of pop culture, but I am unable to propose one. "Pop music", "pop art", "pop fashion", *15* "pop telly"; it's true that in each case the adjective colours the noun, and, at the same time, suggests some common ground, some common meaning, but to map out that ground, to pin down that meaning, is like trying to stare fixedly at a spot before the eyes. There is no adequate *20* hold-all sentence. I will proceed by degrees.

Both popular and pop culture are of working-class origin, and both arose out of a given situation both social and economic. The principal difference is that popular culture was unconscious, or perhaps unselfconscious would *25* be more exact, whereas pop culture came about as the result of a deliberate search for objects, clothes, music, heroes and attitudes which could help to define a *stance*.

From this it can be said that, whereas the older popular culture stood for the spirit of acceptance, pop culture rep-*30* resented a form of protest. Superficially, and given our current prejudices, this would suggest an advance but, initially at any rate, I don't think that this was the case. Popular culture may have had a vacuous sentimental side to it, an easy tendency to respond to stock stimuli with *35* stock responses, but there was a wry toughness, a *flamboyant* and warm vulgarity which came across as a form of courage. On the other hand the protest in early pop had neither target nor aim. It was *against* a great deal, but *for* nothing. It was parasitic rather than creative, and moti-*40* vated by material envy. The explanation for this un-promising start lies in another important difference between the two cultures. Popular culture, although naturally subjected to regional differences and increasingly corrupted by the early mass media and the spread of *45* *gentility*, had grown slowly and naturally from a settled if frequently deplorable environment. Early British pop was confined entirely to *cosmopolitan* working-class adolescents. The soil it sprang from was poor and sour, enclosed on one side by a brief and inadequate education, and on *50* the other by conscription into the forces. The seed had been planted during the war when circumstances had

broken down the old working-class patterns, and it was
fertilized by the big money from dead-end jobs. It is
hardly surprising that its first flowering should have
55 seemed rank if vigorous. It was called Rock 'n' Roll.

My own *conviction* is that pop music has always formed
the heart of pop culture, and that the rise of Tommy
Steele in the middle 50s is the first British pop event. If I
am right, it would seem right to start with the music.

60 But before doing this it seems to me important to
sketch in other less central factors which have nevertheless
affected the development of pop culture or, in their turn,
been changed by it. For whereas the old popular culture
altered very slowly and appealed throughout its long
65 history to basically the same class, pop has rapidly permeated all strata of society, and at the same time succeeded in blurring the boundaries between itself and
traditional or high culture.

It is of course true that in the past many artists and
70 critics belonging to high culture have taken an interest in
popular culture. Toulouse Lautrec for example painted the
music halls, George Orwell broke new ground, and incidentally founded a minor industry, by examining the neg-
lected byways of popular culture . . . but for these and
75 people like them popular art acted as raw material. The
pop *intellectual* doesn't raid pop culture. He hopes to
create pop art, and tries to live the pop life; to use a Negro
expression, he is trying to pass.

Yet because pop has won converts in certain traditional
80 strongholds it would be *naïve* to imagine that it has conquered universally. On the contrary, the opposition is both
powerful and widespread, and includes not only those
reactionaries who reject all modern culture, but many left-
wing critics who suspect a deliberate plot to brainwash the
85 working class young. . . . The jazz world too rejects pop
music more or less completely, and although financial envy
should be taken into account, this is by no means the main
ground. The folk world, too, is extremely suspicious,
believing, and with considerable justification, that pop
90 constitutes a permanent seductive threat to many weak
but talented adherents of the *ethnic* canon.

Furthermore, a large section of the nation is either unaware of the existence of pop culture or thinks of it, if at

all, as a noisy fringe of show biz or the source of jokes
95 about electric guitars and long hair; and finally a considerable amount of traditional popular culture still exists,
although admittedly mostly for the benefit of the old or
middle-aged. Yet despite the *hostility* or indifference it
would be absurd to try and play down the effect of pop
100 culture on our society as a whole. Not only has it attracted
people from every class and of every level of intelligence,
but it has had the effect of a stone thrown into the middle
of a pond. The ripples round the edge may be faint, but
they are there.

(a) Using no more than 200 of your own words give the differences and similarities the writer considers to exist
between "popular culture" and "pop culture". (15 marks)

(b) State in your own words the opposition the passage
indicates there is to "pop". (10 marks)

(c) Replace each of the following words used in the passage
by *either* a word *or* phrase which could be substituted
without change of meaning:
(i)   etymology (line 8);
(ii)   stance (line 27);
(iii)   flamboyant (lines 35—6);
(iv)   gentility (line 45);
(v)   cosmopolitan (line 47);
(vi)   conviction (line 56);
(vii)   intellectual (line 76);
(viii) naïve (line 80);
(ix)   ethnic (line 91);
(x)   hostility (line 98). (10 marks)

(d) Keeping the context of each phrase closely in mind
explain *clearly and briefly*, what is meant by:
(i)   . . . in each case the adjective colours the noun
(lines 15—16);
(ii)   . . . both arose out of a given situation both social
and economic (lines 22—3);
(iii)   . . . an easy tendency to respond to stock stimuli
with stock responses (lines 34—5);
(iv)   . . . It was parasitic rather than creative (line 39);
(v)   . . . pop has rapidly permeated all strata of society
(lines 65—6). (10 marks)
(45 marks)
(R.S.A. Stage III.)

21. Read the following article from a popular newspaper and then answer the questions which follow it.

The Patients Association is a plucky little David that has taken on the Goliath of the medical profession.

Its latest report describes GPs as operating a "medical Mafia" — an unwritten code that blacklists "difficult" patients. They're the ones who complain. The ones who expect courtesy, efficiency and competence.

The ones who expect the right to change to another doctor when they don't get those things.

The Mafia make sure that no other doctor in the area will take "difficult" patients. Suddenly, their lists are full.

Or they refuse to take a patient who is already registered with a doctor in the area.

Shock

And if a complaint is made, it has to be lodged within eight weeks.

But when a member of the family has died or has been found to have a serious disease — such as cancer — eight weeks is not enough to recover from the shock. Let alone organize a complaint.

You cannot be legally represented at the hearing of your complaint. But your doctor will have the highly experienced Medical Defence Union advising him.

You cannot complain about your GP to the Health Services Commissioner — the Ombudsman. He only deals with complaints about *hospital* doctors.

Stop

The stones fired from the sling of the Patients Association will not injure their target, because the medical profession has closed ranks to deny the allegations in the report. Predictably.

But we should all stop treating doctors with automatic awe and respect.

As a profession, they are secretive, defensive and patronizing.

(a) Suggest reasons why this article is written in very short paragraphs and in short sentences and parts of sentences.

(b) (i) Why has the writer used the David and Goliath metaphor?

(ii) Why is this metaphor not completely suitable?

(c) What is illogical about the first sentence in the second paragraph?

(d) State *in one sentence* who the "difficult" patients are, according to the article.

(e) In your opinion are all patients who complain likely to be "difficult"?

(f) Write out a "paragraph" from the article which consists of only a fragment of a sentence.

(g) Explain what the writer means by "Suddenly their lists are full".

(h) What is the disturbing implication contained in the seventh paragraph?

(i) Who is the Ombudsman?

(j) Comment on the placing of the word "only" in the sentence: "He only deals with complaints about *hospital* doctors".

(k) "The stones fired from the sling . . .". Replace "fired" with a more suitable word.

(l) Substitute for "Predictably" a group of words which could be attached to the sentence which ends "in the report".

(m) What in your opinion is the meaning of the phrase "As a profession"?

(n) Judging from your own experience, do you agree that the impression given of doctors is a fair one?

(o) State the meaning of the following words as they are used in the passage:
plucky
courtesy
allegations
automatic
patronizing

22. Read the following passage and answer the questions below it.

The big bully boy

As that great big bully boy they call bureaucracy grows in its arrogant strength each year, so grows the need for the Ombudsman.

It is reassuring to know that ordinary folk have a friend to referee their fights against the mighty machine.

At least it should be reassuring.

But what happened last week?

In a sad report, Ombudsman Sir Idwal Pugh revealed that the Inland Revenue refused to agree with a recommendation from him and he indicated there was nothing much more he could do about it.

The case concerned a couple who had paid £644 too much tax. They had been mulcted by the State. The Ombudsman looked into it and decided that the tax authorities were to blame.

Injustice

The couple, said Sir Idwal, had suffered injustice "and that injustice has not been remedied".

But the taxmen say: "We do not agree that there was mishandling." And then they add this bureaucratic classic: "The Ombudsman can make recommendations but we are not bound to accept them."

Really? Then perhaps Parliament should give the Ombudsman not just the power to make recommendations but the power to issue orders.

To all fair-minded people the issue is clear. The taxman owes this couple £644. He should post them the cheque tomorrow.

(Editorial, *News of the World*, 1 August 1976.)

Answer the following questions. The answers to (a), (b), and (c) should be expressed in complete sentences.

(a) To whom in your opinion is the writer of this article referring when he uses the expression "ordinary folk"?
(b) What is the "mighty machine" referred to?
(c) Comment on the suitability of the metaphor from boxing.
(d) "Bureaucracy", half French and half Greek in origin, means "civil servants" or "red tape" or "government by officials". State the words ending in "cracy" which mean, approximately:
  government by the people
  government by one man
  government by the rich
  government by the Church
  government by the best people
  government by deserving people
  government by technicians or technologists
(e) Express in your own words "this bureaucratic classic".

(f) Supply words or phrases which could be used to replace the following words in the passage:

arrogant

indicated

mulcted

bound

23. Carefully read this passage from *The Guardian* and then answer the questions which follow it.

Anyone for Menace?

Martin Walker on a cracking start to the violent season.

Britain's most popular weekend recreation — spectator sport violence — got off to a cracking start to open the new season yesterday.

Motor sport fans surged into an early lead with five arrests, 10 injured policemen, a burned-down discotheque, and a blazing car and caravan at Silverstone. Somewhere nearby there was a motor-cycle grand prix.

But the football fans came back with a determined assault on Grimsby. The brave lads did so well that ten of their number had to be transferred to the cells in Scunthorpe, because the Grimsby lock-up was bulging at the bars. For the last day of this popular three-day event, 28 youths will appear in court this morning.

The plucky cricket fans are still in the sports-rowdy championship after scoring a national first at the Oval on Saturday. It was the first time the umpires stopped a test for crowd-stopped-play. Four hundred fans surged onto the pitch as England's last recognized batsman, Captain Tony Greig, was clean-bowled by the West Indies fast bowler Michael Holding.

But the greater experience of the soccer fans told in the end. There were 12 arrests at the Rochdale—Blackburn game, 10 at the Bury—Preston match, and a wrecked carriage on the Liverpool—London train carrying Liverpool fans to a pre-season charity match with Southampton.

It is a measure of these supporters' dedication to the game that they lose no opportunity for training. Other fans may be content to wait until the real season starts — but Liverpool likes to get in early.

(The start of an article in *The Guardian* of 16 August 1976.)

(a) The writer pretends that spectator violence is itself a sport. Quote any two sentences or phrases he uses to maintain this pretence.

(b) What is likely to be the writer's real attitude to spectator violence? Answer in one sentence.

(c) Quote two words from anywhere in the passage used ironically or sarcastically.

(d) Define in one sentence a charity match.

(e) What is "the game" referred to in the sixth paragraph?

(f) Supply words or phrases which could be used to replace the following as they are used in the passage:

   fans

   determined

   surged (para. 4)

   dedication

(g) Why in your opinion is there so much spectator violence?

24. Read the following editorial and answer the questions based on it.

Tito's Chinese Friends

Peking's reddest carpets are now spread out for the Yugoslav Foreign Minister, Mr Tepevac, as they were last week for another visitor from Eastern Europe, President Ceausescu of Rumania. China is as *assiduous* in cultivating Russia's Communist neighbours as she is in developing relations with the West. Mr Ceausescu's visit is rather a routine affair, although the welcome accorded, and accepted, was this time unprecedentedly effusive. He thus reasserts his position as the canny *maverick* among Russia's satellites, although he has recently found it necessary to toe Moscow's line more obediently in economic, diplomatic and military matters. His visit is significant, but Mr Tepevac's even more so.

The accusations of "deviationism" and "reformism" that Peking hurls at Moscow look like hair-splitting compared with the *evolution* that has taken place in Yugoslavia. Yet Yugoslav policy is being accorded nothing but *eulogies*, with special emphasis on her "glorious resistance to the interference and threats from the two super-Powers". In fact, as China well knows, Yugoslavia is in no danger from America. It is precisely because of increasing

Russian designs against Yugoslavia that Peking sought the present visit and is making the most of it.

Tensions between the country's national groups may be *aggravated* rather than *assuaged* by forthcoming increased decentralization. The Serbs are afraid of losing their preponderance, the others want more *autonomy*. Hard-line Moscow-type Communists blame the country's problems on to economic and political liberalization. Russia, who, at the time of her invasion of Czechoslovakia *toyed* with the idea of dealing with Tito simultaneously, thus bringing Yugoslavia back into the satellite fold and getting control of the Adriatic ports, is *intriguing* busily and hopefully. This brought a sharp protest from Belgrade last week. At last month's constitutional congress President Tito, who at 79 seemed to be faltering, made a vigorous come-back. While he is going strong he is Yugoslavia's best all-purpose *deterrent*. For the rest, China's obvious concern with any major upset to the balance of power anywhere is a factor increasingly to be reckoned with.

(Editorial from *The Daily Telegraph* of 15 June 1971.)

(a) State the meaning of *eight* of the following words as they are used in the passage: assiduous, canny; maverick; evolution; eulogies; aggravated; assuaged; autonomy; toyed with; simultaneously; intriguing; deterrent.

(b) State in your own words the meaning of:
  (i) unprecedentedly effusive
  (ii) to toe Moscow's line
  (iii) hair-splitting

(c) State why a capital letter is used in "West".

(d) "glorious resistance to the interference and threats from the two super-Powers." Who is being quoted?

(e) "Tensions between the country's national groups . . .". Which country?

(f) What point is emphasized by the inclusion in the last sentence of the passage of the word "anywhere"?

(g) "Satellites" is applied in this passage to countries closely linked to Russia. State another use of the word "satellite", either literal or metaphorical.

25. Study the following passage carefully and then answer the questions which are based on it.

The attempt to rehabilitate the memory of Benedict

Arnold, the alleged American Revolutionary War traitor, reported in *The Times* last week, was apparently just the tip of a counter-revolutionary iceberg. The latest news from the rebellious colonies is the establishment of the Committee for Reunion with England.

The Committee regards the 200th anniversary of the Declaration of Independence with dismay, and has issued its Declaration of Reunion with England. It calls for the immediate petitioning of the Queen and Parliament for forgiveness.

In words that may not have thrilled Thomas Jefferson, the reunionists declare that 200 years of crises are the inevitable festering of a grievous mistake: the American Revolution. Corruption in high places, the putrescence of American political institutions, and the decay of the country's moral fibre originated in the self-serving and the extremist acts of the hot-headed, rebellious founding fathers, they say.

The corruption, violence and injustice could have been avoided if the radicals had been patient enough to work within the British system. The slave trade was abolished in the British Empire in 1807, "two score and sixteen years" before the Emancipation Proclamation, they add. There would have been no Civil War, no Reconstruction period, no Ku-Klux-Klan.

"World Wars I and II would never have occurred. Germany would never dare attack a British Empire that included both sides of the Atlantic Ocean. The American Revolution not only betrayed America, but also Mother England, nay the entire civilized world . . .

"For 200 years we have been deceived and bullied into believing that violent, hot-headed men like Patrick Henry, George Washington and Thomas Jefferson were heroes, but the real heroes of that period were the American Loyalists, the Tories who could see what terrible things the Revolution would cause . . .

"Mother England is kind and just. If we apologize now and promise not to rebel any more, she will go easy on us. Amnesty will be offered to the rebel leaders and the present officials of this rebel government . . .

Contributions are requested and should be sent to the committee's headquarters at 16 East Main Street,

Richmond, Virginia 23219. Presumably sinking pounds will be accepted, although they may suggest that reunion is not such a good idea after all.

(From an article in *The Times* by Louis Heren.)

(a) Supply words or phrases which could be used to replace the following words in the passage: rehabilitate; hotheaded; Emancipation; amnesty.

(b) Supply a prefix which could take the place of "counter" (para. 1)

(c) Explain what the author means by "the tip of a counter-revolutionary iceberg".

(d) In paragraph 3 the author uses the word "festering". Write down two other words which he uses to convey the idea of rottenness.

(e) "Germany would never dare attack" (Para. 5) Comment on the tense use.

(f) Explain why "sinking pounds" may suggest that reunion is not such a good idea after all.

(g) Answer either (i) or (ii)
  (i) "two score and sixteen years" — of what famous speech might this unusual way of saying "fifty-six" remind Americans?
  (ii) Name any two of the present "rebel leaders".

Chapter 13

Metaphors and similes

Metaphors and similes, especially when they are fresh, vivid, and particularly appropriate, enliven both speech and writing. Whether they are thought up carefully to emphasize or illustrate a point, whether they are used spontaneously, whether they are used without the speaker or the writer realizing that he is using them, the way in which metaphors and similes are used is an indication of the user's imaginativeness and of his command of English. That is one reason why questions on metaphors and similes are set in many examinations.

Metaphors

A metaphor is a word or group of words used not in its literal (real, actual) sense, but as a means of indicating an appropriate comparison. Here are some examples:

- He roared down the road on his motor-bike.
- As she stood on the tarmac, the scream of the jets almost deafened her.
- He smiled at her warmly but she gave him an icy stare.
- Petrol prices have rocketed.
- There will be no whitewash at the White House. (Richard Nixon)
- A blanket of snow covered the valley.
- He hared off down the road.

- He considers himself a <u>bright spark</u>.
- The small child lost in the department store could see only a <u>forest of legs</u>.
- After forgetting his wife's birthday he found himself <u>in the doghouse</u>.
- You must <u>take the bull by the horns</u>.
- Is the Concorde going to turn out to be <u>a white elephant</u>?

- Don't <u>count your chickens before they're hatched</u>.
- The protest movement <u>had run out of steam</u>.

In the examples given above no actual roaring, high or low temperatures, rockets, whitewash, blankets, hares, etc., are involved. The words are being used not literally but metaphorically. The noise being made by a swiftly accelerating motor cycle is being compared to the roar of a ferocious animal, the unfriendliness of the girl's stare to the coldness of ice, the speed at which the price of petrol has increased to the rapidity of a rocket's ascent, and so on.

It will be noted that single words (nouns, verbs, adjectives, and even adverbs), phrases and whole sentences may be used metaphorically. Sometimes we find a metaphor sustained for a whole paragraph. Indeed, it could be said that a book like *Animal Farm* by George Orwell is one enormous metaphor.

Similes

Similes are groups of words which explicitly indicate similarity. The comparison made by a simile is usually introduced by "like" or "as". Here are some examples:

- As mad as a hatter.
- As dead as a doornail.
- As keen as mustard.
- Like a bull in a china shop.
- He doth bestride the narrow world like a Colossus. (Shakespeare)
- Trying to get any response from the class was like trying to strike a match on a blancmange.
- A computer is like a brain in some respects.
- An atom, consisting of electrons moving round a nucleus, resembles a miniature solar system.

Questions on metaphors and similes

In comprehension questions candidates are sometimes asked to explain a metaphor or simile or comment on its suitability. Examples of such questions will be found in Chapter 12. In other questions candidates are asked to use certain words or phrases metaphorically. Occasionally the word "figuratively" is used instead of "metaphorically". It means much the same thing.

Exercises

1. Explain what is wrong with all of the following sentences:
   She sat with her eyes literally glued to the television.
   When I told him the news he literally exploded.
   You are, quite literally, driving me up the wall.
   There were literally millions of people in the hall.
   We were literally flooded with applications for the job.

2. Choose four of the following words. For each construct two sentences, using the word literally in the first and metaphorically (non-literally) in the second.
   sweep; iron; whitewash; cream; cultivate

3. Write sentences with the following words used metaphorically:
   plough; veil; shroud; carpet; herald; fireworks; snowball; boomerang; iron; ice-breaker

4. Write sentences in which the following words are used as metaphors:
   forest; jungle; oasis; desert; mountain; iceberg; tide; flood; hail; rain

5. Write sentences in which the following words are used as verbs:
   fox; dog; fish; badger; crow; wolf; hog; ferret; hound; ape

6. Complete the following sentences with suitable metaphors:
   All that the nervous actor was aware of was a . . . . of faces.

From the attic window she could see a . . . . of television aerials.

A . . . . of protest greeted the Government's decision.

The wind was . . . . . . eerily in the trees.

7. Choose five of the following phrases and for each of those you choose:

   (a) Write one sentence to show what is meant by the phrase; AND

   (b) write one sentence to explain what special characteristic of the animal is being used to add significance and force to the phrase:

      a panda car; a zebra crossing; cat's eyes studs; a jumbo jet; a cub reporter; a caterpillar track on a tractor; the bull's eye of a target; a wild-cat strike; a clothes horse; a bulldog paper-clip.

      (R.S.A. English Language II.)

8. Write sentences in which the following words are used figuratively:

      trickle; stream; current; torrent; storm

9. Use the following expressions metaphorically:

      Iron Curtain; hawk; dove; sacred cow; grass roots; summit; carrot and stick; carbon copy; shark; vulture.

10. State the meaning of the following figurative expressions and put each of them into a suitable sentence:

      a bolt from the blue; the tip of the iceberg; a flash in the pan; on the shelf; a whale of a time; to bark up the wrong tree; to carry the can; to let the cat out of the bag; cook his goose; in the soup.

11. State the meaning of the following expressions as applied to people:

      a cold fish; a wet blanket; a live wire; a chip off the old block; a minx; a rough diamond; an ass; a wolf; a bright spark; a battle-axe.

12. All of the following expressions could be used metaphorically. Try to think how each could be used.

conveyor-belt; factory; ghost; heresy; tower (verb);
umbrella; flotsam and jetsam; guinea pig; pain in the neck;
lukewarm; league; David and Goliath; Mecca; Waterloo;
coals to Newcastle; the pot calling the kettle black;
antennae; headache; hangover; scalp; nightcap; sandwich
(verb or adjective); pall; heart; satellite; autumn; seed;
wreath (verb); bombshell; plant (verb); reservoir; background; army; cat's paw; pawn; bible; landmark; camouflage; window-dressing; explosion; bottleneck; ceiling;
postscript; wallflower; war-paint; thirst; hunger; harvest;
bellow (verb); fossil; wrinkle; flame; ember; butterfly;
drone; bonus; dwarf (verb); root; face-lift; cup of tea;
medicine; magnet.

13. The following sentences contain metaphors or similes
which, for varying reasons, are open to criticism. Improve each
sentence in any way that you consider necessary.
  (a) The dress was as green as grass.
  (b) Production bottlenecks must be ironed out as soon as
      possible.
  (c) When he heard that he had passed the examination he
      was as pleased as Punch.
  (d) The new legislation is intended to pave the way for more
      motorways.
  (e) The play, described by the announcer as a thriller, was as
      dull as ditchwater.
  (f) The attacking troops were met by a cloud of machine-
      gun bullets.
  (g) We must explore every avenue and leave no stone un-
      turned until we find an acceptable formula.
  (h) We thought the cold war was thawing out but now, with
      this latest crisis, it seems to be hotting up.
  (i) Each speaker at the Agricultural Conference was an
      expert in his field.
  (j) The Government's target was an inflation rate of 8% by
      the end of the following year and it was hoped that the
      target would not only be reached but passed.
  (k) With his new sports car he swept Susan off her feet.
  (l) Instant coffee has never really been my cup of tea.
  (m) The Chancellor ran the gauntlet with his carefully
      balanced package. (ITV News, 22 July, 1976, on the
      British Government's economy measures.)

   (n) The Government are concerned at the health of sterling — that plague of economic planners. (ibid.)

   (o) The Chairman of the company behind the project regards the deal as "a toe in the ocean" which in time may open the flood-gates for an invasion of British productions in a hitherto unexplored territory. (Newspaper report.)

14. Use each of the following words in two sentences. In the first sentence use the word literally; in the second use it figuratively. For example, "profile":

      The famous detective's profile could be seen silhouetted against the gaslit window.

      Every week the *Sunday Mail* carries a profile of a well-known politician.

      windfall; nightmare; dynamite; juggle; marathon; skeleton; eclipse.

15. Explain the meaning of the following figurative expressions and write sentences to illustrate the use of five of them:

(a) to have two bites at the cherry	(f) to get one's skates on
(b) scraping the barrel	(g) blanket coverage
(c) some of his own medicine	(h) muscle in
(d) to be left holding the baby	(i) the thin end of the wedge
(e) to carry the can	(j) the lion's share

16. Many of our traditional similes are colourful and interesting and even some of those which seem nonsensical have vigour, for example, "as right as rain". Nevertheless, we may not want to rely on traditional similes. Write out the following sentences with the underlined similes replaced by others which you think might be suitable.

   (a) He looked as happy as a <u>sandboy</u>. (e.g. as a person who had just won. . . .)

   (b) Her teeth were as white as <u>snow</u>.

   (c) The look she gave him was as cold as <u>charity</u>.

   (d) The idea of political union is now as dead as <u>a doornail</u>.

   (e) He's as smart as <u>paint</u>.

17. Illustrate the metaphorical use of ten of the following:

      passport; ton; ounce; feeler; crocodile; pump; funnel; comb; shield; wrinkle; axe; reprieve; gag; sugary; soft soap; peanuts; chickenfeed: evaporate; crystallize; herald.

N.B. The metaphorical use of some of these words may be restricted to conversation or journalism.

18.
- (a) Find out the meaning of the following expressions:

Onomatopoeia	Epigram
Bathos	Paradox
Syllepsis	Hyperbole
Mixed metaphor	Transferred epithet
Alliteration	Personification

- (b) Find an example of each of the above in the following sentences. Each is exemplified by one sentence.
  - (i) The only thing that we can change is the past.
  - (ii) Hamlet wondered whether it was nobler in the mind to suffer the slings and arrows of outrageous fortune or to take arms against a sea of troubles.
  - (iii) I lit a rather thoughtful cigarette.
  - (iv) We were knee-deep in requests for information and snowed under by paper-work.
  - (v) The bacon was hissing and sizzling and crackling.
  - (vi) Famine is stalking the land and we shudder before his gaze.
  - (vii) The post-prandial petulance of the pampered pekingese perturbed me greatly.
  - (viii) He arrived in a luxurious Cadillac and a furious temper.
  - (ix) The English country gentleman galloping after a fox — the unspeakable in full pursuit of the uneatable. (Oscar Wilde.)
  - (x) "She walks in beauty like the night of cloudless climes and starry skies; and all that's best of dark and bright meet in her aspect and her eyes. Another bit of bread and cheese," he said to the lad behind the bar.

    (From *The Inimitable Jeeves* by P. G. Wodehouse.)
- (c) Make up your own examples of:
  - onomatopoeia
  - bathos
  - personification
  - alliteration
  - hyperbole

Chapter 14

Vocabulary exercises

1. Use each of the following words in a sentence which shows that you know its meaning. The references in brackets are to pages in this book on which the word is used.

eradicate	(3)
allude	(6)
adept	(10)
carnivorous	(18)
strenuous	(45)
discern	(47)
exult	(46)
imperiously	(47)
affluent	(56)
consecutive	(56)

2. Use each of the following words in a suitable sentence which shows that you know its meaning. The references are to precis exercises in which the words are used.

misnomer	(B9)
assertion	(C1)
obsolete	(C3)
specific	(C4)
orientation	(C4)
incentive	(C6)
amenities	(C8)
incipient	(C9)
inference	(C11)
proficient	(C13)

3. Show that you understand the meaning of the following words by using each of them in a sentence. The references are to the Comprehension exercises in this book.

radical	(1)
yardstick	(1)
arduous	(2)
predicament	(2)
imply	(5)
sceptical	(5)
indigenous	(7)
diversify	(8)
ambiguous	(10)
reverberate	(11)

4. Use each of the following words in a sentence which shows that you know its meaning. The references are to the Comprehension exercises in this book.

sonic	(15)
chauvinistic	(15)
annihilate	(17)
exhilaration	(17)
layman	(18)
proletariat	(18)
arbitrary	(19)
etymology	(20)
permeate	(20)
ethnic	(20)

5. Write sentences in which the following names of parts of the body are used as verbs:

foot; stomach; thumb; finger; eye; nose; shoulder; elbow; mouth; knuckle.

6. Use a good dictionary to find the meanings and origins of the following words:

tawdry; quixotic; machiavellian; gerrymander; malapropism; spoonerism; fabian; hector; tantalize; jeremiad.

7. The popular usage of words (the sense in which many and perhaps most people use and understand them) can certainly change their generally accepted meaning, the meaning to be found in dictionaries. Already there may be some dictionaries

which give as the first meaning of "nice": "pleasant, attractive". When "nice" is used in its "correct" sense (e.g. "There is a very nice distinction between murder and manslaughter") most people find it very difficult to suppress the idea of pleasantness.

However, there are a number of words which, although they are widely used in conversation, have kept their distinct and different literary meanings. It is worth noting that the meaning of such words in colloquial speech is often vague.

Write sentences which show that you know the accepted literary meanings of the words underlined below. If you find this exercise difficult or impossible it may be a sign that you do not very much reading.

1. My friend told me that the film was <u>fabulous</u> but when I discovered that it was <u>chronic</u> I was absolutely <u>livid</u> and decided that she had been trying to <u>aggravate</u> me.
2. The match was so <u>putrid</u> that I left after half an hour.
3. The restaurant looked rather disreputable but I managed to get a fairly <u>decent</u> meal there.
4. We promise you that you'll have a <u>fantastic</u> time at one of our self-catering villas on the Costa del Sol!
5. I felt so <u>lousy</u> that I took the day off.
6. The weather was so <u>ghastly</u> that we never left the hotel for a week.
7. My <u>alibi</u> for arriving late was that the car wouldn't start.
8. He is rolling in it and lives in a very <u>salubrious</u> part of London.
9. I had a <u>great</u> time last week.
10. He is rather a peculiar <u>individual.</u> (But Charles Dickens used the word in this way.)

8. The following sentences contain words used incorrectly. Identify the wrong word in each sentence and replace it with the correct word.

1. All day long the cat laid on the mat.
2. I brought five pounds' worth of goods at the supermarket.
3. I've bought my transistor radio so we can listen to the commentary.
4. This particular model is in fact rather unique; only thirty-seven exist in the whole of Britain.
5. The notorious film-star was constantly pursued by a mob of newspaper correspondence.

6. The motor trade is particularly susceptible to seasonable variations.
7. It is high time that capital punishment was reintroduced into schools.
8. It was, said the speaker, the Government's fault that prices had rocketed and he went on to say that they were trying to use the drought as an alibi.
9. Lying on the grass and looking up at the trees, I noticed that there were less apples than usual.
10. The President of the Club strongly refuted suggestions that the umpires were biased against players from overseas.
11. The economies of Algeria and France were competitive rather than complimentary.
12. Since I cannot attend for interview on the date you suggest, perhaps you would be good enough to suggest an alternate date.
13. Whatever you do, don't loose your temper.
14. If you have no dependents, write "None".
15. Please bring your references with you when you attend for interview.
16. This was all together a new idea to him.

9. All of the following words appeared in *The Sun* newspaper on 28 July 1976, and they were all used correctly. How many of them do you know?

1. incompatible
2. destitute
3. vagrant
4. bluff (adj.)
5. obsessive
6. insolvency
7. intrepid
8. corruption
9. negligence
10. reprieve
11. rebuke
12. perverse
13. sub judice
14. unanimously
15. psychiatrist
16. decree nisi
17. prejudice
18. affiliate
19. aligned
20. custody
21. integrity
22. obscure (adj.)
23. accelerate
24. rapacious
25. infelicitous
26. redundancy
27. obese
28. addictive
29. hypothesis
30. hypothetical
31. turbulent
32. venue

33. dilemma	42. motivation
34. raucous	43. crestfallen
35. innuendo	44. irreparable
36. bonanza	45. savour
37. unobtrusive	46. dynamic
38. anatomical	47. aura
39. oblivion	48. zest
40. pentathlon	49. belligerence
41. inhibiting	50. rile

10. Arrange the following words into ten groups, each group to consist of three synonyms — words of similar meaning.

alleviate, merriment, financial, sly, dog, sharpness, joyfully, happy, enthusiastic, insignia, eager, joy, mitigate, artful, merrily, pecuniary, shadow, avid, symbol, merry, monetary, acuteness, cunning, happily, joyful, happiness, follow, relieve, keenness, sign.

11. Many English words have come to us from Latin, often via French but sometimes directly. Here is a short extract from Vergil's *Aeneid*, an epic poem written about 25 BC.

"Huc omnis turba ad ripas effusa ruebat,
Matres atque viri, defuncta corpora vita
Magnanimum heroum, pueri innuptaeque puellae,
Inpositique rogis iuvenes ante ora parentum:
Quam multa in silvis autumni frigore primo
Lapsa cadunt folia . . ."

Here is a translation:

Hither all crowded and rushed streaming to the banks, mothers and men, and great-spirited heroes dead and done with life, boys and unwedded girls and children laid on the funeral pile before their parents' eyes: as numerous as the falling leaves in the forests at the first cold touch of autumn . . .

By referring to the above texts and, when necessary, consulting a dictionary, find the English words with the following meanings:

(a) a vehicle for *all* types of people
(b) tumultuous, riotous
(c) of a river bank
(d) gushing
(e) woman managing the domestic affairs of a hospital

- (f) full of manly strength
- (g) dead, no longer in existence (of organization, club, etc.)
- (h) applied to the body (sometimes literally!)
- (i) forming a body
- (j) united body of persons
- (k) bodily, material
- (l) full of life
- (m) great-hearted, generous
- (n) a brave person
- (o) childish
- (p) wedding
- (q) of children (often in a derogatory sense)
- (r) cold, unemotional
- (s) container for keeping things cold
- (t) first
- (u) leaves on trees
- (v) before, in front of, or next to (The answer is a prefix.)

12. Sort the following 30 words into fifteen pairs of synonyms:
suitable; soothe; smooth; level; exhaustive; chief; tiring; principle; Gallic; droop; air; leader; sea; rule; eligible; legible; look; chronometer; main; thorough; standard; French; readable; calm; unruffled; exhausting; vapour; watch; gas; flag.

13. Trace the derivation of the following words:
boycott; morse; martinet; cardigan; guillotine; sandwich; macadam; saturnine; jovial; martial.

14. Write sentences to show that you know which is the verb and which the noun in each of the following pairs:
(a) advise, advice (b) practise, practice (c) devise, device (d) license, licence (e) prophecy, prophesy.

15. Write sentences in which the following words are used correctly:
- (a) lay (as a past tense)
- (b) lain
- (c) born
- (d) borne
- (e) effect (noun)
- (f) effect (verb)

    (g) affect
    (h) except
    (i) accept
    (j) lose
    (k) loose
    (l) principal (adjective)
    (m) principal (noun)
    (n) principle
    (o) marshal
    (p) martial
    (q) complement
    (r) compliment
    (s) imply
    (t) infer